PUTTING WALES FIRST

T0284961

Putting Wales First
The Political Thought Of Plaid Cymru

Volume 1

Richard Wyn Jones

Translated by Tom Ellis with Lowri Edwards and
Richard Wyn Jones

UNIVERSITY OF WALES PRESS
2024

© Richard Wyn Jones, 2024

Originally published in the Welsh language as *Rhoi Cymru'n Gyntaf: Syniadaeth Plaid Cymru, Cyfrol 1* (2007) © Richard Wyn Jones

All rights reserved. No part of this book may be reproduced in any material form (including photocopying or storing it in any medium by electronic means and whether or not transiently or incidentally to some other use of this publication) without the written permission of the copyright owner except in accordance with the provisions of the Copyright, Designs and Patents Act 1988. Applications for the copyright owner's written permission to reproduce any part of this publication should be addressed to The University of Wales Press, University Registry, King Edward VII Avenue, Cardiff CF10 3NS

www.uwp.co.uk

British Library Cataloguing-in-Publication Data
A catalogue record for this book is available from the British Library.

ISBN 978-1-83772-183-2
e-ISBN 978-1-83772-184-9

The rights of authorship of this work have been asserted in accordance with sections 77 and 79 of the Copyright, Designs and Patents Act 1988.

Typeset by Geethik Technologies
Printed by CPI Antony Rowe, Melksham

Contents

Preface to the English translation   vii
Introduction   ix

PART ONE – NATIONALISM

1   Nationalism, National Movements and Wales   23
    Understanding nationalism   24
       Nationalism, the old and the new   31
       Nationalism, the self and violence   37
    National movements   46
       The development of national movements   51
       The ideology of national movements   55
    Wales – in the shadow of the firstborn   63

PART TWO – NATIONALISTS

2   A Passionate Love for a Stable Civilisation: The Saunders Lewis Era   79
    Seizing the agenda   82
    Principles of Nationalism   92
       Historiography   97
       Nonconformism   103
    Laying the foundations   106
    Holding on   117
       One language or two?   117
       'Three acres and a Welsh-speaking cow'   119

Dominion status   126

A flash in the pan   131

3   'A reconciliation with her fair past': The Gwynfor Evans Era   139

I was rejected …?   144

The inheritance: the core ideas of 'Saunders' a 'Gwynfor'   151

Fundamental policies: the inheritance and its evolution   158

The Welsh language   158

Economic policy   169

Constitutional objectives   180

Aros Mae   198

The End of Britishness   216

4   More than *Dal Ati*? The Era of the Two Dafydds   220

Turning Left: The End of the 'Third Way'   226

Political philosophy   227

Strategy   230

Radical Wales   243

A parliament and Europe – again   269

Wigley, Ceredigion and the paradox of the 1990s   287

Index   307

Preface to the English Translation

It's been a long gestation. While I had always intended to produce an English-language version of the Welsh-language original published in 2007, I determined that it could await completion of Volume Two of the study. But given that Plaid Cymru had entered government for the first time shortly after Volume One had been completed, and bearing in mind that this has proven to be a key (and often dangerous) moment in the development of previously fringe political parties, there appeared every reason to pause before continuing with that second volume.

So things would have remained except for Tom Ellis, the former Labour and SDP member of parliament for Wrexham. Tom had reviewed the book on publication, enjoyed it, and decided that it should be available in English. He wrote to me unbidden and very generously offered to translate it himself. Naturally, I readily agreed, and he went on to complete the task before his untimely death in April 2010. It is doubly unfortunately, therefore – and the source of great regret – that the translation has subsequently sat, unread on my shelf.

By the time Plaid Cymru had completed its first spell in government in May 2011, I was already committed to other writing projects that have been succeeded by yet further opportunities and commitments. Completing Volume Two – and publishing the English version of Volume One – has never been a priority. Until now. Having decided it was past time to return to it, I realised that there was no particular merit in awaiting the publication of Volume Two before proceeding with the English translation of Volume One. I was subsequently fortunate that Lowri Edwards was willing to cast her professional eye over the manuscript. As a final step, I have worked through the translation myself. The aim throughout this process has been to retain at least some of the flavour of the original whilst rendering it as readable as possible in its new and very different linguistic context.

In preparing the final version for publication I was faced with the dilemma of whether to engage with any relevant literature that has appeared since the original version of this book was published in 2007. Rightly or wrongly, I have decided that I should not run the risk of embarking on a process that might easily lead to the extensive rewriting – rather than translation – of Volume One. I will engage with more recent literature where appropriate in Volume Two. Any changes have therefore been kept to a minimum.

In addition to Tom Ellis and Lowri Edwards, I am grateful to the following for their assistance and support in facilitating the publication of this book: Liz Bowen for her kind permission to use the cover image; the School of Law and Politics at Cardiff University; all my colleagues in the Wales Governance Centre at Cardiff, but especially Ed Gareth Poole and Lucy Hammond, both of whom have been particularly generous with their time and expertise; Jerry Hunter; Siwan Ifan; and the excellent staff of the University of Wales Press, including Llion Wigley, Adam Burns, Steven Goundrey, Elin Williams and Dafydd Jones.

Richard Wyn Jones
Fagerstrand
February 2024

Introduction

This is the first of two interconnected volumes focused on Plaid Cymru. A wise commentator once suggest that any attempt to trace the development of a political party is bound to involve writing the history of the country that is its host from the perspective of that party.[1] These volumes are concerned with only one aspect of the development of the Plaid Cymru, namely its political thinking. They contain very little discussion of its internal structures or organisation. Elections are rarely mentioned. In short, many of the most basic elements of the daily life of any political party are more or less absent from the pages that follow. Yet the fact that the study has expanded to two volumes should make it clear to the reader that understanding the ideological development of Plaid Cymru has necessitated an engagement with wider questions and trends in Wales and beyond.[2]

Intellectual history of the kind offered in *Putting Wales First* appears to be a rather unfamiliar genre to many Welsh readers. We are, apparently, more comfortable with memoirs and autobiographies, volumes of literary criticism and more conventional (and broader) historical narratives. Because of this, it is

---

[1] 'The history of any given party can only emerge from the complex portrayal of the totality of society and State (often with international ramifications too). Hence it may be said that to write the history of a party means nothing less than to write the general history of a country from a monographic viewpoint, in order to highlight a particular aspect of it.' Antonio Gramsci, 'Political Parties', *The Modern Prince* (New York: International Publishers, 1957), p. 149.

[2] In fact, the overall project will have given rise to three books, namely a two-volume study of which this forms the first part, as well as a third book: Richard Wyn Jones, *The Fascist Party in Wales? Plaid Cymru, Welsh Nationalism and the Accusation of Fascism*, trans. Dafydd Jones and Richard Wyn Jones (Cardiff: University of Wales Press, 2014).

appropriate to offer an explanation of the rationale for these volumes as well as provide an introduction to their overall structure. It is also important to shed some light on the perspective that has shaped the analysis.

* * *

To engage with and take seriously the political thinking of Plaid Cymru is to challenge two, deeply rooted preconceptions. The first is the assumption that Welsh politics is incapable of acting as an incubator for political ideas of any real substance. Or in the words of another commentator, 'There is scarcely any Welsh political thought worthy of the name.'[3] When it is recalled that these words were penned by none other than Kenneth O. Morgan, the doyen of contemporary Welsh historiography, it is no small matter to disregard them. A different prejudice becomes apparent when scrutinising the enormous academic literature on nationalism. Whatever the particular pathologies of Welsh politics, the belief of some of the leading experts in the field of nationalism is that the specific ideas of the movements that are the object of their studies are both insubstantial and ultimately unimportant. Thus, according to Eric Hobsbawm, nationalism is the belief of the 'lesser-examination passing classes'.[4] Due to the derivitive, simplistic and shop-worn nature of nationalist thought, Ernest Gellner considered that the ideas of specific individuals in nationalist ranks are of no particular importance or interest. 'If one of them had fallen,' he said, 'others would have stepped into his place... No one was indispensable. The quality of nationalist thought would hardly have been affected much by such substitutions. Their precise doctrines are hardly worth analysing.'[5] Which is to say that it was of no real importance whether it was Saunders Lewis or Gwynfor Evans who led Plaid Cymru and gave direction

---

3 Kenneth O. Morgan, *Democracy in Wales from dawn to deficit* (Cardiff: BBC Wales, 1995), p. 8.
4 Eric Hobsbawm, *Nations and Nationalism since 1870: Programme, Myth, Reality* (Cambridge: Cambridge University Press, 1990), p. 118.
5 Ernest Gellner, *Nations and Nationalism* (Oxford: Blackwell, 1983), p. 124.

to its political thinking. The party would have continued to plough the same ideological furrow, come what may.

Both preconceptions are mistaken. With regards the alleged shortcomings of Welsh political thought, there can be no doubt that the most prominent structural feature of this country's politics in the democratic era, namely 'one-party dominance', has militated against intellectual creativity in the ranks of the dominant party itself.[6] There is certainly little to excite those interested in political thought in the publications of the Liberal Party in the first quarter of the twentieth century, or in the publications of the Labour Party during the second half of that century.[7] But if intellectual atrophy is one of the characteristics of dominant parties in one-party dominant political systems as those parties focus on the more mundane questions of maintaining status and power, this is surely only one side of the coin. The other is that those parties that find themselves marginalised within such systems may well find themselved emphasising (even overemphasising) the ideational dimension of politics. Put another way, since those parties have little or no institutional power, is there not a tendency for their members to focus their energies on trying to secure some measure of ideological power and influence? There are without doubt interesting intellectual trends in the socialist movement in Wales in the period before the Great War – one need only recall the discussions among trade unionists in Tonypandy's Aberystwyth Restaurant that gave rise to *The Miners' Next Step* – which were later to resurface at various points in the Communist

6 There is an innovative discussion of 'one-partyism' in relation to the Welsh Labour Party in Iain MacAllister, 'The Labour Party in Wales: The dynamics of one-partyism', *Llafur*, 3 (1) (1980), 79–89. More generally on 'one–party dominant regimes' see T. J. Pempel (ed.), *Uncommon Democracies: The One-Party Dominant Regimes* (Ithaca: Cornell University Press, 1990).

7 In his discussion of Welsh Liberalism in the first decades of the twentieth century, Kenneth O. Morgan notes that Liberal politicians remained 'sunk in the politics of nostalgia and ... wedded to the old themes' such as temperance and disestablishment – this despite the enormous social changes that were underway in Wales at the time. This contrasted with the situation in England where the Liberal Party was responding to the same changes by adopting a more radical ideological programme, namely 'New Liberalism'. Kenneth O. Morgan, 'The New Liberalism and the Challenge of Labour: The Welsh Experience, 1885–1929', in his *Modern Wales: Politics, Places and People* (Cardiff: University of Wales Press, 1995), p. 64.

Party in Wales.[8] Meanwhile, Plaid Genedlaethol Cymru, or the Welsh Nationalist Party – Plaid Cymru after 1945 – has often been very active in intellectual terms. As will become clear in these volumes, the ensuing debates encompassed not only fundamental questions about the relationship between the nation and the individual, but also a very wide range of policy areas. It is, of course, a matter for the reader to weigh up the quality of those various contributions; whether or not there is anything of lasting value that might be distilled from them is another question to ponder. Nevertheless, there is ample evidence that there was at least one element in Welsh political life that has taken political thinking seriously. My own view, at least, is that the legacy they have bequeathed is not an insubtantial or insignificant one: *pace* Kenneth O. Morgan, this is political thinking that deserves to be taken seriously.

I also believe that there is enough evidence in these volumes to demonstrate that the exact authorship of these ideas was no trivial matter. Rather, the different personalities and associated preconceptions and prejudices of the specific authors of the ideas associated with Plaid had a major impact on the form and contents of its political thinking. So, to presage one of the arguments of the current volume, while it can be argued that a preoccupation with historiography and the 'national story' is one of the general characteristics of nationalist thinking, Saunders Lewis and Gwynfor Evans advanced very different versions of the history of Wales, with different implications for public perceptions of the party. Individuals matter, especially so in the context of small political parties, which is exactly what Plaid Cymru has been throughout most of its existence – despite the intellectual stature of some of those associated with it. Of course, individuals – all of us – are to some extent a reflection of our wider social circumstances. But we are more than that. It is certainly a grave mistake to assume that any given individual's point of view is simply a reflection of a particular constellation of class and community interests and characteristics. We can think for ourselves and, to some extent at

8 Unofficial Reform Committee, *The Miners' Next Step* (Tonypandy: Unofficial Reform Committee, 1912).

least, transcend the circumstances which have helped form us. Or as Karl Marx once said, it is men that make history but not in circumstances of their own choosing. These volumes proceed on the basis that political ideas matter and attempts to trace the development of the political thinking of an exceptionally determined group of people who, ultimately, helped change the course of Welsh history.

* * *

There are two parts to the present volume. Part One, Nationalism, introduces the understanding of nationalism on which the remainder of the study is based. It is included primarily because because nationalism is a phenomenon that seems particularly prone to misunderstanding – it is a subject on which almost everyone appears to have a strong opinion even if it is rarely based on deep consideration. In Wales, the most significant contemporary political tradition – namely the Labour tradition – has tended to condemn nationalism in the name of 'internationalism', arguing that the former is an expression of narrow-mindedness, parochialism, or worse. In stark contrast, Welsh nationalists tend to regard their nationalism as simply the natural expression of an age-old sense of national community. As we shall see, both understandings are insufficient; indeed, both are best regarded as a manifestation of the ubiquity of nationalist assumptions (British nationalist assumptions, in the case of the mainstream of the Welsh Labour Party). It is also here that we discuss the relationship between nationalism and political ideologies as they are understood more conventionally, namely as socialism, liberalism, and conservatism. Finally, we discuss some of the implications for Wales and Welsh nationalism of the fact that England was the modern world's 'firstborn': it was in England that the first modern state took shape, it was England that saw the first society based on a capitalist economy, and it was in England, too, that nationalism first developed.

As all of this suggests, the discussion in Part One is rather general in character and, in places, quite abstract. I make no apologies for seeking to deal with complex matters even as I have attempted to be as clear as I can in writing about them. Nonetheless, those readers solely interested in matters related to Wales may wish to move straight to Part Two (in the hope that they will then feel inspired to return to the first part of the book on completion of the rest!).

Part Two of the book, Nationalists, traces the development of Plaid Cymru's political thought from its beginnings until the establishment of the National Assembly for Wales in 1999. That is achieved by focusing in turn on the ideas of the four most significant leaders in the party's history to date. Chapter 2 is devoted to a discussion of Saunders Lewis's political thought. Gwynfor Evans is the subject of Chapter 3 while the two Dafydds, Dafydd Wigley and Dafydd Elis-Thomas, share the focus in Chapter 4. The justification for devoting so much attention to the party's leaders is the fact that they played such a central role as both architects and advocates of their party's worldview and policy programmes. This was absolutely the case for Saunders Lewis who, as we shall see, completely dominated the party during his period as president. It was also true to a very significant extent during Gwynfor Evans's extended period as leader. There is, nonetheless, something of a shift towards the latter part of his presidency, in part as a result of the growth of Plaid Cymru. As such, neither Dafydd enjoyed or desired the same level of ideological ascendancy over their party as their two most important predecessors. This despite the fact that Dafydd Elis-Thomas displayed a real and creative interest in political ideas, and that I also present a case for considering Dafydd Wigley to be a more significant political thinker than is generally realised. Thus the focus on the dominant figures is perhaps a little more strained and artificial by the time our discussion arrives at the 1970s. That said, the truth of the matter is that there are limitations to every alternative structure that might have had been adopted. I remain confident that Part Two sheds new and revealing light on the development of the political thinking of Plaid Cymru.

This is not the appropriate place to provide more than a very brief preview of the contents of the Volume Two of the study.

Suffice it to say that its focus shifts from specific individuals to a discussion that is more thematic in nature. That book will also contain a detailed accounting of the development of Plaid Cymru's political thought since the establishment of a devolved Welsh parliament; by far the most significant institutional development in Welsh politics since the so-called Acts of Union.

* * *

There is no perspective-less history or social science. Alarm bells should ring when any writer claims to be objective. It is a pretence that masks – or even seeks to conceal – different values and preconceptions. Of course, any worthwhile writer will strive to rise above these prejudices. Nevertheless, as *Putting Wales First* discusses issues and events that engender strong feelings, and as some readers may well attribute those arguments and analyses with which they disagree to the author's own predelictions and presumptions, it is appropriate to briefly state what I understand to be the basis of the worldview reflected in these pages.

Antonio Gramsci is said to have once decribed himself as 'a Sardinian without complications'. While I make no claim to be free of complications, as far as my sense of national identity is concerned it is quite straightforward. In the words of Gareth Siôn's epic state-of the-nation poem about Wales in the 1980s, '*Wyf Gymro*' – 'I am Welsh'. Full stop. I am a member of that part of my generation that is completely immune to the charms of Britishness. This not because we have consciously rejected British identity, but because our background and upbringing has ensured that we never felt any affinity with it in the first place. A Welsh national identity is not necessarily to be valorised over a British one – even if I happen to believe that it retains more creative and progressive possibilities because it is not weighed down with the same institutional sclerosis and all the class and national prejudices that are the legacy of the 'glorious history' of the United Kingdom. My point is rather this: I engage with Plaid Cymru's political thought as someone who is, to a significant extent, a product of that party's success in influencing the worldview of a proportion of the people of Wales. Indeed, one way of interpreting this study – if, one hopes, the least interesting – is as an effort to critically examine the political culture that shaped its author.

The reference to Gramsci points to a further influence. These volumes were written from a broadly left-of-centre perspective. Tom Nairn is surely correct when he argues that any serious engagement with nationalism must entail rejecting Marxism in its most overbearing form – that secular religion which, at one time, claimed to understand the past, present and future of everyone and everything. Neither can it be denied that the left now finds itself in a deplorable intellectual state. Nevertheless, there remains lasting value in the approach to understanding history and society that emphasises the influence of material processes and tries to understand their complex interrelationship with the cultural and political spheres. Neither does acknowledging the complexity of the contemporary world or the grave shortcomings of the left invalidate efforts to build a world in which individuals, nations and the environment are treated with dignity and respect. Even if it remains more influential in Wales than in many other places, this attitude is now distinctly unfashionable. We can debate whether the reluctance of the Welsh to cast aside the ideals of the left reflects the inevitable small 'c' conservatism of minoritised cultures, or rather the ability of the people of the fringes to resist the various intellectual whims that bedazzle the (allegedly) sophisticated core. Be that as it may, these volumes reflect the assumption that a materialist perspective helps us make sense of the past and will again form the basis of an emancipatory politics, whether or not that is expressed through the medium of the political party that is their subject.

* * *

This study is the result of many years of work and it is high time to publicly thank those individuals and organisations that have provided support during this period. First, I would like to acknowledge my heavy debt to my department, the Department of International

Politics at the University of Wales, Aberystwyth. I am particularly grateful to it for allowing study leave so that I could focus on a long-term research project away from the (increasing) demands of teaching and administration. Two organisations in Norway were kind enough to offer me shelter during these periods. The fact that they did so despite the fact that I was researching a subject considered by many (in the UK, at least) to be of marginal interest and writing in a minority language, shows that old-fashioned commitment to learning for its own sake remains alive and well in one corner of Europe. *Tusen takk* to Sverre Lodgaard and his colleagues at the *Norsk Utenrikspolitik Institutt* and to Hanne Marthe Narud and her colleagues at the *Institutt for Statsvitenskap* at the University of Oslo. A grant from the Higher Education Funding Council for Wales allowed me to complete the book and I am also grateful for its generosity.

During my years on the staff in Aberystwyth the enthusiasm and interest of the students I have had the privilege of teaching has been a constant inspiration. Many of the ideas found in this study first saw the light of day in various lectures and seminars. I am also indebted to the various organisations that gave me the opportunity to present these ideas to a wider audience. Special thanks, therefore, to the officers of the Philosophy Section of the Guild of University of Wales Graduates, to Duncan Tanner and his colleagues at the University of Wales, Bangor, to the Centre for European Research (ARENA) at the University of Oslo, to the School of Welsh at Cardiff University, and to Geraint H. Jenkins and the Centre for Welsh and Celtic Advanced Studies. I owe a considerable debt to Geraint H. Jenkins. As well as being able to take advantage of the general support that he has extended so generously to so many younger scholars, he invited me to contribute an article on 'Saunders Lewis a'r Blaid Genedlaethol' (Saunders Lewis and the Nationalist Party) to the fifteenth volume in the *Cof Cenedl* series published in 1999. It contains early versions of some of the arguments presented in Chapter 2. Some of the arguments in Chapter 3 were first aired in an article titled 'Syniadaeth Wleidyddol Gwynfor Evans' (The political thought of Gwynfor Evans) in volume 63 of *Efrydiau Athronyddol*. I am grateful to the editors Walford Gealy and John Daniel. It was Simon Brooks, during his time as editor of *Tu Chwith*, who first invited me to write about Dafydd Elis-Thomas. Even if little of the contents of that original article has survived – it was published in the summer 1996 issue as 'O Sosialaeth Gymunedol i *Quango Wales*: Ymdaith ddeallusol hynod Dafydd Elis Thomas' – the invitation was nonetheless important in allowing me to get my bearings.[9] The subject's own (characteristic) willingness to engage positively to my rather harsh treatment of him was another inspiration.

A number of other colleagues and friends were also important sources of support on the journey. In particular, I would like to thank Non Gwilym, Peter Jackson, Charlie Jeffrey, Rhys Jones, James Mitchell, Elin Royles, Steve Smith, Dafydd Trystan, Lee Waters, Daniel Williams and Michael Williams. Special thanks is due to Gwenan Creunant who was a constant source of sage advice and encouragement. The incomparable John Davies – 'Bwlch-llan' to generations of his former students – was another crucial inspiration. Although I have tried to acknowledge my debt to other scholars in various footnotes, I fear that I have not given him due recognition. In truth, I learned more about the subject of this study chatting with John in the *Coopers* than in any book or classroom.

Other friends were kind enough to offer to read parts of the book before publication and offer valuable suggestions for improvements. I especially thank Anwen Elias, Meredydd Evans, Rhys Evans, Geraint Gruffydd and Marion Löffler. It should be stressed that they bear no responsibility for any remaining deficiencies. Thanks also to Dyfed Elis-Gruffydd for his work as copy-editor. I am particularly indebted for those who helped locate material for the study, and specifically to the late Phil Williams and Ann Williams who allowed me to loan a collection of Plaid Cymru pamphlets for a (very) extended period. Three booksellers, Dafydd Jones, Dafydd Timothy and Gwilym Tudur, were also willing to go

9 Richard Wyn Jones, 'From "Community Socialism" to Quango Wales: The Amazing Odyssey of Dafydd Elis Thomas', trans. Meg Elis and Richard Wyn Jones, *Planet: The Welsh Internationalist*, 119 (1996), 59–70.

far beyond the call of duty on my behalf. I also owe a great deal to Aled Elwyn Jones for his invaluable help in preparing the book's index and for his detective work on my behalf at the National Library. It is a pleasure to thank the staff of the University of Wales Press – and especially Sarah Lewis – for their help and patience, as well as the anonymous reader who read the book on behalf of the press and provided constructive and supportive comments. The book would not have been completed without the support of my friend Jerry Hunter, now of Penygroes and Bangor University. He has read, debated, encouraged, poked and prodded for two decades. Beyond that, he provides a model of what scholarship can be – both Welsh *and* international in its location; both Welsh *and* international in its horizons.

Most of all, I would like to thank my family. When Eli adopted this Welshman she had no inkling that Saunders, Gwynfor, D. J. and Noëlle and the rest were part of the package! She has been amazingly tolerant and I will be forever grateful to her for that, and for her unwavering support. Eirig and Owain are still too young to understand exactly what their father does 'at work', nonetheless their laughter and mischief has been a tonic.

A final word about my parents. Devolution was always a big dream in our household. My father's heart was broken by the result of the 1979 St David's Day referendum and he could hardly bring himself to get involved in politics after that. But in the summer months of 1997, he began to hope that there might yet be a dawn after such a long, dark night. In the early hours of 19 September, the two sat expectantly awaiting the results of a second referendum. As they were announced, it appeared increasingly likely that the Welsh were about to choose to continue to cower in the shadows on the fringes of history. My father retired to bed. But my mother is not one to lose faith. She waited to see John Meredith fighting unsuccessfully to hide a broad smile as he assured the viewers of S4C that the final result from Carmarthen might yet change everything. My father was roused from bed and, following that last declaration, they both drank a toast to the new Wales with a small glass of sherry. This book is for them in that wonderful, indelible moment.

Part One

Nationalism

1

Nationalism, National Movements and Wales

Viewed from an international, comparative perspective, the fact that a nationalist movement developed in Wales must be regarded as wholly unsurprising. The key question is rather why that movement has not enjoyed greater success. Indeed, given the importance of nationalism as a global phenomenon, it might well be argued that this is the only historiographical question of universal importance to arise from the Welsh experience. After all, there were few other European nations where the prospects for a successful nationalist movement were better than in nineteenth-century Wales. Many other nations (both large and small), succeeded in demanding and gaining their freedom based on much more meagre resources than those available to Wales. Miroslav Hroch observed this in his influential work, *The Social Preconditions of National Revival in Europe*:

> For Wales ... all the features of the 'classical' definition [of a successful prospective-nation] were valid in the full extent: it had a compact area of settlement, and old-established and distinctive cultural unity, a modernized literary language, its territory even formed an economic whole, comparable with a national market – and despite this we cannot speak of a full-developed Welsh nation. At the same time it would be possible in contrast to instance a series of nations from which some of these features were absent, but which nevertheless became constituted into national units with an independent existence.[1]

1 Miroslav Hroch, *The Social Preconditions of National Revival in Europe: A Comparative Analysis of the Social Composition of Patriotic Groups among the Smaller*

Why, then, was the 'national revival' in Wales so weak? So weak that it took until 1997 for the Welsh to agree to the establishment of a rather feeble National Assembly, and only then by the tiniest of majorities; so weak that the Welsh language remains fragile and imperilled.

I make no claim to have provided a definitive answer to these questions here. Even if I possessed the necessary intellectual resources to attempt such a task, it would require a very different book in order to do so. Nonetheless, before we focus on the form of Welsh nationalism manifested in the political thought of Plaid Cymru, some general observations about the nature of nationalism and national movements – as well as the more specific situation of Wales – are in order. This will serve to highlight a number of themes that recur in subsequent chapters. In addition, it will help to make clear the theoretical and conceptual underpinnings of this study, allowing the reader an opportunity to assess their validity.

Understanding nationalism

Nationalism is a modern phenomenon, rooted in the transformation from the Middle Ages to industrial society; from feudalism to a world in which capitalism forms the basis of the economic and social order and whose political system is organised around the sovereign state. Nationalism is the political and cultural manifestation of this transformation. It has provided a means of coming to terms with changes that have revolutionised every single aspect of human life, not least those worldviews that help to make sense of it.

Key to understanding the varied forms taken by nationalism is that this process has always been uneven and unequal: the impact of modernisation on communities has varied (and continues to

European Nations, trans. Ben Fowkes (Cambridge: Cambridge University Press, 1985), p. 4. Note Hroch's assumption that full national development is synonymous with the establishment of a nation state. The validity of this assumption is subject to debate – and was most certainly not the *rhetorical* position of Plaid Cymru's leadership during the period under consideration in what follows.

vary) enormously, across both time and space. In some places, particularly in those regions associated with the origins of the process, it was a relatively gradual development. Indeed, such were the advantages attaching to primacy that, in these comparatively advantaged regions at least, it is tempting to understand modernisation as a 'social evolution'. Yet even here, the danger with this framing is that it tends to sanitise a process that was, even at best, callous and ugly. The cruellest and most destructive aspects of modernisation were most evident in regions that underwent the process at a later stage. In those places – for example, in those parts of Africa or the Americas on which the 'West' decided to bestow its 'civilisation', or among the rural peasantry that Stalin and Mao chose to honour with a role in their demented schemes – modernisation came at a terrifying pace. Here people were dragged by their ears – some of them kicking and screaming – into the relentless and merciless currents of the modern world. As these examples suggest, the nature of those areas that, in their turn, became subject to the inescapable logic of the modern world varied greatly: varied linguistically and ethnically, of course, but varied also in terms of the ways in which power – be that military, economic, political or cultural power – was distributed within and across them. In all of these different and complex contexts, the effect of unequal modernisation was to create, or sometimes intensify, social divisions. It is from this endowment that nationalism developed.

Those acquainted with the academic literature on the subject will know how much we owe Ernest Gellner for this understanding of nationalism. There is no evidence that he had any particular interest in Wales. In fact, to the contrary. In 1991, he managed to deliver an entire lecture on nationalism before an audience in Aberystwyth without uttering a single word about Wales or its situation.[2] Nevertheless, anyone wishing to study nationalism

---

2 The lecture can be found in Ernest Gellner, *Encounters with Nationalism* (Oxford: Blackwell, 1994), pp. 20–33. The occasion was the E. H. Carr Memorial Lecture. In this context, it is interesting to note that (apart from one insignificant reference in a footnote) Carr himself failed to mention Wales in his own influential book on nationalism, *Nationalism and After* (London: Macmillan, 1945). He had

– including those seeking to understand the particularities of Plaid Cymru's political thought – are greatly indebted to him.

Gellner's great contribution was to have made it much it more difficult for commentators (at least those concerned with intellectual respectability) to continue to string together the tired old clichés that have tended to characterise – and bedevil – the debate on nationalism. He undercut the pretensions of those 'anti-nationalists' who seek to contrast the primitive, illogical and unacceptable nationalism of others with their own normal and civilised patriotism.[3] Equally, he undermined the moralising of the same ilk who claim to rise above any base feelings of nationalism by claiming a higher internationalism and cosmopolitanism. More than anyone else, Gellner made clear how nationalism permeates *all* aspects of *every* modern society. He demonstrated that every successful state has come to rely on a sense of nationalism. In fact, following Gellner's reasoning, and as will become clearer in due course, we see that every important modern political ideology – liberalism, conservatism, socialism, communism, fascism – in practice if not in theory, are all reliant on nationalist assumptions and preconceptions. As David McCrone's excellent discussion of the subject makes clear, 'Nationalism is the *sine qua non* of modern societies.'[4] It is Gellner that we need to thank for this key insight.

It should be stressed that Gellner was not drawing attention to the omnipresent nature of nationalism because he was a nationalist himself, nor was it because he saw the growth and spread of nationalism as beneficial and positive. In fact, in many ways it was quite the opposite. He hankered after the Austro-Hungarian Empire and warned against the consequences of the dissolution

even less excuse than Gellner, given that he held the Woodrow Wilson Chair in the Department of International Politics at Aberystwyth between 1936 and 1947.

3 It is worth emphasising this point: the constant efforts to differentiate between patriotism, on the one hand, and nationalism on the other, are of no analytical value. It is better, rather, to see such efforts as *part* of the politics of nationalism – as a (more or less conscious) process of validating certain viewpoints and institutions, while seeking to render others as invalid. This argument is, of course, commonly deployed by advocates of various state nationalisms against representatives of national minorities regarded as posing a threat to the integrity of those states.

4 David McCrone, *The Sociology of Nationalism: Tomorrow's Ancestors* (London: Routledge, 1998), p. 72.

of the Soviet Union. In the context of the current discussion, it is interesting to note Tom Nairn's suggestion that, by the end of his life, Gellner had become an admirer of the United Kingdom: 'It was as if a part of the Habsburg mantle (which he was quite fond of praising) had fallen upon Windsordom.'[5] His work challenges the prejudices of nationalists just as much as those of their opponents.

One of the dearest beliefs of nationalists is that their own form of nationalism, at least, is completely natural. Alongside this, we tend to see those same nationalists insisting that other forms of nationalism are unnatural – especially other forms of nationalism which seek to lay claim the same people and territory that they have claimed as their own. Witness the way that some Welsh nationalists argue that the British 'nation' is not a true nation, and that therefore British nationalism is not a valid or coherent position. Gellner's argument was that *all* forms of nationalism are just as unnatural as each other (if indeed the use of terms such as 'natural' and 'unnatural' is helpful in this context). Each form of nationalism is a 'construction', to use a currently fashionable academic term. Thus, while nationalism *in general* is an integral and inevitable part of the modern world, there is nothing inevitable about the development and survival of any *specific* expression of it (that is Danish, French, Eritrean nationalism, etc.). We shall return later to the implications of this crucially important point.

To continue for the moment with our discussion on nationalism at a general level, it is Gellner's belief that nationalism arises from the fact that a shared linguistic and cultural context is essential in an industrial society (note that Gellner tends to equate industrialism with modernity). In pre-industrial societies it did not matter if the language of the court was different from that of the people, nor was it of real importance if the language and culture of people of different classes within society differed from each other. The life horizons of the overwhelming majority were hyperlocal, and the relationships between people of differing status and class tended to be rather formal and formalised in character. In modern

---

5   Tom Nairn, 'The curse of rurality: limits of modernisation theory', in John A. Hall (ed.), *The State of the Nation: Ernest Gellner and the Theory of Nationalism* (Cambridge: Cambridge University Press, 1998), p. 134 n.

society, however, an individual's geographical and social position is more open and subject to change. In comparison with the pre-industrial age, modern society is thus comparatively egalitarian.[6] The only way people can move around within – and through – a society like this is via the existence of a common cultural context which enables everyone in society to communicate freely and (comparatively) unambiguously with each other.[7] This common cultural framework – and above all a common language, spread across the whole of society by means of a common education system – is the basis for a feeling of nationhood and nationalism. According to this interpretation, the growth of literacy and the development of nationalism are intertwined; this is the glue, so to speak, that holds modern society together.[8]

While agreeing with Gellner's general emphasis on nationalism as a manifestation of modernisation, others have emphasised the importance of other aspects of that process beyond industrialisation per se. Michael Mann, for example, stresses the centrality of the development of capitalism and the growth of the modern centralised state.[9] An important driver for both was the revolution in military technology and, relatedly, fighting techniques which transformed the nature of warfare in Europe over a period of around a century after 1540. In the wake of these developments, warfare would require a very different kind of state – more centralised and much larger both in terms of its bureaucracy and budget. It also placed a premium on the state's ability to communicate effectively across its own territory. The consequences of this change were, in turn, a strong push towards the creation of a literate society and the sprouting of the first shoots of nationalism.

6 Gellner, *Nations and Nationalism*, p. 25.
7 Gellner, *Nations and Nationalism*, p. 141.
8 Benedict Anderson emphasises the importance of the growth of the printing press and print culture (print capitalism) in the same process. See *Imagined Communities: Reflections on the Origin and Spread of Nationalism*, rev. edn) (London: Verso, 1991). For the Welsh context see Jerry Hunter, 'Cyfrinachau ar dafod leferydd: ideoleg technoleg yn ail hanner yr unfed ganrif ar bymtheg', in Angharad Price (ed.), *Chwileniwm: Technoleg a Llenyddiaeth* (Caerdydd: Gwasg Prifysgol Cymru, 2002), pp. 36–53.
9 Michael Mann, *The Sources of Social Power, Vol. 1: A History of Power from the Beginning to AD 1760* (Cambridge: Cambridge University Press, 1986).

Liah Greenfield also identifies the origins of nationalism as lying in the sixteenth century, but in her case, it is England specifically (rather than Europe more generally), that is regarded as the point of origin. According to her influential analysis, it is vital that we recognise the catalytic role of Protestantism if we are to understand this initial expression of what will eventually become a global phenomenon (we return to the implications of this argument for our understanding of the Welsh case in the latter part of this chapter).[10] In contrast, David Bell identifies eighteenth-century France as the birthplace of nationalism. Indeed, Bell is bold enough to offer a precise date and place of birth, namely a speech by Jean-Paul Rabaut de Saint-Etienne to the National Assembly of revolutionary France on 21 December 1792.[11] He is not the only one to regard events in France in 1792 as being of particular significance in the development of nationalism. For German poet, Goethe, the Battle of Valmy at the end of September of that year was the critical moment. On seeing French volunteers fired with national, revolutionary zeal withstand Prussia's professional forces, he claimed to be bearing witness to the beginning of a new era in history – the national era.[12] From Nairn's perspective, however, the key elements were 'the combined shocks engendered by the French Revolution, the Napoleonic conquests, the English industrial revolution, and the war between the two super-powers of the day, England and France. This English-French "dual revolution" impinged upon the rest of Europe like a tidal wave.'[13]

These various interpretations, as well as others like them, differ in interesting and significant ways. Yet, in the present context, there is little to be gained from overemphasising these differences. The development of the modern state and capitalism (commercial and industrial), and indeed the growth of Protestantism,

10 Liah Greenfeld, *Nationalism: Five Roads to Modernity* (Cambridge, MA: Harvard University Press, 1992), pp. 27–88.
11 '[I]t marks, as well as any single event can, the historical moment at which it became possible to speak of nationalism in France': David A. Bell. *The Cult of the Nation in France: Inventing Nationalism, 1680–1800* (Cambridge, MA: Harvard University Press, 2001), p. 3.
12 James J. Sheehan, *German History 1770–1866* (Oxford: Clarendon Press, 1989), p. 222.
13 Tom Nairn, *The Break-up of Britain*, 2nd edn (London: Verso, 1981), p. 96.

were all interconnected and interdependent processes. Indeed, Gellner himself seems to have accepted the power of arguments such as Mann's and Greenfield's by the time he wrote his last short book on the subject, *Nationalism*.[14] In that work, to borrow the words of Brendan O'Leary, one of Gellner's shrewdest critics, 'bureaucratic centralisation (and its standardising implications) and "Protestant-type" religions (with their egalitarian and high-culture diffusing properties) are granted their due as semi-independent agents in the generation of nationalism'.[15] What is important for the current discussion, therefore, is the common ground between these various scholars: all regard nationalism as an integral part of the modernisation process.

It is the uneven nature of modernisation that has ensured the proliferation of nationalism as a global phenomenon. Even as it ensured an element of egalitarianism *within* societies caught in its flow by undermining what Gellner described as 'the rigid, absolutised, chasm-like differences typical of agrarian societies', modernisation opened up enormous chasms *between* these societies and other places and peoples.[16] In such a context, nationalism becomes a means of trying to inspire subordinated societies to transform their own status *by modernising themselves*. Peoples are thus united, inspired, and often forced to mobilise, on the basis of those ethnic and national differences (both real and imagined) that make them different and unique. The whole process is summarised by Nairn in the following terms:

> uneven development has invariably generated an imperialism of the centre over the periphery; one after another, these peripheric areas have been forced into a profoundly ambivalent reaction against this dominance, seeking at once to resist it and to somehow take over its vital force for their own use. This could only be done by a kind of highly 'idealist' political and ideological mobilization, by a

14 Ernest Gellner, *Nationalism* (London: Weidenfeld and Nicholson, 1997).
15 Brendan O'Leary, 'Ernest Gellner's diagnoses of nationalism: a critical overview, or, what is living and what is dead in Ernest Gellner's philosophy of nationalism?', in Hall (ed.), *The State of the Nation*, pp. 72–3. See Gellner, *Nationalism*, pp. 25–30.
16 Gellner, *Nations and Nationalism*, p. 25.

painful forced march based on their own resources: that is, employ-
ing their 'nationality' as a basis.[17]

Old communal ties – or, more often than not, reformed or (re)im-
agined versions of them – are called upon as a means of survival
in the modern world.

As well as crystallising the political geography of the growth
of nationalism, this quotation also serves to draw our attention
to a number of other aspects related to its development. We now
turn to a brief consideration of two of the most important: the
relationship between nationalism and that which nationalists
seek to promote, namely the nation (*Nationalism, the old and the
new*); and what Nairn regards as the fundamental ambiguity of
nationalism (*Nationalism, identity and violence*).

Nationalism, the old and the new

Since it was first sung in the early 1980s, 'Yma o Hyd' has become
nothing less than a second national anthem for Welsh nationalists.[18] Although the subject of Dafydd Iwan's song is the history
of Wales, the general sentiment it conveys can be regarded as a
crystalline expression of the essence of nationalist historiography
right across the world. Indeed, its feat – as previously achieved
in Saunders Lewis's play, *Buchedd Garmon* – is to distil the nationalist perspective on history to its very essence. Its emphasis is
on ancestry, inheritance, and tradition; on the living connections
between past and present embedded in the national community.
Above all, it conveys how the hardships and sufferings of ancestors imposes a moral obligation on those living in the present day
to ensure that the nation survives into the future, doing so 'despite everyone and everything' ('er gwaethaf pawb a phopeth').

The (numerous) critics of nationalism tend to be scornful of
such notions. For them, the idea that there exist lasting, even
timeless national connections is so much stuff and nonsense.

---

17 Nairn, *The Break-up of Britain*, pp. 340–1.
18 It should be noted that these words were originally written long before the
song's more recent adoption (largely through the efforts of Welsh football supporters) as an informal second national anthem, apparently equally beloved by
those who do not consider themselves to be nationalists.

Rather, they regard the whole idea of the nation as a relatively recent creation by nationalists themselves. Eric Hobsbawm, for example, views the whole phenomenon from a rather crude, vulgar-Marxist perspective. For him and others of like mind, nations and nationalisms were – and are – a means by which the bourgeoisie reinforce their grip on power. By yoking the working class to the socio-political interests of those who rule society, nationalism binds them to a political programme which runs counter to their true, objective interests. On this view, the popular commitment to the nation is a case of 'false consciousness' – an example of mass self-delusion on an epic scale.[19]

Ernest Gellner, too, tended to stress the newness of nations – especially when seeking to tweak the tail of nationalists! In one of his earliest and best-known statements on the matter, he asserted that: 'Nationalism is not the awakening of nations to self-consciousness: it invents nations where they do not exist.'[20] However, he did not view this presumed fact in the same negative light as Hobsbawm. He argued rather that inventing and promoting the concept of the nation had played an all-important role in

[19]   Eric Hobsbawm's scathingly critical attitude towards nationalism and nationalists permeates his work – it is obvious not only in his essays on nationalism per se, such as those collected in *Nations and Nationalism since 1780*, but also in his more general essays, for example in *The Age of Extremes: The Short Twentieth Century 1914–1991* (London: Abacus, 1995). As a man of Jewish descent with deep roots in central Europe, it is both unsurprising and understandable that he is particularly conscious of and watchful for the devastating possibilities that can lurk under the mantle of nationalism. Nevertheless, it seems that a more recent and directly personal animus is also at work here, especially in relation to his attitudes towards Welsh nationalism and nationhood. In his autobiography – *Interesting Times* (London: Penguin, 2002), pp. 233–45 – the historian makes clear his resentment at the inhabitants of the small village of Croesor in Eifionydd, where for many years Hobsbawm rented a summer residence from the Portmeirion estate. Despite the local inhabitants welcoming Hobsbawm and his family into their midst, they are chastised for allowing their growing Welsh nationalist consciousness to sour their relationship with those bohemian intellectuals who spent their summers in the area. Suffice it to say that the villagers themselves remember things very differently. In an article in the *Guardian* (14 September 2002) to mark the publication of the autobiography, it was revealed that Hobsbawm and his wife were by then owners of a holiday home near Hay-on-Wye where they were attempting, in the words of a friend, to 'reproduce the urban intelligentsia in a Welsh wilderness'. Wales is so much easier without the Welsh. I am grateful to my friend, Rhys Jones, for a discussion about his own childhood memories of Hobsbawm's presence in his home village.

[20]   Ernest Gellner, *Thought and Change* (London: Weidenfeld and Nicolson, 1964), p. 168.

resisting imperialism – a force that, without challenge, could easily have generated a global form of apartheid. Nevertheless, he was also clear that no particular respect should be accorded to the fictionalised romanticism that characterises nationalist history.

It should be emphasised that many scholars who accept that national*ism* is a modern phenomenon, nonetheless, reject Hobsbawm's and Gellner's assertions regarding the fictional nature of nationalist history. According to Nairn, for example, 'The kind of remaking which features in modern nationalism is not creation *ex nihilo*, but a reformulation constrained by determinate parameters of the past.'[21] While there is, without doubt, a 'creative' element to nationalist historiography, and often even an element of deliberate fabrication, nationalism also remains a modern interpretation and expression of ancient ties and relationships. It is the very existence of such ties (however fragile) that gives nationalist rhetoric its purchase and appeal. Hroch, too, rejects suggestions that the concept of 'nation' has no substance beyond the fever dreams of nationalists themselves:

> The basic condition for the success of any national agitation … is that its argument at least roughly corresponds to reality as perceived by those to whom it is directed. National agitation therefore had to (and normally did) begin with the fact that, quite independently of the will of the 'patriots', certain relations and ties had developed over the centuries which united those people towards whom the agitation was directed. They formed a community united by inward ties, and they were at least vaguely aware of this.[22]

That is to say, notwithstanding the dreaming, the romanticisation and, yes, the invention, that characterises the nationalist approach to history, it is nonetheless the case that national ties

21 Tom Nairn, *Faces of Nationalism: Janus Revisited* (London: Verso, 1997), p. 104. This, too, is the argument presented by Prys Morgan in a splendid essay published, ironically, in a volume co-edited by Hobsbawm: see Prys Morgan, 'From a death to a view: the hunt for the Welsh past in the Romantic period', Eric Hobsbawm and Terence Ranger (eds), *The Invention of Tradition* (Cambridge: Cambridge University Press, 1983), pp. 43–100.
22 Miroslav Hroch, 'Real and constructed: the nature of the nation', in Hall (ed.), *The State of the Nation*, pp. 99–100.

existed before the emergence of nationalists. Indeed, they were an indispensable part of the elements brought together in the 'new retrospect' on any given country's history generated by its nationalist historians.[23]

That said, it is a mistake to fall into the anachronistic trap of believing that our ancestors in the pre-modern era viewed the nation in the same way as it has later been viewed in the age of nationalism. This is particularly clear in Jerry Hunter's luminous study of national identity amongst the Welsh in the sixteenth century, *Soffestri'r Saeson* (The Sophistry of the English).[24] Depending on the context, the main protagonist of that work, Elis Gruffydd, considered himself to be a Welshman, a Briton and an Englishman, doing so without suffering any of the psychological anguish which modern nationalists would assume to be present in such circumstances. We must be wary of positing a simple, linear relationship between attitudes in earlier periods and those in our own time. Having said that, it cannot be denied either (as Hunter demonstrates) that national consciousness and patriotism, including with regards Wales and Welshness, not only existed but had considerable significance long before the dawn of the modern age, whatever date we choose to ascribe to that development.

How exactly, then, might we distinguish between nationalism and the feeling of patriotism and national pride that was clearly present in the pre-modern era? To my mind, there are three significant differences. The first difference is of perspective and worldview. In the modern age, the world is seen above all as a world of nations. The nation, or to be more precise, the national territory, is the fundamental unit we use to interpret and understand the divisions and inter-relationships between different

---

[23]   This is Tom Nairn's term: see Nairn, *Faces of Nationalism*, p. 71. More generally on this theme, see the work of Anthony D. Smith, in particular *The Ethnic Origins of Nations* (Oxford: Basil Blackwell, 1986) and *Nationalism and Modernism: A Critical Survey of Recent Theories of Nations and Nationalism* (London: Routledge, 1998).

[24]   Jerry Hunter, *Soffestri'r Saeson: Hanesyddiaeth a Hunaniaeth yn Oes y Tuduriaid* (Caerdydd: Gwasg Prifysgol Cymru, 2000).

parts of the world.[25] Clearly other collective units exist, a number of them having survived from previous eras including 'civilisations' and 'faith communities'. Others, like 'class', have acquired a new significance in the modern age. Nonetheless, the nation is a fundamental organising principle of the modern era. This can be seen most clearly, perhaps, with reference to those revolutionary regimes that have claimed to reject reactionary 'old world' categories and install a new worldview in their place. To note one example from many: even in its early revolutionary days, the nation was an all-important category in terms of the internal organisation and administration of the Soviet Union.[26] In more elevated language, the nation is fundamental to the 'ontology' of the modern world; the 'community of fate' that is the nation is key to our comprehension of and involvement in that world.[27]

Secondly, national ties are conceived in a fundamentally different way in the modern world. For nationalists, the nation is an abstract community with each member enjoying a direct, unmediated relationship with his or her nation – and in this sense, at least, the nation is a community of equals. We are not members of the nation by virtue of our role as retainers of some or other noble family. Similarly, even if some leadership figures can play an all-important symbolic role, no individual or family personifies or embodies the nation as such. It is to the nation per se that we are loyal. Nothing stands between us as individuals and our nation, and in this regard, nationalism is one of the cornerstones of democracy.

The third characteristic of nationalism follows directly from this. As O'Leary has pointed out, the essence of nationalism is 'a theory of political legitimacy' which holds that 'the government must be conational with and representative of the governed'.[28] To

---

[25] Rogers Brubaker borrows the words of Pierre Bourdieu when he describes how, in the modern age, 'the nation' became one of the social world's main 'principle(s) of vision and division'. See *Nationalism Reframed: Nationhood and the National Question in the New Europe* (Cambridge: Cambridge University Press, 1996), p. 3.

[26] See Brubaker, *Nationalism Reframed*, pp. 23–54.

[27] The description of nation as a 'community of fate' (*Schicksalsgemeinschaft*) is from Otto Bauer's work: see Otto Bauer, 'The nation', in Gopal Balakrishnan (ed.), *Mapping the Nation* (London: Verso, 1996), pp. 39–77.

[28] O'Leary, *Ernest Gellner's diagnoses of nationalism*, p. 55.

be sure, there are pre-modern cases of the argument being made that only a co-national could legitimately rule a given country. In the Welsh context, we might recall the declaration by the men of Eryri in the bleak winter of 1282 that they would never pay homage to a foreign king, while the Arbroath Declaration (1320), which insisted that Scotland would never suffer foreign rule, has acquired considerable symbolic importance in the politics of con-temporary Scotland.[29] However, it is only in modern times that this presumption has become a cornerstone of political legiti-macy. As nationalism acquired the status of 'common sense', it became impossible to imagine a person or persons of one nation being accepted as ruling another except in the context of a system of government, such as federalism, that is specifically designed to allow for such an arrangement. A Frenchman as president of Germany; a Korean as emperor of Japan: any such scenario would be unimaginable in the age of nationalism.

The fate of modern-day monarchies offers ample evidence of how politics became nationalised and nationalist. The ways in which even England's royal family found it necessary to, in effect, disown its own Germanic heritage and anglicise itself dur-ing the Great War, is a familiar story. But consider those exam-ples of newly independent European nations that established their own monarchies by inviting a member of another nation's royal family to become their king. To establish themselves suc-cessfully, the new monarch and his successors were expected to learn the language and adopt the (supposed) customs and traits of the country adopting them – often even changing their names in the process. Is it too fanciful, perhaps, to interpret all of this in terms of a symbolic marriage with the nation? Be that as it may,

---

[29] R. R. Davies, 'Law and society in thirteenth-century Wales', in R. R. Davies, Ralph A. Griffiths, Ieuan Gwynedd Jones and Kenneth O. Morgan (eds), *Welsh Society and Nationhood: Historical Essays Presented to Glanmor Williams* (Cardiff: University of Wales Press, 1984), p. 52; William Ferguson, *The Identity of the Scottish Nation: A Historic Quest* (Edinburgh: Edinburgh University Press, 1998), pp. 41–3. What is significant for the future about both the declaration of the men of Eryri and the Declaration of Arbroath is the fact that their authors make it clear that they would not accept foreign rule even if their political leaders assented to this. Loyalty to the nation was, thus, placed above loyalty to princes or to individual kings.

the point is this: in order to continue as institutions in the modern age, monarchies have had to adapt to the new national order.

Two of the main political principles of nationalism are an expression of these characteristics, namely self-government and citizenship. The first claims that the nation should decide its own constitutional status, while the second emphasises the right of each member of the nation to partake in the process of determining and shaping its future (and so, it should be noted, has democracy as its logical corollary). It is during the era of nationalism, and because of its influence, that citizenship and self-government have come to be considered as normal, common-sense practices and principles. These have become accepted – rhetorically at least – by advocates of many different kinds of political ideology, and in this sense, nationalism can be regarded as a progressive force in the modern world. But, alas, it is not exclusively a force for good. The central role of nationalism in modern-day politics is also linked with the frequent attempts that have taken place to create national uniformity within the boundaries of the 'national territory' (since rarely do cultural and political boundaries coincide precisely). This has led in turn to all manner of evil up to and including 'ethnic cleansing' and genocide.[30] Nationalism is a dialectical phenomenon containing within it both emancipatory potential and grave dangers.

Nationalism, the self and violence
The inherent ambiguity of nationalism – its power to inspire both the constructive and the destructive – derives from the same source, and that is its intertwining with belonging and identity. National identity is the most significant expression of human identity – be that individual or collective – in the modern age. It is national identity, rather than say class or religion, that has established and marked the boundaries of culture, of civil society and of state politics. Neither can it be doubted that – thus far, at least – it is only the feeling of belonging to a national community

30 Michael Mann, 'Explaining murderous ethnic cleansing: the macro-level', in Montserrat Guibernau and John Hutchinson (eds), *Understanding Nationalism* (Cambridge: Polity, 2001), pp. 207–41.

that has been able to generate over the long-term the sense of social solidarity that is a prerequisite for a progressive and civilised political and social order.[31] But the truth about identity (*any* identity), as noted by J. R. Jones, is that 'one cannot know about belonging without having a sense of not belonging'.[32] In other words, in order to understand who we or what we are, we must know who or what we are not. An element of polarisation is therefore unavoidable. And often, 'not belonging' has presaged persecution as the 'other' has been made scapegoat.

Which brings us to a dimension of nationalism that is the source of considerable unease to its wisest and most intellectually honest advocates, namely its undeniable potential as an appallingly cruel and destructive force. Love of country has inspired cultural masterpieces beyond number, from the music of Beethoven to the architecture of Gaudí and the poetry of T. Gwynn Jones. Nationalism has also been the indispensable foundation stone for one of the most enlightened social systems in the history of humanity, namely the welfare states of Scandinavia. But this is very far from the whole story. One need only to think of Bosnia, Kosovo, Rwanda and the two world wars, to name just a few potential examples, to confirm that nationalism can also inspire monstrous cruelty and almost apocalyptic levels of death and destruction.

As noted, self-proclaimed 'anti-nationalists' have responded to the perturbing dualism inherent in nationalism by seeking to hide behind a façade of purity. *They* are the nationalists, they say, not *us*. If those kinds of people had their way, we would suffer the same fate as Northern Ireland or the Balkans or some other benighted place. But we are different; we are morally superior. 'Patriotism' is the name given to the altogether more sensible and wholesome alternative position that is routinely juxtaposed with nationalism. But in Wales, another alternative has also been influential, and that is internationalism. Space precludes detailed engagement

---

31 See David Miller's defence of the nation's political and social value in his important book, *On Nationality* (Oxford: Oxford University Press, 1999).
32 J. R. Jones, *Gwaedd yng Nghymru* (Lerpwl: Cyhoeddiadau Modern Cymreig, 1970), p. 14: 'na ellir gwybod am berthyn heb ymglywed â pheidio a pherthyn'.

with that sacred cow.[33] Suffice it to note a fact that has become ever more apparent since the demise of the Soviet order, namely that internationalism in its communist guise ('proletarian internationalism') proved to be the obedient servant of the Russian empire's national interests. Unfortunately, this was the case even during the Spanish civil war, often regarded (certainly in Wales) as the most honourable example of proletarian internationalism-in-action.[34] Similarly, the Labour Party's version of internationalism has tended to act as little more than buttress for Anglo-British nationalism in all its dreary parochialism. None of which is to belittle or devalue the best instincts associated with internationalism – the readiness to show solidarity with others in their anguish as well as joy, and the desire to interact with them as equals. But taking these values seriously means acknowledging the base hypocrisy of so many of the actions that have been justified under the banner of internationalism. It also means accepting that, conceptually speaking, the assertion of an absolute difference between internationalism and nationalism makes no sense. Indeed, as the Welsh experience confirms, self-proclaimed nationalists have displayed those better instincts as often as, if not more often than, those who self-consciously reject such 'narrow-mindedness' in the name of an internationalist cosmopolitanism.[35]

For those unprepared to embrace the easy but ultimately fake moral certitudes of the anti-nationalist stance, the situation is not so simple. Those who understand the pull of national ties but who also recognise their inherent dangers, require another means of making sense of the dual nature of nationalism. The standard way of doing so is to seek to distinguish between different types of nationalism – dividing the sheep from the goats, so to speak.

Several different ways of doing so have been suggested. Lenin, for example, sought to differentiate between nationalisms intent

[33] But see Tom Nairn's essay, 'Internationalism: a critique', reprinted in *Faces of Nationalism*, pp. 25–46. While his target is the Scottish left, many of Nairn's observations are relevant to Wales, even if, understandably, he does not deal with some of the specifically Welsh dimensions of this view.
[34] For a fuller discussion of attitudes in Wales towards the Spanish civil war see Wyn Jones, *The Fascist Party in Wales?*, pp. 49–60.
[35] See Will Kymlicka, *Politics in the Vernacular: Multiculturism and Citizenship* (Oxford: Oxford University Press, 2001), pp. 203–20.

on liberating subordinated nations and those nationalisms that chauvinistically celebrate the superiority of dominant states. While the first was regarded as acceptable within specific limits, the latter was viewed irredeemably reactionary and repugnant. This evaluation of the relative merits of different kinds of nationalism was turned on its head by scholars such as Hans Kohn and John Plamenatz. Both regarded 'western nationalism', which they associated with the stable states of western Europe, as progressive, rational and liberal. In contrast, they viewed 'eastern nationalism' – that is, the type of nationalism that had developed among more marginalised peoples – as irrational, reactionary and dangerous. A more recent and more sophisticated variant of the latter argument has been propounded by Rogers Brubaker, who differentiates between 'liberal nationalism' and its feral cousin 'closed nationalism'.[36]

At present, however, there is no doubt that the most influential of the various attempts to categorise and differentiate between types of nationalism is that which distinguishes between 'ethnic' and 'civic' nationalisms. At the root of the difference between the two are different understandings of the nature of the ties that bind the national community together. Ethnic nationalism regards the nation as primordial and permanent, with ties of blood forming the very essence of the national bond. On this understanding, the nation may be regarded as an extended family or tribe. We are inevitably born into a nation and, as a result, inherit its faults and challenges, its privileges and strengths. To seek to reject or otherwise evade our national destiny is to risk being psychologically scarred. This is that nation that is the subject of Welsh poet T. H. Parry-Williams's best-known poem, *Hon*: the nation that cannot be escaped ('ni allaf ddianc rhag hon').

36 V. I. Lenin, 'The rights of nations to self-determination', in *Lenin: Collected Works*, vol. 20 (London: Lawrence and Wishart, n.d.), pp. 393–454; Hans Kohn, *The Idea of Nationalism: A Study in its Origins and Background* (New York: Collier Books, 1967); John Plamenatz, 'Two types of nationalism', in Eugene Kamenka (ed.), *Nationalism: The Nature and Evolution of an Idea* (London: Edward Arnold, 1976), pp. 22–36; Rogers Brubaker, *Citizenship and Nationhood in France and Germany* (Cambridge, MA: Harvard University Press, 1994).

In contrast, civic nationalism stresses that what binds the national community together, above all else, is institutional ties. The feeling of belonging to a nation is something that arises from the experience of living together within the orbit of different social, cultural and political institutions. Rather than being primordial and permanent, this nation must be continually created and re-created. It is an understanding of nationhood beautifully encapsulated by another Welsh poet, Waldo Williams (translated here by Tony Conran), who asks:

> Being a nation, what is it?
> Keeping house in a cloud of witnesses.[37]

There is no nation unless a population 'testifies' to its existence through the practices of their daily lives.[38] The voluntary element of this process is all-important since it implies that, in principle at least, the nation can be inclusive. One is not part of a nation merely because of an accident of birth; one can also actively choose to be a part of a given national community.

The appeal of being able to distinguish and draw a line between ethnic and civic nationalism should be immediately apparent. During the twentieth century, countless millions of innocent and defenceless people – Armenians, Jews, Roma, Tutsis – were slaughtered solely because of their ethnic heritage (or their 'blood'). To seek to fortify human society against such atavism requires no justification. It is no surprise, therefore, that the ethnic/civic division has developed great rhetorical significance. Modern nationalists tend to label their own point of view as 'civic'. This is as true of Dafydd Wigley's form of Welsh nationalism and of Gordon

---

37 Pa beth yw cenedl? / Cadw tŷ mewn cwmwl tystion.
38 There is a striking resemblance between Waldo Williams's portrayal of the nation and Ernest Renan's famous discussion in his essay 'Qu'est-ce qu'une nation?' (1882), one of the first attempts to address the concept of the nation in a systematic way. As he sought to crystallise those factors that ensure the continued existence of the nation, Renan employed the metaphor of a 'daily plebiscite'. On this view, without the members of a nation desiring and witnessing its existence, there is no nation: see Ernest Renan, 'What is a nation?', trans. Martin Thom in Geoff Eley and Ronald Grigor Suny (eds), *Becoming National: A Reader* (New York: Oxford University Press, 1996), p. 53.

Brown's form of British nationalism. Wigley is emphatically clear that Plaid Cymru's nationalism is a civic nationalism. Meanwhile Brown, while claiming that British national identity is civic and ultimately progressive in nature, strongly implies that Scottish and by extension Welsh nationalism represent something altogether more regressive.[39]

Whatever the rhetorical uses and abuses of the civic/ethnic classification, and indeed the real analytical value associated with it – clear from Liah Greenfield's influential book, *Nationalism: Five Roads to Modernity* – it is also important to recognise that, in reality, nationalisms are never as simple or as easily corralled. Rather, the overwhelming majority, if not all, forms of nationalism, manifest as a complex mixture of both the civic and the ethnic. Take Scotland, for example, a country that for many represents a classic example of civic nationhood and nationalism. The focus of Scottish national identity is institutional, it is claimed: the foundation of what makes the country different are its historic estates; its educational, legal and religious systems – institutions which flourished despite the union with the Crown and, later, with the English.[40] Yet, even if we aver that this general analysis is correct, one need only spend a short time in Scotland to realise the centrality of ethnic markers to its national life. They are highly visible – often in ways that are strikingly kitsch. And despite the fact that nationalist intellectuals have railed at length against tartanry, the romanticism of the lost cause and so forth, the SNP has not been shy in seeking to turn these Braveheart-ish features to its own advantage.[41]

---

[39] See, inter alia, Dafydd Wigley's remarks in the House of Commons on 8 December 1997 (*Hansard*, column 705): 'We regard all the people who live in Wales as citizens of Wales and all are equal irrespective of race, creed, colour or language. Plaid Cymru is a national party, but our nationalism is a civic nationalism.' For Brown's treatment of Britishness, see the discussion in Richard Wyn Jones, 'On process, events and unintended consequences: national identity and the politics of Welsh devolution', *Scottish Affairs*, 37 (autumn 2001), 34–57.

[40] See, for example, Lindsay Paterson, *The Autonomy of Modern Scotland* (Edinburgh: Edinburgh University Press, 1994) and David McCrone, *Understanding Scotland: The Sociology of a Nation* (London: Routledge, 2001).

[41] For a bracingly scornful example, see Tom Nairn's essay, 'Old and new Scottish nationalism', in his volume, *The Break-up of Britain*, pp. 126–95.

Shifting our attention to Wales, one could easily construct an argument to the effect that Welsh national sentiment is fundamentally ethnic in character. After all, the Welsh language has long been the key marker of Welsh distinctiveness. Given that language is normally considered to be an ethnic characteristic, and that the survival and revival of the language has long been a central concern for the national movement, should not Welsh nationalism therefore be categorised as a form of ethnic nationalism? Yet, it must also be recognised that the creation of Welsh civic institutions has always been one of the principal aims and achievements of Welsh nationalists – a national university, a national library, a national parliament. Would it not be reasonable to argue, therefore, that they are civic nationalists after all? Waters are further muddied when we consider the attitude of avowed British unionists – hence British nationalists – such as Neil Kinnock. Part of the latter's argument against devolution in 1979 was that Welsh nationhood should continue to be a 'matter of hearts and minds, not bricks, committees and bureaucrats'.[42] That is to say, while he had no objection to the continuation of Welshness in its ethnic forms (setting aside for the moment his attitude towards the Welsh language), he opposed giving Welshness civic expression. Who, therefore, are the civic and the ethnic nationalists in the Welsh context? The point is, of course, that there can never be a definitive answer to this question as it is based on an ultimately futile attempt to establish a neat binary division that simply does not exist. While invoking the terms 'civic' and 'ethnic' remains a convenient way of drawing attention to different elements in the make-up of any given expression of nationalism, it is a category error to believe that a hard and fast distinction can be drawn between civic and ethnic nationalisms. Life is rarely that simple and nationalism certainly is not – as both Waldo Williams and T. H. Parry-Williams were aware.

Relatedly, it is also far too glib and simplistic to regard civic nationalism as inherently virtuous and ethnic nationalism as

---

42   See Anon. [Neil Kinnock], *Facts to beat Fantasies: The Detailed Reasons for Voting NO in the March 1st Referendum and Answers to the Claims of the Yesmen and Guessmen* (Labour No Assembly Campaign, 1979), p. 6.

its automatic opposite. American nationalism is a paradigmatic example of civic nationalism, with the very essence of US national identity based on loyalty to constitution and flag. Yet, this is also a society in which racism was – and is – rampant, and a state that colonised and ethnically cleansed the continent's native population and continues to act as an imperial hegemon in global affairs. There is, in short, a world of difference between the inclusive rhetoric of ostensibly civic American nationalism and the reality of the practices with which it is associated. By the same token, neither can there be any justification for an 'in principle' condemnation of every effort to maintain and promote ethnic difference. Should Tibetan nationalists really be blamed for their efforts to draw attention to – and resist – the Beijing government's deliberate policy of transforming the demographic profile of Tibet by encouraging immigrants of Han (Chinese) descent to settle there? Should the people of East Timor be condemned for their ultimately successful resistance to the attempts of the multi-ethnic Indonesian state to eradicate their language after its occupation of their country in 1975? The answers to these questions are surely obvious. By the same token, neither should campaigners for Welsh-language rights be branded as reactionaries on the basis that language is considered by many to be a marker of ethnic identity.[43]

The danger of placing too much weight on labels like 'ethnic' and 'civic' is that it can become a substitute for serious analysis rather than a means for its facilitation. It diverts from the essential political and moral task, which is to look beyond the labels applied to given movements – or the ones which they claim for themselves – and consider critically their ideas and their actions and the consequence thereof. For if the analysis of nationalism presented in this chapter is accurate, it must be accepted also that every type of nationalism is multifaceted. Every national identity, like every form of social identity for that matter, depends on defining a specific person or people as 'other': we know who *we*

[43] I should acknowledge that the view taken here is a little different from the one that I adopted in some previous works which utilised the civic/ethnic framework rather uncritically. Ned Thomas's characteristically wise remarks on the subject ('Never say ethnic: the political culture of devolution', *Planet: The Welsh Internationalist*, 136 (1999), 35–8) served as an important corrective.

are, at least in part, because we believe that *we* are not like *them*. Every form of nationalism appeals to continuity and tradition, and thus looks back while looking forward. Every nationalism draws on the resources of the past and the present, be that in the form of institutional or ethnic connections, to unite and fortify for the future. It need hardly be emphasised that there are dangers inherent in all of this. Those considered to be different from us may also be regarded as being our inferiors – even as barbarous or *Untermensch*. Similarly, while nationalist historiographies generate the romanticised and idealised tea towel versions of national histories routinely used to separate tourists from their money, they can also be used to justify – indeed demand – monstrous behaviour in the here and now.

The creative and constructive possibilities of nationalism go hand in hand with the destructive and detrimental. The danger of any attempt to differentiate between 'good' and 'bad' forms of nationalism at the conceptual level is that we lose sight of the fact that all nationalism is inherently ambiguous. Nairn made the point in his own inimitable style: 'the huge family of nationalisms cannot be divided into the black cats and the white cats, with a few half-breeds in between. The whole family is spotted, without exception.'[44] To acknowledge this point is not of course to imply that that every nationalism is equally problematic or objectionable. Such an argument would be both illogical and ahistorical. It does, however, signal the need for watchfulness.

Scholars and other analysts must avoid adopting analytical frameworks that oversimplify or otherwise smooth out the contradictions of nationalism. Even more importantly, perhaps, politicians as well as citizens need to be wary of the dangers inherent in nationalism. The evidence collated in this volume demonstrates that Plaid Cymru's leaders have always been aware of what we

[44] Nairn, *Break-up of Britain*, pp. 347–8. Unfortunately, it seems that Nairn was to lose sight of the implications of this all-important insight. In an essay in *Faces of Nationalism* (1997) he presented a more reassuring image of the evolution of nationalism suggesting that the emphasis on the ethnic was some kind of historical aberration and that nationalism was becoming more civic in character ('From civil society to civic nationalism: evolutions of a myth', pp. 73–89). For once, Nairn was guilty of over-simplifying.

might term the duality of nationalism and have sought to rein in its destructive potential. Saunders Lewis asserted that 'Welsh nationalism is a Christian, moderate and conditional nationalism'.[45] While the commitment to Christianity has waned in an increasingly secular Wales, nonetheless a balance has continued to be struck between an emphasis on the national community and the rights of individuals, on the one hand, and the demands of humanity, on the other. Indeed, as will become apparent, it has been regularly argued that it is *only* through its contribution to the life of the individual as well as humanity as a whole that nationalism can ever be justified. Nevertheless, only the blindest of optimists could believe that the situation in Wales could not deteriorate if its nationalists – be they Welsh or British nationalists – choose to think and act differently.

National movements

The term 'British nationalism' is one that remains awkwardly unfamiliar to most. While we are all long accustomed to hearing about Welsh and Scottish nationalism, British nationalism is seldom mentioned except, perhaps, in the context of the thuggish British National Party. Certainly, leaders like Tony Blair, Gordon Brown and Margaret Thatcher are very rarely referred to as British nationalists, despite the ways in which the rhetoric of 'the nation' permeates their speeches and public pronouncements. Thus, even while insisting on the political relevance of Welsh nationhood and arguing that Wales should have equal status with other countries are both regarded as examples of Welsh nationalism, regarding Britain and Britishness in a similar way are seldom regarded as manifestations of British nationalism. This even as both Labour and Conservative politicians continually seek to rally 'the nation', 'our nation' or 'this nation of ours' to achieve some purpose or other (to create a new spirit of entrepreneurship,

---

[45] '[C]enedlaetholdeb Cristnogol, cymedrol ac amodol ydy cenedlaetholdeb Cymreig': Saunders Lewis, *Cymru Wedi'r Rhyfel* (Aberystwyth: Gwasg Aberystwyth, 1942), p. 21.

to create a new country, to fight terror and so on); and despite the fact that politicians of both major parties never tire of calling in aid 'the national interest' while insisting that Britain should enjoy a leading role in European and global politics. On the theoretical level, it is impossible to justify using the term nationalism in the Welsh context without equally acknowledging its presence in the British. But of course, this is not how it works in everyday discourse. Understanding why this is the case – why the popular and indeed scholarly treatment of Welsh and British nationalisms tends to be so different – is key if we are to recognise the role and significance of nationalism in modern society.

In Britain, British nationalism enjoys 'common sense' status (this is not true across the United Kingdom as a whole: Northern Ireland is different). Its fundamental assumptions – that Britain is a nation, and that it is therefore 'natural' for it to be the pre-eminent political unit for its population – are considered so obvious as to be beyond argument. Michael Billig called this type of nationalism 'banal nationalism' – nationalism that has permeated so deeply into the life of society that the members of that society are hardly aware of its existence. In this discussion of the particularities and peculiarities of banal nationalism in Britain and the United States, Billig notices how, '[i]n so many little ways, the citizenry are reminded of their national place in the world of nations. However, this reminding is so familiar, so continual, that it is not consciously registered as reminding.'[46] Generally speaking, the nationalism of established, stable states is the world of the small, unremarkable things. It is the world of the possessive pronoun – *our* country, *our* people, *our* nation; the world of sports coverage – again, '*our* hopes in the Olympic games this year'. It is the world of the familiar lines of borders on the TV weather map. The world of the barely noticed flag flying above a public building (the central image of Billig's study). It is only on specific occasions – at times of national celebrations or, of course, international tension – that it all becomes more

46   Michael Billig, *Banal Nationalism* (London: Sage, 1995), p. 8.

self-conscious. Otherwise, this form of nationalism is simply the taken-for-granted backdrop to daily life.

Whatever their other differences, the preconceptions of British nationalism are common ground for the overwhelming majority of politicians, commentators and citizens. For them, Britain Was, Britain Is, Britain Will Be. The same is true for the politics and society of France, Sweden, Mexico and so on. Nationalism is the foundation for modern-day politics across the global. As O'Leary correctly notes: 'The claim can be made ... that self-professedly modern political doctrines, liberal, socialist or conservative are parasitic upon nationalist assumptions; and that the political success of these doctrines in argument and political struggle rests upon these assumptions.'[47] With the possible exception of anarchism, in the modern era every political ideology, and most certainly every successful political ideology, operates with rather than against the grain of nationalism.[48] The most important boundary of political organisation reflects nationalist presumptions; the same presumptions shape political rhetoric. Modern politics is national and nationalist.

British nationalism's 'common sense' status is a measure of its power. Its hegemonic status is underlined by the fact that while members of the national parties in Wales and Scotland are labelled 'nationalists' – a term with negative connotations in the minds of many – the designation is almost never applied to leaders or members of British political parties. Britishness is the norm; part of the natural order of things. Only those eccentrics – or worse – who seek to challenge its hegemonic, common-sense status are obliged to justify themselves. Many have grappled with the task of explaining how a particular set of ideas or presumptions have come to shape and determine a society's views so fully that they

47 O'Leary, 'Ernest Gellner's diagnoses of nationalism', p. 67.
48 It might well be argued that the only non-national ideology to gain a foothold in twentieth-century Wales was the revolutionary syndicalism that inspired the authors of *The Miners' Next Step*. Yet, in the writings of Niclas y Glais (T. E. Nicholas) from the same era, syndicalist ideas are linked to Welsh nationalist aspirations. See, inter alia, 'Y ddraig goch a'r faner goch: cenedlaetholdeb a sosialaeth', *Y Genhinen* (January 1912), 10–15 and 'Gornest Llafur a chyfalaf', *Y Genhinen* (April 1912), 123–7. In Niclas's view, at least, there was no contradiction between his revolutionary beliefs and his nationalism.

become accepted at the subconscious level as part of the natural order of things. One of the shrewdest was Antonio Gramsci.

As a revolutionary, Gramsci was interested not only in how some ideas become hegemonic, to the point where they embed themselves and attain the status of common sense, but also in those processes that can lead to the undermining of one hegemony and the establishment of another in its place. Gwyn A. Williams's brilliant essay on 'The Sardinian Marxist and Wales' crisis' provides a comprehensive account of Gramsci's ideas on these issues.[49] In the present context, we need only touch on two aspects: first, the importance he places on the role of intellectuals in the process of creating and re-creating hegemony; and secondly, his emphasis on the way that the ideational and the material combine (in the form of what he calls an 'historic bloc') in order to successfully create and sustain a particular hegemonic order.[50]

As veins are to blood, so are intellectuals to ideas: it is via intellectuals that ideas permeate society. Crucial for understanding Gramsci's analysis is to recognise that he considered that the category of 'intellectual' encompasses a much broader group than is commonly imagined. It is not only those perched in university 'ivory towers' that should be considered as playing the social function of intellectuals – which in broad terms means playing an educative leadership role in shaping and driving public opinion, values and actions. Rather, teachers and journalists, broadcasters and health visitors, poets and politicians, as well as the holders of a wide array of other roles, should also all be regarded as intellectuals. The majority reproduce the 'governing' ideas of

---

[49] Gwyn A. Williams, 'Marcsydd o Sardiniwr ac argyfwng Cymru', *Efrydiau Athronyddol*, 47 (1984), 16–27. The essay reflects the historian's life-long interest in Gramsci's life and ideas, an interest which surfaces regularly throughout his work. He focuses specifically on Gramsci in the aforementioned essay as well as in 'The concept of *Egemonia* in the thought of Antonio Gramsci: some notes on interpretation', *Journal of the History of Ideas*, 21 (4) (1960), 586–99, and *Proletarian Order: Antonio Gramsci, Factory Councils and the Origins of Italian Communism, 1911–1921* (London: Pluto Press, 1975), but the influence of Gramsci's thinking permeates Williams's masterpiece *When was Wales? A History of the Welsh* (London: Penguin, 1985).

[50] Antonio Gramsci, *Selections from the Prison Notebooks*, ed. and trans. Quintin Hoare and Geoffrey Nowell Smith (London: Lawrence and Wishart, 1971), pp. 5–23, 323–77.

the day, doing so quite unconsciously. That is to say that they do not support a particular social arrangement or other as the result of a considered decision. The reality is rather more mundane. Consider, for example, one of the means whereby Britishness is presented (and reproduced) as representing part of the natural order. Sports commentators and correspondents do not naturalise a sense of belonging to or identification with Britishness as part of some deliberate strategy – or just to annoy the nationalists of the Celtic fringe! They are rather merely repeating and thus, in turn, reinforcing, the common-sense assumptions that have influenced them.

But in addition to playing a key role in sustaining hegemony, intellectuals also play a central role in the process of undermining one hegemony and its replacement with another. Through gradual, incremental activity, intellectuals committed to different ideas and values or to a particular cohort within society – be that a social class or a national group – can undermine the naturalised, common-sense status of a current hegemony. That can in turn open the door to its replacement by their own 'anti-hegemonic' position. It is important to note that the emphasis here is on the possibility of such a development. There is nothing inevitable about it. History is replete with examples of intellectuals working hard to install alternative ideas that have never managed to acquire hegemonic status. To understand why some of these attempts succeed and others fail, we need to turn to the inter-relationship between the ideational and the material.

Gramsci used the term 'historic bloc' to refer to the combination of cultural-moral and political-economic leadership that, in his view, is the basis of any successful hegemony. To be influential, an ideology must promote the political-economic interests of a specific section of society. It will only become a hegemonic force if there is some more or less credible way of presenting it as being of benefit to society as a whole. If on the other hand, ideas are regarded as undermining (perceived) material interests, then no matter how attractive they may otherwise be, they will have little or no influence. The relevance of these observations becomes clear as we now turn from considering nationalism in its 'banal' form, to deliberate efforts to promote nationalism amongst stateless nations. In other words, to the politics of national movements.

The development of national movements
Through his comparative studies of national movements amongst the stateless peoples of nineteenth-century Europe, Miroslav Hroch developed a typology for their development that has since been accepted by scholars as varied as Eric Hobsbawm, Tom Nairn and John Davies.[51] Hroch distinguishes between three phases in the activity of every national movement, phases to which he refers in his characteristically utilitarian way as Phases A, B and C. Phase A is characterised by scholarly activity: in this period, knowledge is collated and a narrative is developed about the linguistic, cultural, social, economic and historical character-istics of the national group, generating a foundation on which a more extensive national consciousness may be developed. In the Welsh context, the Morrises of Ynys Môn and Iolo Morganwg can be regarded as key figures in this phase. The foundation laid down in Phase A is built on in Phase B, as efforts are made to dis-perse national consciousness and sentiment throughout the gen-eral population, with intellectuals (in the wider Gramscian sense) playing a central role in the evangelising work. Emrys ap Iwan and Michael D. Jones may be regarded as all-important figures in the Welsh national movement's Phase B. Phase C develops once a substantial proportion of the target population begins to feel and emphasise the significance of their national identity – this is when nationalism develops into a truly mass phenomenon; this is when it becomes a hegemonic force.

There is nothing inevitable about the success of a national movement. Indeed, only after reaching Phase C can it be said that the future of the nation in question is secure. Before that, there is

---

51 Hroch, *The Social Precondition of National Revival*; E. J. Hobsbawm, 'Some reflections on nationalism', in T. J. Nossiter, A. H. Hanson and Stein Rokkan (eds), *Imagination and Precision in the Social Sciences: Essays in Memory of Peter Nettl* (London: Faber and Faber, 1972), pp. 385–406; Hobsbawm, *Nations and Nationalism since 1780*, pp. 11–12; Nairn, *The Break-up of Britain*, pp. 81–113; John Davies, *Hanes Cymru* (London: Allen Lane, 1990), pp. 400–1.

a real possibility that the prospective nation ends up as little more than regional 'colour' within a larger nation. As Hroch makes clear: 'We know of several cases in which the national movement remained in Phase B for a long time, sometimes down to the present'; amongst them he notes Wales and Brittany.[52] When discussing cases like these, Hroch claims that the failure of attempts to move to Phase C reflects a failure to link the national project with a credible political/economic programme.

> Where the national movement in Phase B was not capable of introducing into national agitation, and articulating in national terms, the interests of the specific classes and groups which constituted the small nation, it was not capable of attaining success. An agitation carried on under the exclusive banner of language, national literature or ... history, folklore and so on, could not by itself bring the popular strata under the patriotic banner: the road from Phase B to Phase C was closed off.[53]

Which is to say that the failure of a national movement to ensure that the bulk of their 'co-nationals' share the same aspirations, is a reflection, in its turn, of the failure to combine the ideational and material in a successful 'historic bloc'. Without this, there is no prospect of the national consciousness that they are seeking to promote attaining hegemonic status and, eventually, morphing into the 'banal' common sense nationalism characteristic of stable states.

To be clear, use of the world 'failure' in this context is not tantamount to blaming the leaders and members of a particular national movement for their national project's inability to attain the promised land of national revival. Although their ideas and activities undoubtedly impact the prospect for their cause – sometimes in critical ways, as was possibly the case in Brittany – context

---

[52] Hroch, 'Real and constructed', p. 98. The establishment of the National Assembly for Wales in 1999 can be construed as confirmation that Wales finally attained Phase C. Even so, Hroch's judgement was correct in relation to the nineteenth century – the period under consideration in his work – as well as for most of the twentieth century, for that matter.

[53] Hroch, *The Social Preconditions of National Revival*, pp. 185–6.

and circumstance also play a fateful role. 'Man makes history, but not in circumstances of his own choosing.' Sometimes, they overwhelm even the most capable and committed. For Hroch, the precise location of the relevant prospective nation in the broader modernisation process is crucial. In particular, he differentiates between three historical periods – Periods 1, 2 and 3 – emphasising societal characteristics rather than dates per se, given that the various processes to which he draws attention happened at different times in different places.

Period 1 is the early modern period characterised by the struggle against absolutism, the bourgeois revolution and the development of capitalism. Period 2 emerges after the triumph of capitalism as a socio-economic system. One of the key features of this period is the growth of the working class. Hroch also refers to a third period, one characterised by global integration both in terms of the economy and the means of mass communication. In his view, this period post-dates the First World War. Given that his focus is on the nineteenth century, he does not therefore engage with Period 3 in his own analysis of national movements. But in principle, of course, there is nothing to prevent us from doing so – especially if we conclude that there are good reasons to believe that all-important aspects of Wales's economic life had reached Period 3 status well before the Great War.

Overlaying his schema for the phases that characterise the development of national movements onto these different periods in the process of modernisation, Hroch undertakes a comparative study of the development of European national movements, seeking to identify common patterns and, ultimately, explain why some movements succeeded while others failed. This resulting discussion is rich and suggestive, and it will not be possible to do it justice in the confines of the present study. Nonetheless, it is worth dwelling on one of his most important conclusions because of its obvious relevance to our present purposes.

Hroch's study shows how difficult it was for those national movements that attained Phase B after the beginning of Period 2 to then push on successfully and reach Phase C. Why? Because in these circumstances, nationalists struggled to (successfully) link the material interests of their target audience to the national cause they were seeking to promote. Instead, class politics tended to take root, offering an alternative route for promulgating and achieving material benefits; a route that was rather different from the one that nationalists were seeking to traverse. The importance of class politics in twentieth-century Wales confirms that we were not an exception to this general pattern. This is further confirmed by the more sophisticated discussions of the demise of the Cymru Fydd movement which stress the class as well as the national dimensions to its failure.[54] As will become apparent in the remainder of this study, Plaid Cymru in turn has experienced great difficulty in rendering its national vision for the future of the country relevant to the daily lives of its inhabitants.

That said, Hroch's analytical framework raises an issue pertinent to the Welsh case that he does not directly address in his own work. Hroch's main focus is on successful national movements. He gives no serious consideration to those cases – like Wales – where Phase B in the development of the national movement becomes very elongated. But, surely, in such cases it is likely that the 'achievements' of Phase A will begin to be eroded by the alternative understanding of the national past that support the dominant state nationalism? As a result, the national movement in question will necessarily need to devote significant energy and attention in trying to re-establish – or at best defend – the claim that a nation exists at the sub-state level. Which is to say that a long, drawn-out extended Phase B might well mean that a national movement will find itself engaging with the type of activities that, in Hroch's schema, are characteristic of Phase A. If this suggestion is correct, then it illuminates one of the more arresting features of Plaid Cymru's intellectual activity during Saunders Lewis's and Gwynfor Evans's leadership periods, namely its insistent emphasis on claiming that Wales is a nation and – relatedly – its consistent efforts to try to increase awareness of Wales's literary and

---

[54] Emyr Wynn Williams, 'The politics of Welsh home rule 1886–1929: a sociological analysis' (PhD thesis, University of Wales, Aberystwyth, 1986). Also, Dewi Rowland Hughes, 'Y coch a'r gwyrdd, Cymru Fydd a'r mudiad Llafur Cymreig (1886–1896)', *Llafur*, 6 (4) (1994), 60–79.

cultural traditions as a means of redeeming that claim. For while a strong historiographical emphasis is characteristic of nationalist thought, this seems to have been particularly pronounced in the case of Plaid Cymru. This not only because of the character and temperament of the leaders involved, but because the (relative) absence of Welsh national institutions and structures – and a resulting lack of awareness of Welsh history – meant that it could not be taken for granted that the necessary foundations (Phase A) were in place for the development of the national party.

The ideology of national movements

The scholarly discussion of nationalism and national movements exhibits a striking paradox. On the one hand, it is generally accepted that intellectuals play a central role in the growth of nationalism. In terms of Hroch's phases, Phase A of any national movement is in essence all about scholarly activity. Scholars, and in particular those studying the humanities – be they historians, linguists, literary specialists, archaeologists, collectors of folk literature, sociologists, anthropologists, and so on – establish the foundations of a national narrative. Hroch's own empirical studies demonstrate that intellectuals played a central role in Phase B of the development of national movements in stateless nations across Europe. It is certainly the case that the most prominent figures associated with Phase B of the national movement in Wales – Michael D. Jones, Emrys ap Iwan and T. E. Ellis – were intellectuals in the broad sense of that term. Yet, at the same time, there is also something of a consensus in the relevant literature that there is little intellectual substance to nationalist thought. Benedict Anderson's verdict, for example, is that nationalism is characterised by 'philosophical poverty and even incoherence'.[55] He is far from alone in this judgement.

How is it that movements in which intellectuals play such a prominent role have, to all appearances, produced so little of intellectual substance? Hobsbawm's characteristically disdainful judgement is that nationalism was promoted by second- or

---

[55] Anderson, *Imagined Communities*, p. 5.

third-rate intellectuals – 'the lesser-examination passing class-es'.[56] It should therefore come as little surprise that they pro-duced so little of value. This view stands in stark contrast to that of Brendan O'Leary who argues that we are faced with a mis-understanding – a category error – rather than a paradox. What Anderson and others of like mind have failed to appreciate is that some of the foremost political thinkers of the Western tradi-tion were in fact nationalists. O'Leary refers specifically to Jean-Jacques Rousseau, Edmund Burke, J. S. Mill, Friedrich List and Max Weber as thinkers of incontrovertible stature who should all be regarded as 'nationalist grand thinkers'.[57] Given his emphasis on analysing and understanding the history and culture of differ-ent societies, and the need for the work of revolutionaries with the grain of these national particularities, there is a case for add-ing Gramsci's name to this list.[58] While he may indeed have cast off the Sardinian nationalism of his teens, there is no doubt that he continued to experience the gravitational pull of the nation for the remainder of his life.[59]

O'Leary is surely right to draw our attention to the centrality of nationalist assumptions and presumptions to the ideas of some of the most prominent political thinkers. He is also substantially correct in his diagnosis of why this has not been more generally recognised. He argues that the failure to treat nationalist thought with the respect that it merits is a reflection in turn of the prej-udices of (so-called) cosmopolitan observers who refuse to take seriously ideas aimed at narrower, more 'parochial' audiences.[60] Hobsbawm's sneering dismissal encapsulates and exemplifies this attitude. But this is not the whole story either. There is more than simple prejudice at work here and understanding the other

56   Hobsbawm, *Nations and Nationalism since 1780*, p. 118.
57   O'Leary, 'Ernest Gellner's diagnoses of nationalism', p. 87 n.; see also pp. 66–71.
58   For a suggestive observation to this effect see Roman Szporluk, 'Thoughts about change: Ernest Gellner and the history of nationalism', in Hall (ed.), *The State of the Nation*, p. 33. Even if we resist the conclusion that Gramsci was a na-tionalist thinker, there is no denying the nationalism of Irishman James Connolly.
59   Giuseppe Fiori, *Antonio Gramsci: Life of a Revolutionary*, trans. Tom Nairn (London: Verso, 1990).
60   O'Leary, 'Ernest Gellner's diagnoses of nationalism', p. 68.

reasons that help explain the failure to recognise the importance of nationalism within the canon of western political thought also helps draw our attention to some of the most significant features of nationalist-inflected political thinking.

There can surely be no doubt that thinkers listed by O'Leary are considered among the pantheon of the greats. But setting aside their nationalism for a moment, what exactly is the common ground between them? Burke the conservative philosopher, Rousseau the proto-Socialist and Mill the Liberal hero; Mill the early feminist and Rousseau who regarded women as fundamentally inferior; Rousseau the romantic and Weber who unmasked the process of rationalisation that characterises modernity; Burke who would rather the poor wretches of Speenhamland be allowed to starve than see his laissez-faire principles undermined, and List with his emphasis on governmental interventionism in order to secure a healthy economy? Frankly, very little. Needless to say, if Gramsci – or Connolly – is added to their number, then the differences between them only multiplies and any common ground appears even more illusory.

This serves to draw our attention to two, inter-related points. First, most political ideologies exist in symbiotic relationship with nationalism. Which is to say that most political ideologies – and certainly, the overwhelming majority of successful ones – take the presumptions of nationalism for granted. This, in turn, reflects the way in which these presumptions have become part of the 'natural' order of things in the modern era. In general terms, it is accepted that it is the 'nation' that establishes the boundaries for the most significant political community. Different ideologies compete for influence within these boundaries. In this sense, and in the modern era at least, the struggle for ideological supremacy is a competition between different forms of nationalism – liberal nationalism, conservative nationalism, social-democratic nationalism and, in practice if not always in theory, Marxist nationalism.[61] All this has far-reaching implications as we move from

[61] The academic debate concerning 'liberal nationalism' has helped illuminate this key point. See, for example, Yael Tamir, *Liberal Nationalism* (Princeton: Princeton University Press, 1993).

the abstract level to a more concrete consideration of Welsh politics. For it should be apparent that – analytically speaking – it is
unhelpful to think of ideological contention in Wales as a case of
socialism vs conservatism vs liberalism vs nationalism. Rather we
find different combinations of socialism and nationalism competing with different combinations of conservatism and nationalism,
and so forth. The dramatis personae include those who are both
socialists and British nationalists, such as Ness Edwards and Neil
Kinnock, and others who are socialists and Welsh nationalists,
like Phil Williams and Dafydd Elis-Thomas. We find (some) conservative Welsh nationalists like Saunders Lewis and many more
conservative British nationalists, for example Nicholas Edwards.
No matter the rhetoric, few if any have reached the stage while
adopting a completely non-nationalist standpoint – and certainly
no one of significant import.

The second point follows on directly from this. Nationalism
cannot be regarded as a complete political ideology in its own
right.[62] While establishing the boundaries of a political community is of course of fundamental importance, this does not in itself
provide guidance on political questions such as the appropriate
level of income tax, how to organise and finance higher education, whether or not hunting with dogs should be allowed, and
so on. Yet nationalist parties, which are key to making the leap
between Phase B and Phase C, cannot avoid adopting a stance
on these matters. This not only because so much day-to-day
political discourse revolves around these questions, but – more
fundamentally – because nationalism's ability to become a mass
force depends on the ability of its advocates to link their national
project to some sort of socio-economic transformation that is perceived to be beneficial by a significant proportion of the population. Ultimately, a nationalist party has no option but to develop a
position on such matters, even when it might prefer not to.

Acknowledging that every national movement is a combination of nation-specific elements as well as other ideas and ideals

---

[62] This notwithstanding the fact that various nationalists, Welsh nationalists
among them, have sought to claim otherwise – as discussed in the following chapters.

(ideologies) means acknowledging that each case is *sui generis*. There is no means of creating a single, all-encompassing account of the political thinking of national movements. Viewed from a theoretical perspective, we must expect that different national movements vary just as much as the various 'nationalist grand thinkers'. Further, we should also expect substantial variation within the different movements themselves. Having said that, it remains possible to draw out several common features that characterise the nation-specific elements of the thinking of national movements. It is helpful to enumerate those before we begin to focus more specifically on the political thought of Plaid Cymru.

According to Anthony Smith, the nationalist credo contains three central elements.[63] The first is an emphasis on the *unity* of the national territory; an emphasis on the need to treat that territory as an organisational unit along with an associated tendency to argue that the presumed unity of the nation transcends other divisions, be they class, linguistic, cultural, geographic, urban-rural or other divisions. This element of nationalist thinking is epitomised in one of the slogans of Cymru Fydd, the late nineteenth-century national movement that preceded Plaid Cymru: 'Cymru'n Un' (Wales as One).[64] It has remained a constant theme in the rhetoric of its successor.

The second element of Smith's trinity is the emphasis on national identity. Nationalists tend to lay great stress on those elements of a nation's identity that they believe are constant features throughout the various twists and turns that will inevitably affect any people and territory. It is these which serve to link its past, present and future. This is an argument that tends to presuppose that a nation has its own distinctive characteristics. In the case of stateless nations, this is accompanied by the belief that these characteristics are being smothered or diluted as a result of the domination of a larger nation (and its state). In Wales, for example, our 'radical tradition' has often been held to be the political manifestation of our national character which will only be fully expressed

---

63   Anthony D. Smith, *Nationalism* (Cambridge: Polity, 2001), p. 9; also pp. 24–8.
64   Dewi Rowland Hughes, *Cymru Fydd* (Caerdydd: Gwasg Prifysgol Cymru, 2006).

through the attainment of self-government. Thus, according to Lloyd George during his time as a Welsh nationalist, 'were self-government conceded to the people of Wales she would be a model to the nationalities of the earth of a people who have driven oppression from her hillsides and initiated the glorious reign of freedom, justice and truth'.[65] As his words suggest, the emphasis on national self-government completes the trinity. This is the belief that the nation, and only the nation, has the legitimate right to decide how it should be governed. National movements usually favour the creation of a national sovereign state for their nation, although there are examples where they have supported less far-reaching forms of self-government, including federalism or devolution.

History – or to be precise, historiography – is the main weapon utilised by nationalists to assert their nation's identity and unity, and to establish the foundations of their claim to its autonomy. In his various discussions of nationalists' attitude to history, Tom Nairn regularly refers to the Roman god Janus.[66] Janus is a two-faced god that faces in two directions at once. The same is true of nationalism (the 'modern Janus' according to Nairn). Nationalism calls on the resources of the past to prepare the ground for living in the future. That is the whole point of nationalist historiography: it emphasises continuity and significance of the nation's memory as a means of uniting, strengthening and surviving though the whirlpools and eddies of uneven development. To accuse nationalists of 'living in the past' is therefore to completely miss the point. Even if an element of eccentricity and downright crankism appears to manifest in every form of nationalism and in all national movements, and is particularly apparent in context of claims and beliefs about the nation's history, it is not for its own sake that history is important to nationalists. Rather, the past is relevant because of its indispensable contribution to the future.[67] Nationalism does not live in the past, it rather uses

---

65 Quoted in Hughes, *Cymru Fydd*, p. 103.
66 See Nairn, *Break-up of Britain*, pp. 317–50, and *Faces of Nationalism*, *passim*.
67 A similar point was made by Gellner, in the language of classical sociology. Nationalism, he said, adopts the phraseology of the *Gemeinschaft* in order to create a *Gesellschaft*.

the past to inhabit the present and build for the future. It is an attitude and approach encapsulated in another of the slogans dear to late nineteenth-century Welsh nationalists, 'Cymru Fu, Cymru Sydd, Cymru Fydd' (Wales Was, Wales Is, Wales Will Be).

There is no doubt that the national narrative established by nationalist historiography presents only a fragmented, incomplete picture of the history of 'the nation'. As Renan noted, a successful national story relies on forgetting as well as remembering.[68] Indeed, as the historian R. F. Foster demonstrates in a particularly suggestive account of nationalist historiography in nineteenth-century Ireland, in the hands of nationalists history tends to mimic the structure of fairy tales.[69] Nor can it be denied that exaggeration, self-deception, fabrication and even downright lies have also featured in nationalist historiography – especially before history developed the kind of disciplinary standards that have served to curb such behaviour.[70] This is not to suggest, however, that nationalist historiography is necessarily more prone to the phoney and the deceptive than any other form of historiography. Karl Klaus defined historians of all kinds as prophets facing backwards.[71] This striking image draws our attention to one of the characteristics of historical writing recognised by most authorities on the subject, namely that *any* historical narrative connecting and attributing significance to past events is bound to reflect the worldview of the historian and, more generally, those of the present day. It is unavoidable; 'objectivity' in any simple definition of that word is impossible. In the words of Alun Llywelyn-Williams, we are 'ourselves inevitably a part of history ... In the end, therefore, no matter how objective our

---

[68] 'The essence of a nation is that all its individuals have many things in common, and also that everybody has forgotten many things': Renan, 'What is a nation?', p. 45.

[69] Foster relies on the Russian literary critic Vladimir Propp's analysis of such stories: see R. F. Foster, *The Irish Story: Telling Tales and Making It Up in Ireland* (London: Penguin, 2002), pp. 4–8.

[70] Thus, Renan's additional observation, 'Forgetting, I would even go so far as to say historical error, is a crucial factor in the creation of a nation ...': Renan, 'What is a nation?', p. 45.

[71] Quoted in James Wood, 'Bobbery', *London Review of Books*, 20 February 2003, 13.

attitude may be, all history will be an interpretation of the past ... and it cannot be other than this.'[72]

Historiography is, therefore, a crucial element of the thought of those national movements that, like Plaid Cymru, seek to enter the 'final' Phase by overthrowing the official national narrative embodied in and made banal through the institutions of the state from which they are trying to gain freedom. For this reason, it will form a recurring theme throughout this book. Another aspect of the discourse on nationalism discussed here – again, an aspect which seems to be a common feature of every national movement – is the emphasis placed on other nations as an example either of what the nation could become if it adopts the nationalists' preferred solutions, or its fate if it does not.

One of the accusations heard most frequently about nationalists is that they are 'parochial'. There are few accusations with less substance. The empirical evidence demonstrates that nationalist leaders and thinkers are, more often than not, people with direct knowledge – both biographical and intellectual – of the wider world beyond their nation. Hroch's studies demonstrate that the patriotic activities of national movements during Phase B of their development tend to be centred on the 'most market-oriented parts of the territory occupied by the oppressed nationality'.[73] Wales was no exception to this general pattern. Nationalist thinkers thus tend to be acutely conscious of the reality of 'uneven development' even if they do not necessarily use this specific terminology describe it. The example of other nations is also an all-important means, not only of imaging a better future for their nation within this process, but of trying to communicate that vision to a wider audience.

The model chosen as an appropriate example for the nation to follow – the exemplary nation, so to speak – reflects the wider values and beliefs of the nationalists concerned. Which is to say that there are many possible nations that the 'subjugated' nation might seek to emulate, and one of the principal factors influencing

[72] Alun Llywelyn-Williams, *Nes Na'r Hanesydd? Ysgrifau Llenyddol* (Dinbych: Gwasg Gee), p. 12; translation.
[73] Hroch, *The Social Preconditions of National Revival*, p. 172.

the choice between them is precisely the type of economic and social policies and values they are regarded as embodying. For example, as will be discussed in more detail in the second volume of this study, while left-wing thinkers within Plaid Cymru pointed regularly towards Scandinavian countries as an example of what the Wales of the future might become, those of a different ideological disposition looked in other directions.

As we consider the role of other nations in the ideational matrix of national movements, we return once more to the Janus-like nature of nationalist thought. Nationalist ideology not only uses history as a resource in the present and for the future. It also looks beyond the nation's borders to discover examples which might assist in triggering a national 'awakening' within them. Two faces, then, looking backwards and forwards both through space and time.

Following this general discussion on the nature of nationalism and national movements, we must now consider the specific politico-economic context that has formed Welsh nationalism and within which it has sought to manoeuvre. Specifically, we shall turn our attention to the nature of that remarkable and unique state of which Wales is a part, namely the United Kingdom of Great Britain and Northern Ireland.

Wales – in the shadow of the firstborn

'For Wales, see England.' The familiar words of one of the entries in the 1888 edition of the *Encyclopaedia Britannica*; words that have enraged many a proud Welsh person during the intervening period. What is less well known is that those readers who turned to the entry on England would not have received much by way of enlightenment there either, since it contained next to no information about Wales.[74] Wales was belittled, patronised and then ignored. In this respect, the attitude of the editors of the *Encyclopaedia* can

[74] I owe this observation to John Davies.

be seen as emblematic of an attitude towards Wales and the Welsh that has been perpetuated within sections of the English elite (in particular) to this day. Nevertheless, the uncomfortable truth is that it is also a phrase that contains within it a kernel of truth. Very little in the political, social and, indeed, cultural history of this place can be understood without reference to its relationship with our neighbour to the east. The relationship with England, multi-layered in its complexity but, above all, profoundly unequal, is key to understanding the formation of modern-day Wales.

Wales is hardly alone in this regard. Indeed, if the account of the development of the modern world sketched in this chapter is correct, we cannot hope to understand the condition of *any* people without understanding their relationships with other populations around them. This is obviously the case for those small nations living in the shadow of larger and more powerful neighbours. Catalunya, for example, cannot be understood without engaging with its relationship with France and Spain, and to get to grips with Finland requires an appreciation of its relationship with Russia and Sweden. But the argument is equally relevant for the great powers themselves. In an international order in which everything is interconnected and interdependent – even while some are more dependent than others – we cannot separate the story of any given country from its relationship with others. That means that to understand a France, a Spain or a Russia, we need to locate each within a complex web of wider political, economic and cultural relationships.

What makes Wales's position special is not its status as a small nation lurking in the shadows of a much larger country, but, rather, the singularity of England and the British state. England is no ordinary nation; neither does Britishness constitute a conventional sense of national identity.[75] It is also undeniably the case that the British state has certain characteristics that set it apart from other developed states. These characteristics stem, above all, from the fact that, in terms of modernisation, England was

---

[75] For an in-depth discussion of national identities in England see Ailsa Henderson and Richard Wyn Jones, *Englishness: The political force transforming British politics* (Oxford: Oxford University Press, 2021).

the firstborn.[76] It was in England that nationalism first took root. The English state was the first to begin to take on the form of a recognisably modern state. And it was in England that a modern capitalist economy first became successfully embedded. This precedence had an enormous influence on the development of England/Britain, and in its wake has driven and coloured the entire Welsh experience.

The nature of the British state, together with the social order that it supports, has been the subject of particularly lively intellectual debate reaching back to the early 1960s. That was when a group of left-wing intellectuals associated with the journal *New Left Review* began to use ideas and concepts that were (then) largely alien to the British intellectual tradition to interrogate the economic, political and cultural foundations of that same tradition. The originality of the 'Nairn-Anderson' thesis – so-called after its main proponents, Tom Nairn and Perry Anderson – lay in the fact that it traced the causes of Britain's contemporary economic and social malaise back to the economic and social roots of the early modern state.[77] While many at the time rejected their analysis, nevertheless, as the country's problems became ever more apparent, its general form – if not all of its specific contents – became influential across the political spectrum. Even right-wing observers began to recognise that the origins of Britain's problems were to be found somewhere deep in the entrails of its society and governing system.[78] More latterly, discussions of

76   This is a deliberate echo of the title of Liah Greenfeld's chapter on England in *Nationalism*: 'God's firstborn: England', pp. 27–87.

77   Anderson's original contributions were republished – with revisions and a further discussion – in his *English Questions* (London: Verso, 1992). See the preface as well as chapters 1 and 4, in particular. Nairn's most muscular statement of the thesis is to be found in the first chapter ('The twilight of the British state') of *Break-up of Britain*. Nairn's discussion of the nature of Labourism is also of fundamental importance (see 'The nature of the Labour Party (Part I)', *New Left Review*, 27 (September/October 1964), 38–65 and 'The Nature of the Labour Party (Part II)', *New Left Review*, 28 (November/December 1964), 38–62) as well as his discussion of the monarchy in *Enchanted Glass: Britain and its Monarchy* (London: Vintage, 1994).

78   Martin J. Weiner, *English Culture and the Decline of the Industrial Spirit, 1850–1980* (Cambridge: Cambridge University Press, 1981) and Corelli Barnett, *The Audit of War: The Illusion and Reality of Britain as a Great Nation* (London: Macmillan, 1986) are perhaps the most influential of these studies.

English and British identity have begun to multiply – which may well be read as a sign of the considerable uncertainty that has arisen as the previously self-evident Greatness of Britain has ever more obviously been called into question by the European integration and devolution processes.[79]

Even so, there is little in the abundant literature of recent decades to compare with the breadth and depth of the Nairn-Anderson analysis. Theirs is a body of work that traverses a very wide terrain ranging from the nature of capitalism in Britain and the characteristics of England's intellectual culture, to the distinctive features of 'Labourism' (their term for the governing ideology of the Labour Party and the British Labour movement) and the role of the monarchy in modern Britain. Almost every aspect offers insights relevant to those who would better understand Wales. In the present context, however, we can do no more than draw attention to a few points that are of direct relevance to the development of the Welsh national movement. Our starting point is the maintenance of Welsh distinctiveness.

In her seminal work, *Britons*, Linda Colley notes that in the nineteenth century, there were more differences between Wales and England than between Scotland and England, this despite the fact that Scotland had remained an independent state until 1707: 'Possessed of its own unifying language, less urbanised than Scotland and England – and crucially – less addicted to military and imperial endeavour, it [Wales] could strike observers from outside as being resolutely peculiar to itself.'[80] Unfortunately, she does not develop this perceptive remark any further. Nonetheless, her comments are a means of drawing our attention to one of the most striking features of Wales's history, and a feature that is of central importance in trying to understand Welsh nationalist politics.

Despite having been conquered in 1282, formally colonised in 1284 and incorporated into the English state in the sixteenth

---

79 Amongst the most notable of these studies are Linda Colley, *Britons: Forging the Nation, 1707–1837* (London: Pimlico 1994); Norman Davies, *The Isles: A History* (London: Papermac, 2000); Simon Schama, *A History of Britain*, vols 1–3 published in turn by the BBC in 2000, 2001 and 2002.

80 Colley, *Britons*, p. 394.

century, Wales remained different and, indeed, alien (both linguistically and culturally) from the rest of Britain's population
until the nineteenth century and even beyond. If we reverse this
perspective, the same point can be expressed in a different way:
even though it took possession of Wales so early in its development, the English/British state never felt the need to try to enforce
uniformity across its territory by assimilating the Welsh into the
majority culture. This differs markedly from the practice of two
other states that were, in their own ways, forerunners of the
modern state, namely France and the United States. In the first,
a determined effort was made to forge French citizens from the
linguistically and culturally diverse populations that inhabited
the 'national territory', while the second was built on the genocide of the native population.[81] As already noted, these efforts
to assimilate and otherwise enforce uniformity were far from the
exception – they are rather entirely characteristic of politics in the
modern, national era.[82] In contrast, although it cannot be denied
that some attempts were made to force the Welsh to assimilate,
there was no consistent policy aimed at effacing difference and
ensuring uniformity – this notwithstanding the role of the 'Welsh
Not' in nationalist folklore.[83] Indeed, as Hywel Teifi Edwards
demonstrated, rather than being the result of *direct* coercion from
the state, the most enthusiastic pressure in favour of assimilation
was generated by the Welsh themselves.[84]

How can this be explained? Should the English/British state be
regarded as particularly enlightened or compassionate? Hardly.
The Scottish Highlands experienced the terrible fury of that state

[81] In the case of France, see Eugen J. Weber's classic study, *Peasants into Frenchmen: The Modernization of Rural France 1870–1914* (London: Chatto and Windus, 1977). On the massacre of north America's native population see James Wilson, *The Earth Shall Weep: A History of Native America* (London: Picador, 1998).
[82] Michael Mann, *The Dark Side of Democracy: Explaining Ethnic Cleansing* (Cambridge: Cambridge University Press, 2004).
[83] It is a fact that the 'Acts of Union' had set linguistic demands on the holders of governmental and legal posts. It remains the case, however, that only a very small percentage – that is, the elite – of the population was affected by these claus-es. There was no systematic effort to change the language of the majority – neither during the sixteenth century nor later.
[84] Hywel Teifi Edwards, *Codi'r Hen Wlad yn ei Hôl 1850–1914* (Llandysul: Gomer, 1994).

after the 1745 rebellion – as indeed had the Welsh themselves in the wake of Glyndŵr's rebellion centuries before. When the state was under threat, it was more than capable of bestial behaviour. The United Kingdom did not follow in the footsteps of other modern states because it was some sort of humanitarian oasis. The explanation is rather to be found in the form of the state. More specifically, the form of the English/British state reflects the fact that England/Britain pioneered the road towards the modern state. The so-called Acts of Union between England and Wales were in fact among the first steps on that journey. It is this pioneering role that allowed some pre-modern elements to survive that state's formation. This is Nairn's summary of the process:

> Although a developmental oddity belonging to the era of transition from absolutism to capitalist modernity, its anomalous character was first crystallised and then protected by priority. As the road-making state into modern times, it inevitably retained much from the mediaeval territory it left behind: a cluster of deep-laid archaisms still central to English society and the British state. Yet the same developmental position encouraged the secular retention of these traits, and a constant return to them as the special mystique of the British Constitution and way of life. Once the road-system had been built up, for other peoples as well as the English, the latter were never compelled to reform themselves along the lines which the English revolution had made possible. They had acquired such great advantages from leading the way – above all in the shape of empire – that for over two centuries it was easier to consolidate or re-exploit this primary role than to break with it.[85]

So many advantages stemmed from being the 'first mover' in terms of modernisation that the British state was characterised by much greater continuity than other societies that subsequently came to travel along the same road.

The legacy of this earlier age permeates the governmental and social systems of the United Kingdom: in the ways in which

---

85   Nairn, *The Break-up of Britain*, pp. 64–5.

all-important decisions are kept out of the hands of the House of Commons because the government serves the Crown rather than the people; in the fact that the clear separation of powers between the different branches of government considered to be essential in democratic countries does not exist in Britain; in the way that social and economic elites have been absorbed into a worldview that in so many ways continues to reflect the practices and values of the old land-owning class, and so on. Most directly relevant in the present context, however, is the atypical way that the United Kingdom dealt with the challenge of territorial governance.

In most politics textbooks, the United Kingdom is classed as a unitary state. This seems misleading. How can we really classify a state that has three different legal systems operating within it (in Scotland, in Northern Ireland, and with another in England and Wales) as unitary?[86] The same state is also home to two different established churches in England and in Scotland respectively, while two other parts of its territory (Wales and Northern Ireland) have no established church at all. In response, experts on Scottish politics have recently begun to classify the United Kingdom in a different way, drawing on the work of Norwegian academic, Stein Rokkan.[87] According to this alternative typology, Britain is not a unitary state but rather a union state. The characteristics of such a state are described in the following terms:

> The union state does not enjoy direct political control everywhere. Incorporation of parts of its territory has been achieved through treaty and agreement; consequently integration is less than perfect. While administrative standardization prevails over most of the

[86] Indeed, as devolved Wales starts to develop its own public law, it can be argued that there are now – in effect – three and a half legal systems in the United Kingdom. See Richard Rawlings, *Delineating Wales: Constitutional, Legal and Administrative Aspects of National Devolution* (Cardiff: University of Wales Press, 2003), pp. 458–94.

[87] Wales appears regularly in the work of Rokkan, a giant in the world of political studies. As a member of a small nation on the margins of Europe, it perhaps comes as no surprise that he showed an interest in the fate of other marginal nations. But he was also married to a Welshwoman – Elizabeth – which meant that he spent part of his holidays each year in St David's. Following his premature death, Elizabeth returned permanently to Wales.

territory, the union structure entails the survival in some areas of variations based on pre-union rights and infrastructures.[88]

It is immediately apparent that the United Kingdom, with all its peculiarities and anachronistic echoes of bygone eras, conforms far better to this description than it does to that of a modern, unitary state. Had Britain been obliged to undergo the painful transition towards a more thoroughly modern form of state, no doubt the various territorial 'anomalies' just described would all have been swept away and replaced by a more uniform and 'rational' set of arrangements. But due to the advantages of precedence, this never occurred.

Ironically enough, therefore, Britain's shortcomings when measured against the yardstick of contemporary democratic standards – and the fact that, as a state, it never systematically sought to assimilate its inhabitants – are both interconnected and derive from the same source. And of course, the fact of Wales's continued distinctiveness has meant, in turn, that the Welsh national movement had soil in which to take root. Indeed, the very form of the United Kingdom state arguably made it easier for that national movement to take root and grow more successfully than might otherwise have been the case. This because Welsh nationalists have not been faced by a state that makes presumptions of principle, or erects constitutional obstacles, such that change in one part (e.g. gaining a measure of self-government) requires revolutionising the system as a whole. In the union state, concessions can be won piecemeal and incrementally. Compare this with the position facing the nationalists of those small nations that live under the shadow of the French state, a state that has elevated uniformity itself to an ideal and graven image.

That said, the nature of Wales's relationship with the English state (the British state after 1707) should not be idealised or romanticised. It is undoubtedly better for people to be patronised,

88   Stein Rokkan and Derek Urwin, *Economy, Territory, Identity: Politics of Western European Peripheries* (London: Sage, 1983), p. 181. In the Welsh context, Jonathan Bradbury deploys the same terminology in Jonathan Bradbury and John J. Mawson (eds), *British Regionalism and Devolution* (London: Jessica Kingsley, 1997).

scorned and ignored, than to be oppressed in more direct and bloodier ways. Nevertheless, the pathologies of the relationship – in all its multi-layered complexity – continue to cast a shadow over Wales to this day.[89] This can be seen most clearly, perhaps, in the pattern of Wales's economic development.

There is a common tendency in Wales to take pride in our allegedly central role in the Industrial Revolution – it is certainly a sentiment repeated in the writings of some of Plaid Cymru's leaders.[90] Alas, these assertions must be seen as one aspect of the combination of 'collective inferiority complex and national megalomania', which in the opinion of Polish historian Jerzy Jedlicki, is typical of marginal peoples.[91] Rather the evidence suggests that industrialisation was confined to a few comparatively small areas in Wales in the period around 1830 when it was already being felt much more widely in England. Indeed, in an important essay bearing the provocative title 'Was Wales industrialised?', L. J. Williams compares the reliance of nineteenth-century Wales's economy on 'primary production' (coal mining, iron, slate, and so on) and its (relative) failure to develop a manufacturing sector, to the situation of the less-developed economies in the latter-day Third World.[92] As in the case of the latter, Wales's principal role in the international economy was to supply raw materials to other areas: it did not develop into a centre of growth and development in its own right. In this sense, Wales played a peripheral and dependent role in the Industrial Revolution, even if the vicissitudes of the industrial economy had a far-reaching effect on every aspect of life in Wales.[93]

89 Richard Wyn Jones, 'The colonial legacy in Welsh politics', in Jane Aaron and Chris Williams (eds), *Postcolonial Wales* (Cardiff: University of Wales Press, 2005), pp. 23–38.
90 For example: 'Every visitor to Wales should travel to Dowlais Top and look out over Merthyr. Here, with only a breath of imagination, can be seen the birthplace of the modern industrial world': Phil Williams, *Voice from the Valleys* (Aberystwyth: Plaid Cymru, 1981), p. 34.
91 Jerzy Jedlicki, *A Suburb of Europe: Nineteenth-century Polish Approaches to Western Civilization* (Budapest: CEU Press, 1999), p. xiii. I am grateful to Iver Neumann for bringing this book to my attention.
92 John Williams, *Was Wales Industrialised? Essays in Modern Welsh History* (Llandysul: Gomer, 1995) pp. 14–36.
93 See, for example, the striking statistical evidence presented by Brinley Thomas in his justly renowned essay 'Wales and the Atlantic Economy', in *The*

But Wales's economy was even more peripheral than is implied above as a result of one all-important dimension that discussions of the Welsh economic development tend to over-look, namely the peculiarity of economic development in Britain. As Geoffrey Ingham demonstrated: 'it constitutes a unique case ... in which international commercial capitalism has been domi-nant, and has had a determining impact on its class and institu-tional structure'.[94] That is to say, it is the sector of the economy involved in international commerce and banking – 'The City' is the familiar shorthand – and *not* the industrial sector, that has dominated capitalist economic development in the British state. Indeed, the dominance of 'The City' has served to hinder industrial development.[95] Once again, as Anderson and Nairn argued, it was Britain's imperial role that shaped this unique form of modern development. The innumerable advantages that accrued to Britain as a result of her dominant role in her empire and wider international economy – and, relatedly, the central role played by sterling in international trade – meant that invest-ing and re-investing in 'The City' proved to be a simpler, surer way of turning a profit than the longer-term grind of encourag-ing industrial development. It need hardly be emphasised that the role of Wales or of Welsh people in this, the crucial sector of the UK economy, was very minor indeed.

In broad-brush terms, a process of dual marginalisation is observable. Wales was peripheral to industrial development. It tended to supply raw materials to other areas rather than become a centre for growth and development in its own right. But additionally, at a British level, industry played a secondary role to another sector of the economy. Despite the relative limited number employed in it, 'The City' was the most important polit-ico-economic force in terms of driving and promoting economic

Welsh Economy: Studies in Expansion (Cardiff: University of Wales Press, 1962), pp. 1–19.

94 Geoffrey Ingham, *Capitalism Divided? The City and Industry in British Social Development* (London: Macmillan, 1984), p. 6.

95 As well as Ingham's volume, see John A. Hall, 'The tyranny of history: an analysis of Britain's decline', in Armand Cleese and Christopher Coker (eds), *The Vitality of Britain* (Amsterdam: Rozenberg Publishers, 1997), pp. 5–20.

development in Britain. This was (and is) a sector of the economy in which Wales played next to no part.

Wales, of course, was part of the modern world. There was no means by which a territory connected so closely, both geographically and historically, with the pioneer of modernity could avoid that. But Wales was carried by the tide, with neither oar nor sail with which to steer a course. When the current and winds were favourable, Wales experienced periods of prosperity – substantial prosperity, at that. But when cross winds and heavy seas arose – let alone the storms of the Great Depression – Wales could not even attempt to set her own course, let alone find a more sheltered anchorage. There was no deliberate conspiracy at work in all of this, no more than there is a deliberate conspiracy to hinder the development of the global south. Rather, the nature of economic development in Wales was a reflection of structural reality – the fact that Wales was a peripheral part of the first state to resemble a modern state, and a state that succeeded in becoming the strongest imperial power on earth, due in large part to the precedence given to the firstborn.

Naturally enough, the empire was central to the national identity that developed around that state. One of the truly striking features of British identity is its flexibility and ambiguity. These are not uncommon traits for a national identity, of course. Yet, even so, British national identity appears to be more flexible and ambiguous than most. Thus, in England, at least until very recently, those researchers who sought to use quantitative methods to statistically measure national identities were often confounded by the fact that so many respondents regarded English and British identities as synonymous.[96] Many English people appear to regard Britishness as a geographical extension of the English national identity (and nationalism) that was deeply rooted by the seventeenth century. By complete contrast, very few in Wales and Scotland would equate British identity with Englishness. Even if there is no clear consensus about the meaning of Welshness, or indeed Scottish identity, there is nonetheless general agreement

[96] Anthony F. Heath, Bridget Taylor, Lindsay Brook and Alison Park, 'British national sentiment', *British Journal of Political Science*, 29 (1) (1999), 155–75.

that being Welsh or Scottish is not the same as being English, as well as a sense that there is more to being Welsh or Scottish than simply being British (this even if a substantial cohort believe that it is possible to feel both Welsh/Scottish and British simultaneously).[97] The situation is different again in Northern Ireland. There, identifying as British appears to entail adopting a worldview and an associated set of symbolic representations of British identity that most inhabitants of modern-day England, Scotland and Wales find not only incomprehensible but alien.

Once again, it is the fact that the state did not strive to secure internal uniformity that explains this diversity. In the same way and, indeed, as a result of the fact that institutional variation was tolerated, so too was the existence of a variety of different versions of national identity – as long as they did not threaten the continuation of the state order. As Colley makes clear, one of the most important factors holding these various peoples together, especially the inhabitants of England and Scotland, was the empire. '[T]he triumph, profits and Otherness represented by a massive overseas empire', as well as the ways in which the warfare necessary to create and sustain that empire served to unite the population, were the very foundation of Britishness.[98] Colley may be correct in noting that, in the mid-nineteenth century, at least, the Welsh were less likely to participate in these imperial adventures than the English and the Scots. But if so, this was only a matter of degree. And even if the Welsh were comparative latecomers to imperial mania – anti-imperialist sentiment remained a significant element of public life in Wales until the Boer War – this had no bearing on how completely they fell under its spell once they did succumb to its siren call.[99]

97 Dafydd Glyn Jones's essays remind us of the political and social consequences of a period when the Welsh considered Welshness and Britishness to be synonymous. See, for example, Dafydd Glyn Jones, *Agoriad yr oes: Erthyglau ar lên, hanes a gwleidyddiaeth Cymru* (Talybont: Y Lolfa, 2002). Today, however, the evidence from various quantitative surveys strongly suggests that by far the greater part of the inhabitants of Wales consider these to be distinct identities, even if the majority continue to believe that it is possible to be British and Welsh at the same time.
98 Colley, *Britons*, p. 6.
99 See, inter alios, Edwards, *Codi'r Hen Wlad yn ei Hôl 1850–1914*; D. Tecwyn Lloyd, *Drych o Genedl* (Abertawe: Tŷ John Penry, 1987); E. G. Millward, *Yr*

Indeed, was there an element of the typical over-eagerness of the convert in the way that Wales subsequently embraced the symbolism and ideology of imperial Britishness in the twentieth century? Especially, perhaps, in the cringing servility displayed towards the monarchy, an institution that did little to hide its indifference to Wales. More generally, even amongst left-wing Labour supporters, the Greatness of Britain was a matter of pride – something that was to be safeguarded and promoted. Indeed, whatever the other differences between right and left, the self-evident Greatness of Britain was common ground between them. It was taken for granted that Britain had a natural and all-important leadership role to play on the international stage.

This is not the place to discuss the decline of the British Empire – when and how the tide started to turn, and why it ebbed so quickly from then on. These are all matters of great import but, from the perspective of the present study, we need only note that the decline of the empire had far-reaching implications for the state. Because the advantages that had flowed from its pre-eminent international position had proven so influential in shaping its political institutions, its economy and, indeed, its social order, it was inevitable that the eclipse of that power represented an enormous challenge to the whole system. In the second half of the twentieth century – and especially since the 1960s – restoring past glories has been a constant theme in the rhetoric of political leaders like Wilson, Thatcher and Blair. Britain is now the 'old country' which needs to be 'restored' – a change of circumstance that would doubtless have astounded Welsh people in the nineteenth century who were wont to think of Wales and not Britain in such terms. All kinds of remedies were offered to ensure the desired resurrection: the 'white heat' of technology; curbing the power of the trade unions; overcoming the 'forces of conservatism'; reform; the constant obsession with the 'new'; clinging tightly to Europe; or the Commonwealth; or the United States of

Arwrgerdd Gymraeg: Ei Thwf a'i Thranc (Caerdydd: Gwasg Prifysgol Cymru, 1998); Hywel Teifi Edwards and E. G. Millward, *Jiwbilî y Fam Wen Fawr* (Llandysul: Gomer, 1989).

America – even constitutional reform, itself a sure sign that things were serious. Yet the patient's symptoms have proved to be stubborn. The development of the Welsh national movement is also one of those symptoms, and we will now turn our attention to the political thought of that movement.

Part Two

Nationalists

2

A Passionate Love for a Stable Civilisation: The Saunders Lewis Era

Anyone wishing to understand the history or the character of modern Welsh nationalism cannot avoid engaging with Saunders Lewis's signal contribution.[1] It was in his correspondence with H. R. Jones that the foundations were laid for the meeting in Pwllheli on 5 August 1925 when Jones's Plaid Genedlaethol Cymru (the Welsh Nationalist Party) joined forces with Y Mudiad Cymreig (Welsh Society) – a semi-clandestine society of which Lewis was a member – to form the present-day party. There is no doubt that he was the one who decided on the direction – both ideational and organisational – that the party would go on to adopt. A year later, he succeeded Lewis Valentine as the nationalist party's second president and became the main public advocate of its cause. During his period as leader, he ensured that the values and ideas expressed in the party's publications were much closer to his own views than they were – it seems – to the views of most party members and supporters. During the same period, Saunders Lewis was also the main instigator of one of the most consequential and symbolically important episodes in the history of modern Welsh nationalism, namely the 'Fire in Llŷn' (*Tân*

---

[1] There remains no better account of Saunders Lewis's political ideas than Dafydd Glyn Jones, 'His politics', in Alun R. Jones and Gwyn Thomas (eds), *Presenting Saunders Lewis* (Cardiff: University of Wales Press, 1973), pp. 23–78. There is much of interest in D. Tecwyn Lloyd's biography, *John Saunders Lewis: Y Gyfrol Gyntaf* (Dinbych: Gwasg Gee, 1988). Unfortunately, however, the biography is incomplete with this, the first and ultimately only volume, taking the story to circa 1933. It also features more than a little score settling. Robin Chapman's biography of Saunders Lewis – *Un Bywyd o Blith Nifer* (Llandysul: Gomer, 2006) – was published just as this book was being completed.

yn Llŷn).[2] Neither did his contribution end when he finally re-
nounced the presidency in 1939.

Lewis cast a long shadow over the presidency of his successor,
J. E. Daniel (president between 1939 and 1943). In fact, such was
the extent of Lewis's influence over Daniel's political thinking
and, indeed, the ideas of his wife, Catherine Daniel, that, given
our particular interest in the party's ideology, there is no merit
in treating the two presidential eras as distinct in any meaningful way.[3] Not only that, but Saunders Lewis's candidacy in the
famous by-election for the University of Wales's parliamentary
seat in 1943 served to revive the nationalist party during a difficult time in its history. The Welsh Nationalist Party was to remain,
to a very significant extent, Saunders Lewis's party throughout
the years of the Second World War.

Tracing Lewis's influence during Gwynfor Evans's lengthy
period as president is a more complex matter. From an ideological point of view and, more than likely, on a personal level as
well, the relationship between the two was somewhat schizo-
phrenic. On the one hand – as will be discussed in the next chapter – Gwynfor Evans was clearly very significantly influenced by
some of the core elements in Lewis's political thinking. To this
extent, Evans can be considered a disciple of his most prominent
predecessor. On the other hand, considerable tension developed
between the two men (and their camps); a tension that only intensified with the passage of time. Indeed, Lewis's last great political
act, delivering the radio lecture 'Tynged yr Iaith' (The Fate of the
Language) in 1962, came at a time of bitter disagreement in the

---

2 Confirmation of Saunders Lewis's central role in devising and executing
the plan to damage buildings at the proposed RAF bombing school in Penyberth
is given in a revealing letter he sent to Harri Pritchard Jones in 1975. While discussing D. J. Williams's part in the events, Lewis says '[D. J.] went to prison in
1937 without setting anything on fire, without striking a match, without even ap-
plauding the act, but on the sole basis that he decided "Saunders *bach*" should
not be left alone when "he was calling for helpers".' See Harri Pritchard Jones, 'D.
J. Williams', in Derec Llwyd Morgan (ed.), *Adnabod Deg* (Dinbych: Gwasg Gee,
1977), p. 62; translation.

3 For a comprehensive discussion of the political and theological ideas of J.
E. Daniel see D. Densil Morgan's preface to *Torri'r Seiliau Sicr: Detholiad o Ysgrifau
J. E. Daniel* (Llandysul: Gomer, 1993), pp. 9–91. It is to be devoutly hoped that a
study of Catherine Daniel will eventually be produced.

ranks about the party's direction and was, above all, an attempt to undermine Gwynfor Evans's presidency.

As if all of this were not sufficient for Saunders Lewis to claim a central place in any discussion of the political thought of Plaid Cymru, there are two additional factors to consider. First, although it would be impossible to evaluate completely (let alone measure in any accurate way), who could deny the enormous influence of Saunders Lewis's literary work on generations of nationalists? Either directly, through works like *Buchedd Garmon*, or indirectly through the works of others inspired by him – Lewis Valentine's national hymn, 'Dros Gymru'n Gwlad' ('For Wales our Country') is one obvious example – Saunders Lewis's ideas, images and metaphors have become a medium through which Welsh nationalists comprehend the world around them as well as their place in it.

Equally, and on a less exalted note, it can hardly be denied that the accusations of 'fascist' sympathies heard against Saunders Lewis and some of his closest colleagues since the late 1930s even to the present day have cast a long shadow over the party. These accusations – seized on with relish by opponents and enemies – have regularly been a source of deep embarrassment and discomfort to Welsh nationalists.[4] Shadows not only protect and nourish what lies beneath but can also smother and distort – such is the case of the shadow cast by Saunders Lewis over the development of Plaid Cymru.

It is impossible to do justice to every aspect of Saunders Lewis's influence over the nationalist party and on the national movement more generally in the confines of just one chapter – an entire book would hardly suffice. It will be no surprise, therefore, that Saunders Lewis reappears regularly in the rest of this study. This chapter will serve as an introduction to and analysis of Saunders Lewis contribution to the political thought of Plaid Cymru during his period as party president.

There are five steps to the argument. First, we focus on the way that Lewis seized control of the intellectual agenda during the

---

[4] See Richard Wyn Jones, *The Fascist Party in Wales? Plaid Cymru, Welsh Nationalism and the Accusation of Fascism*, trans. Dafydd Jones and Richard Wyn Jones (Cardiff: University of Wales Press, 2014), *passim*.

party's early days. The second step is an analysis of the contents of what must be considered Plaid Cymru's founding document, namely *Principles of Nationalism* (*Egwyddorion Cenedlaetholdeb*) – a speech given by Saunders Lewis at the party's first Summer School in Machynlleth in 1926. Thirdly, we discuss how Saunders Lewis went on to lay the ideological foundations for the party's programme, in the process establishing several features that later came to be regarded as fundamental attributes of the political thinking of Welsh nationalism. As a fourth step we demonstrate the way in which Saunders Lewis retained his grip on the policy agenda when other voices within the party tried to steer a different course, especially after the failure of its first electoral foray when it stood a candidate in Caernarfon in the 1929 general election. Finally, we turn our attention to burning the bombing school at Penyberth, Pen Llŷn, in September 1936 – or more precisely to the wider political failure of that act. For although it has subsequently become a core part of nationalist mythology and folklore, the 'Fire in Llŷn' proved to be something of a damp squib, at least in the eyes of the act's chief instigator. The discussion shows that the failure of party members (let alone the people of Wales) to respond to the leadership offered to them by the perpetrators, was an indication that the gap – in particular, the ideological rift between the members and supporters of the party on the one hand and its leadership on the other – had become too wide to bridge.

Seizing the agenda

Very few Plaid Cymru members today have ever heard of Evan Alwyn Owen. Little mention is made to him in the party's archives after the winter of 1924/5, and except for an obituary by Gwilym R. Jones in the December 1933 issue of *Y Ddraig Goch* – its Welsh-language newspaper – there are very few references to him in anything published by the party.[5] He was not forgotten intentionally. Owen, a former quarryman from Rhyd-ddu, lived

---

5 Gwilym R. Jones, 'Un o sefydlwyr y Blaid: Evan Alwyn Owen', *Y Ddraig Goch*, December 1933, 9.

a life blighted by the twin scourges of tuberculosis and unemployment. He never had the resources – either physical or financial – to match his political vision. Nevertheless, if any individual can be regarded as the founder of Plaid Genedlaethol Cymru, the honour goes to Evan Alwyn Owen. It is worth pausing a moment over Owen's vision for his party – not simply because he deserves a better fate than to be overlooked by history, but more importantly from the point of view of the present discussion, because of the very significant differences between his original vision and the party programme that Saunders Lewis succeeded in installing during 1925 and 1926.

The Welsh Nationalist Party was founded on 21 December 1924 when a group established three months earlier bearing the colourful name Byddin Ymreolwyr Cymru ('The Welsh Home Rule Army') decided on a change of name and direction.[6] The army, which was centred on Caernarfon, was a rather disparate collection of individuals: some were, above all else, supporters of the Welsh language, while others were supporters of 'home rule' in the rather amorphous sense characteristic of the era. There were yet others, however, eager to transplant the attitudes and even methods of Sinn Féin to Wales. It was a member of this latter group that had been the principal instigator of the movement – its subsequent secretary, H. R. Jones.

Despite Jones's enthusiasm, the army was no better organised than many comparable movements of the time such as Byddin yr Iaith (The Language Army) and Cymru Well (Better Wales). These movements and others like them had a short shelf life. That they were formed and re-formed so regularly was a reflection of the deep frustration felt by Welsh nationalists at the time. Yet none took root successfully.[7] Beyond expressing generalised support for the Welsh language and home rule, it

6 There is further discussion on the founding of Plaid Cymru in Gerald Morgan, 'Dannedd y ddraig', in John Davies (ed.), *Cymru'n Deffro* (Talybont: Y Lolfa, 1981), pp. 7–30, and in two essays by J. Graham Jones in volumes 22 and 23 of *Cylchgrawn Llyfrgell Genedlaethol Cymru*.

7 For a revealing account of the patriotic activities of the time see Marion Löffler, '*Iaith nas Arferid, Iaith i Farw Yw: Ymgyrchu dros yr Iaith Gymraeg rhwng y ddau Ryfel Byd*' (Aberystwyth: Canolfan Uwchefrydiau Cymreig a Cheltaidd, 1995).

is hard to discern precisely what 'The Welsh Home Rule Army' was seeking to achieve. Despite its grandiloquent name, neither does it seem to have offered an alternative means of achieving them. Indeed, if the leader of the army, Walter S. Jones (Gwallter Llyfnwy), had had his way, the movement might easily come to an abrupt end.[8] His focus was cultural. He hoped to see a campaign to make the Welsh language obligatory in schools, alongside English, ensuring that all teachers in Wales's primary schools were able to 'lecture' through the medium of Welsh.[9] It was in part, at least, in order to lay the foundations of such a campaign that Jones urged the army to merge with another society, 'Y Tair G' (The Three Gs) (more formally, Y Gymdeithas Genedlaethol Gymreig/The Welsh National Society), formed mainly from students at nearby University College Bangor. Given that 'Y Tair G' boasted such figures as Lewis Valentine and Thomas Parry (later Sir Tom) among its members, it is not hard to see why W. S. Jones regarded a merger as sensible.[10] But not everyone in the army agreed with him.

Jones's proposal was fiercely opposed by the treasurer, Evan Alwyn Owen. He was firmly of the opinion that not only should the movement remain independent, but that it should be transformed into a bona fide political party under the name Plaid Genedlaethol Cymru, the Welsh National or Nationalist Party.[11] Owen expressed his ideas in several letters that he sent to H. R. Jones, an individual who appears to have been of like mind.

8 On Walter S. Jones see Dewi Jones, 'Walter Sylvanus Jones (Gwallter Llyfnwy) 1883–1932', *Trafodion Cymdeithas Hanes Sir Gaerfyrddin*, 50 (1989), 71–85. (I thank Bleddyn Huws for drawing my attention to this essay.) Gwallter was rather fickle in his politics. By 1929 he was campaigning enthusiastically for the Labour candidate in the Caernarfon constituency. In the following year, however, he applied (unsuccessfully) for the post of organiser for the nationalist party following the death of H. R. Jones. On H. R. Jones himself see Gwilym R. Jones, 'H. R. Jones', in Morgan (ed.), *Adnabod Deg*, pp. 31–44.
9 W. S. Jones to H. R. Jones, 2 October 1924 (Plaid Cymru Archive, National Library of Wales).
10 An insight into *Y Tair G* and the milieu that stemmed from it in Lewis Valentine, 'Cyfnod Bangor', can be found in J. T. Jones and Harri Parri (eds), *Cyfrol Deyrnged: I Gofio J. P.* (Caernarfon: Gwasg Tŷ ar y Graig, 1971), pp. 24–35.
11 Plaid Genedlaethol Cymru can be plausibly translated as either the Welsh Nationalist Party or Welsh National Party. When the party adopted an English-language equivalent it chose the former option which is why it is used throughout this study, but cf. the Scottish National Party.

Owen was a man with fire in his belly. 'We have much to learn from the Irish', he wrote in one letter, 'and if we had a few Sinn Feinners in Wales, we would be much better off'.[12] He wrote again to H. R. Jones revealing not only his desire to transform the army into a nationalist party, but also the objective he wanted that party to aim for:

> I am more certain than ever about having a Welsh Nationalist Party, for I am entirely persuaded that it is through that party, and that party alone, that Wales will secure the greatest measure of autonomy: I also see in it – after immersing the inhabitants of Wales in the Nationalist spirit – an excellent means for fighting for total independence.[13]

We shall return to the significance of the reference to 'independence' shortly. But in the meantime, it is important to note that the objective set by Owen for the party was a constitutional rather than a cultural one. Owen's great worry was that uniting with the Bangor students would result in a movement that would prioritise the language over achieving self-government.

In addition, it is clear that Owen was also concerned about the 'character' of any movement that would result from joining forces with 'Y Tair G'. Another letter to H. R. Jones sent only a few days before the meeting on 21 December 1924 – when the army decided to follow the recommendation of its treasurer rather than its leader, and relaunch itself as Plaid Genedlaethol Cymru – contains the following revealing comments:

> After changing the name, I thought we should proceed without delay to call meetings in every area – to get the young men of the valleys to join, and to have a branch in every area, and then a representative on the executive committee of each county – and so on. Without question, that would be the most *gwerinol* way of moving forward. If we want the support of the *gwerin*, we must work our way up in *gwerinol* fashion …

12 Evan Alwyn Owen to H. R. Jones, 2 September 1924 (APC B1); translation.
13 Evan Alwyn Owen to H. R. Jones, 24 November 1924 (APC B1); translation.

Having joined such a society in such a way [here he is referring to the proposed merger with 'Y Tair G'], the *gwerinwr* will not have a voice at all: everything will be in the hands of a small group who will be too respectable to do anything daring. We need new blood, and we need to let young *gwerinwyr* fight and work their way up.[14]

Although he was successful in averting a merger with 'Y Tair G', the great irony is that in the attempt to make Evan Alwyn Owen's great dream of establishing a bone fide nationalist party a reality, many of his fears about that proposed union were realised. For a relatively substantial period of time following its establishment – primarily because of Saunders Lewis's influence – Plaid Cymru placed more emphasis on the language than on self-government. And although no movement of which Saunders Lewis was president could be considered 'respectable' according to the (rather perverse) standards of the time, neither was it a party in which many *gwerinwyr* or 'ordinary people' necessarily felt comfortable.

With Lewis Valentine as its first president, the new party started its work.[15] One of the tasks set for H. R. Jones, who continued as secretary, was to contact other well-known nationalists to

14 Evan Alwyn Owen to H. R. Jones, 15 December 1924 (APC B1); translation. *Gwerin* (and the variations thereof contained in this passage) has long been and remains an important phrase in Welsh-language political and social discourse – one freighted with meaning. There is no direct English equivalent but for illuminating English-language discussions see Prys Morgan, 'The *Gwerin* of Wales – Myth and Reality', in Ian Hume and W. T. R. Pryce (eds), *The Welsh and their Country* (Llandysul: Gomer 1986), pp. 134–52 and Christopher Harvie, 'The folk and the *Gwerin*: the myth and reality of popular culture in 19th-century Scotland and Wales', *Proceedings of the British Academy*, 80 (1991), 19–48. Gwyn A. Williams provides the following precis: 'The gwerin was cultivated, educated, often self-educated, responsible, self-disciplined, respectable but on the whole genially poor or perhaps small-propertied, straddling groups perceived as class in other, less fortunate societies. Welsh-speaking, Nonconformist, imbued with the more social virtues of Dissent, bred on the Bible and good practice, it was open to the more spiritual forms of wider culture and was dedicated to spiritual self-improvement': *When was Wales?* (London: Penguin, 1985), p. 237.
15 The fact that Valentine took on the presidency of the new party and that most of the members of 'Y Tair G' also chose to join the ranks suggests that Evan Alwyn Owen's fears about that society were unfounded. Indeed, considering how isolated Owen was in Rhyd-ddu – something that becomes very clear from his correspondence with H. R. Jones – it seems fair to ask how much he actually knew about it or its membership? What is significant, however, is that Owen insisted on the central importance of establishing a fully-fledged political party with the aim of attaining self-government, and opposed any step that could, in his opinion, lead to a movement with an exclusively cultural/linguistic focus.

secure their membership and create a truly national organisation. These contacts subsequently led to that meeting at Pwllheli that is now regarded as the birthplace of the contemporary party.

Although there is no way of knowing for certain, we can be confident that Saunders Lewis's name was near the top of any list of prospective members drawn up by Jones and his colleagues. Lewis's political views had already been made known via a series of speeches, essays and letters to the press, especially after the summer of 1923.[16] Through these interventions, Saunders Lewis had already established himself as one of the main protagonists of the new wave of Welsh nationalism; a militant nationalism forged in and by the experiences of the Great War. Lewis's public declarations were particularly bold and defiant. As might be expected perhaps, he was berated for them by the press, particularly the English-language press. But Lewis's comments – together with similar remarks by other members of this new generation – also drew the ire of more traditional Welsh nationalists. In an article in the *South Wales Daily News*, Beriah Gwynfe Evans, the former secretary of Cymru Fydd (Young Wales), complained of a situation in which 'De Valera [was] compared and contrasted with Lloyd George, to the latter's disadvantage'.[17] But, of course, for a man like H. R. Jones, such Sinn Féin-ism was not something to shy away from. Here, rather, was excellent raw material for the new party.

When H. R. Jones contacted Saunders Lewis in February 1925 to invite him to participate in the new venture, it is not entirely clear whether he contacted him solely as an individual or whether he was somehow aware that Lewis was already part of Y Mudiad Cymreig. Although Y Mudiad Cymreig was a secret society, given the web of connections that linked the new generation of Welsh nationalists it would not be altogether surprising if the officers of Plaid Genedlaethol Cymru had heard of the existence

16 Lloyd, *John Saunders Lewis*, pp. 218–41.
17 Quoted in Lloyd, *John Saunders Lewis*, p. 241 n. It is hard not to conclude that the willingness of Lewis and Valentine to flout and challenge conventional opinion in the 1920s was connected to their personal experiences in the trenches of France during the Great War. What, after all, was the scorn of respectable society in comparison with the horrors they experienced there?

of some kind of arrangement between nationalists in the south of Wales.[18] Be that as it may, Y Mudiad Cymreig had indeed been meeting occasionally since January 1924. The first meeting was held at the home of G. J. and Elizabeth Williams in Penarth. Their fellow founders were Saunders Lewis and Ambrose Bebb.[19] Over time, others, such as D. J. Williams, Fred Jones and Ben Bowen Thomas, joined them. The Mudiad Cymreig had been intended as a vanguard movement, with its members providing the elite that would give new direction to Welsh nationalism and thus to Wales. Whatever it did in terms of giving Wales direction, Saunders Lewis soon established the direction of the new nationalist party. This because, in replying to Jones's invitation, Lewis stipulated one all-important condition that Jones had to accept before he was prepared to become a member. Quite simply, he insisted that the new party adopt his policy agenda.[20] The acceptance of this condition marked the beginning of a fifteen-year period during which Saunders Lewis succeeded in keeping a tight grip on the party's policies.

In which ways exactly did Saunders Lewis insist on having his own way? First, he wanted to ensure that his understanding of the principle of 'enforcing the Welsh language' (Gorfodi'r Gymraeg) was accepted by the party. For Lewis this meant that every local authority should be compelled to work only through the medium

[18] Although there is no definitive confirmation of this in the Plaid Cymru Archive, D. Hywel Davies's brilliant history of the party's early years seems to imply that H. R. Jones might well have heard of the existence of Y Mudiad Cymreig from Mai Roberts. See D. Hywel Davies, *The Welsh Nationalist Party 1925–1945: A Call to Nationhood* (Cardiff: University of Wales Press, 1983), pp. 47–8. Whether or not this was the case, Mai Roberts is another of those women whose role in the history of the Welsh national movement deserves further study. Not least, Roberts was a direct link between the final period of campaigning for Welsh self-government before the First World War – she was E. T. John's secretary – and Plaid Cymru.
[19] For impressions of the first meeting see Ambrose Bebb, *Lloffion o Ddyddiaduron 1920–1926*, ed. Robin Humphreys (Caerdydd: Gwasg Prifysgol Cymru, 1996), pp. 170–2. There is no hint of the meeting's significance in the letter Saunders Lewis wrote to his future wife, Margaret Gilcriest, recording the occasion: 'I had to sleep on a big couch in the study, but we had a great time all together, talking till dawns and sleeping till noons': Saunders Lewis, *Letters to Margaret Gilcriest*, ed. Mair Saunders Jones, Ned Thomas and Harri Pritchard Jones (Cardiff: University of Wales Press, 1993), pp. 520–1.
[20] Saunders Lewis to H. R. Jones, 1 March 1925 (PCA B2).

of Welsh, and that Welsh should be the medium for education in every school in Wales. In addition, he wanted the party to commit to boycotting Westminster and operate through the local authorities. In all of this, Saunders Lewis was advocating the ideas of Y Mudiad Cymreig, for these were the central elements of the programme that had been agreed by its members. But neither is it clear that H. R. Jones needed much by way of persuasion before accepting them. Although W. S. Jones favoured equal status for Welsh and English, insisting on a monolingual Wales may have been more to the taste of H. R. Jones, who was certainly of a more 'extreme' temperament. Neither would a 'Sinn Féiner' like H. R. Jones have baulked at the commitment to boycott Westminster – this was, after all, at the heart of the Arthur Griffith strategy.[21]

In that case, is it fair to personalise matters by claiming that it was Saunders Lewis who seized the agenda? Would it not be more correct to say that it was the intellectuals of Y Mudiad Cymreig that came to dominate the agenda of the new party? There are at least two reasons for believing that it is legitimate to personalise and focus on Lewis's particular role. First, there is little doubt that Lewis was *primus inter pares* in Y Mudiad Cymreig. Setting aside Ben Bowen Thomas (ultimately, Sir Ben) as a special case, Saunders Lewis certainly was the most 'political' of them all. As such, Saunders Lewis was clearly the principal influence in shaping the Mudiad Cymreig's programme (such as it was).

Even more importantly, it is clear that Saunders Lewis's constitutional vision for the future of Wales was different from that embraced by some of his fellow members of Y Mudiad Cymreig as well as from the views of those that had founded the new party. Yet it was Saunders Lewis's ideas that were incorporated into party policy – and later accepted as party dogma. Above all else, it is in the context of its constitutional policy that we can measure the extent of Saunders Lewis's dominance of the new party, both in its early years and in the decades that followed.

When he recommended the establishment of a Welsh nationalist party, it was Evan Alwyn Owen's intention to create a party

[21] The influence of Sinn Féin on the early Plaid Cymru is considered in greater depth in Volume Two of this study.

that would seek self-government for Wales, leading ultimately to 'Total Independence' (Annibyniaeth Lwyr). H. R. Jones was entirely in agreement with this view. It appears also that at least one of the founders of Y Mudiad Cymreig regarded independence as the ultimate goal. In his diary entry recording the founding meeting at Penarth, Bebb wrote, 'the beginning of the Welsh Nationalist Party and independence for Wales'.[22] Six days after the meeting, Bebb wrote to D. J. Williams to inform him of the existence of the movement and inviting him to become a member. He said, 'Our aim is independence, through every effective means [trwy bob moddion â dal].'[23]

But as a letter he had published in the *Western Mail* in August 1923 had already made clear, Saunders Lewis did not share the same view as Bebb, H. R. Jones and Evan Alwyn Owen on this matter. In that letter, after stressing that Welsh traditions and civilisation needed to be maintained through sustaining the Welsh language and defending the territory of Wales, Lewis went on to outline his constitutional ideas. Since this statement shines a particularly interesting light on his later views – and particularly on the ideas that were to feature in *Principles of Nationalism* – they are worth noting in full:

> Now, if these safeguards of civilisation be impossible without some form of self-government, we must have it, or we must try to win it. But whatever form will provide these safeguards satisfies me, even a 'glorified county council'. What is any government but a glorified county council? And I add that if these safeguards can be assured without any radical change in the relation of Wales and England, then I for my part will be content. I agree that we cannot go back to 1282. But we can in some matters go back to pre-Tudor conditions.[24]

Saunders Lewis did not wish to see Wales becoming an independent nation, because he saw no value in independence as a

[22] Bebb, *Lloffion o Ddyddiaduron 1920–1926*, pp. 171–2; translation.
[23] Quoted in Robin Chapman, *W. Ambrose Bebb* (Cardiff: University of Wales Press, 1997), p. 63; translation.
[24] *Western Mail*, 17 August 1923. Quoted in Lloyd, *John Saunders Lewis*, p. 224.

constitutional condition in and of itself. Indeed, he appears deeply disinterested in constitutional orders of any kind: is not every government just a version of a county council, he asks rhetorically. It is civilisation, rather than constitutional orders, that matters. In 1923, Saunders Lewis's observations were an expression of one man's views. But by 1925, this opinion had become the position of a political party.

There is a letter in the Plaid Cymru Archive which gives some clues as to how this happened. It is a letter sent by Saunders Lewis to H. R. Jones at the beginning of April 1925 in response to a draft of a proposed party pamphlet listing 'seeking self-government for Wales' amongst its objectives.[25] Lewis complained that this formulation was too vague. Indeed, he went so far as to threaten to disengage from the whole venture before it had got properly underway if he was not allowed his own way. 'For my part, certainly, I could not become a member of a movement that from the start is so devoid of ideas [di-syniad] and imprecise.' This threat may go some way towards explaining why there is no reference to self-government in the first list of objectives published by the Welsh Nationalist Party following the Pwllheli meeting; a list that without doubt is testimony to the success of Saunders Lewis's attempt to seize the ideological agenda:

> Purpose: To have a Welsh Wales. That includes:- (a) Ensuring Welsh culture in Wales. (b) Ensuring that the Welsh language is Wales's only official language, and therefore, a compulsory language in all local authority discussions, and a compulsory language for every office and officer in every local authority in Wales. (c) Ensuring the Welsh language as Wales's medium of education from primary School to University.[26]

Poor Evan Alwyn Owen. In the process of turning the nationalist party into an all-Wales national movement, his hopes of establishing a movement that would prioritise constitutional-political over linguistic-cultural matters were dashed. Only at the 1926

---

25 Saunders Lewis to H. R. Jones, 1 April 1925 (PCA B2); translation.
26 Y Ddraig Goch, July 1926, 2; translation.

party Summer School did Saunders Lewis present a definition of self-government that he regarded as acceptable. As we shall see, however, the ideas he presented on that occasion were hardly less vague than the formulation he had rubbished just one year previously. It was not until 1931 that self-government was formally incorporated into the party's official list of objectives.

Principles of Nationalism

Principles of Nationalism – Egwyddorion Cenedlaetholdeb – was the first lecture to be delivered at Plaid Cymru's first Summer School held in Machynlleth in August 1926. It later appeared as the party's first publication. It is, literally, a foundational document in the party's history and in the history of modern Welsh nationalism. It is through this lecture that Saunders Lewis set his mark on the party, moulding it in ways that remain recognisable even today – as these volumes will demonstrate. In both vision and style of argumentation, the lecture is wholly characteristic of Saunders Lewis's political thinking. There is no question that it is a brilliant work on many counts. Even granting that the political speeches of that era tended to offer their listeners more substantial fare than the soundbite laden vacuities to which we have become accustomed, *Principles of Nationalism* must be recognised as being exceptionally ambitious. Its subject is no less than European civilisation and Wales's place within it – past, present and future. It is rich in both reference and allusion and uncompromisingly intellectual throughout. It can be quite fairly regarded as a masterpiece. But it is also a flawed masterpiece. The lecture is replete with sweeping assertions – many of them unsustainable. Some of the historical interpretations it presents are eccentric, to say the least. Despite Saunders Lewis's repeated emphasis on the need to be decisive on essentials, the political philosophy incorporated in the lecture is also ambiguous and confusing – in part presumably because Saunders Lewis regarded himself as rising above such shallow (but, of course, unavoidable) matters as social or constitutional policy. Reading the lecture, one reflects on the brilliance while, simultaneously, wondering how such a statement could ever have been regarded as an appropriate basis to (re)launch Welsh nationalism as a serious political force. Indeed, one might be forgiven for thinking that it rendered what was already likely to be a difficult task practically impossible.

The first part of the lecture consists of a brief outline of the history of Wales. Wales, it is claimed, inherited Europe's Latin civilisation through its place in the Roman Empire. It sought to build its life on the basis of that tradition even after that Empire's final collapse. Although Wales was defeated and subjugated by England by the end of the thirteenth century, in Saunders Lewis's opinion 'no great harm came of it'. For even if it lost 'all shadow of independence', Wales nonetheless retained its freedom to develop its own civilisation in its own way.[27] This apparent paradox reflects the nature of authority in the Europe of the Middle Ages. This was a period in which Europe was united: 'The Christian Church was sovereign in Europe, and Church law was the only final law.' But within this united framework, a number of other levels of authority were acknowledged, and a considerable amount of diversity and plurality was allowed. Linguistic, cultural, legal and political differences were not considered a threat to the fundamental unity of European Christian civilisation, because that unity was 'moral and spiritual'. Thus, even though Wales had been conquered, 'Welsh civilisation was safe, and the Welsh language and the special Welsh way of life and society.'

But since '[M]an's intellect is a frail and uncertain thing', this – for Saunders Lewis – enlightened age came to an end. 'In the sixteenth century, the age of Luther in Germany, Machiavelli in Italy and the Tudors in Britain, the moral unity of Christendom was destroyed, and instead of Christianity another principle came to rule i.e. nationalism.' As a consequence of the growth of nationalism, instead of there being 'one authority in Europe, tens arose', each of them vying for absolute rule within a defined piece of

---

[27]   Saunders Lewis, *Egwyddorion Cenedlaetholdeb*, Plaid Genedlaethol Cymru, Pamffledi'r Ysgol Haf, no. 1 (n.d. [but 1926]). The pamphlet was republished by the party in 1975 with a translation by Bruce Griffiths as *Egwyddorion Cenedlaetholdeb/ Principles of Nationalism* – I draw on that translation in what follows.

territory. In this context, every manifestation of difference came to be considered a threat to the unity of the territory. 'Dictatorship demanded uniformity, one law, one language, monotony.' It is nationalism, therefore – more specifically, the pagan and material nationalism that developed in the sixteenth century – that led to the weakening and undermining of Wales's civilisation.

Based on his analysis, Saunders Lewis argued that Welsh nationalists should oppose the modern, destructive form of nationalism with an alternative form of nationalism 'that is a return to the medieval principle'. The aim of the party, therefore, was 'Not [to] fight for Wales' independence but for Wales' civilisation.' It should stake '[a] claim for freedom for Wales, not independence'. Independence was 'not worth having': Wales should instead seek responsibility for its own affairs or 'self-government'. The constitutional details of such a condition did not concern him. Indeed, if a large measure of devolution (as it is now known) could be secured within the British state, 'Wales may be content to recognise the supremacy of England. That is not the greatest evil. Let us recall the situation between the thirteenth and sixteenth centuries. Today we too can build Welsh civilisation without independence.' The criterion for judging any political order was not abstract constitutional principles, but rather whether or not it allowed Wales to plough its own furrow. If Wales possessed that right, Saunders Lewis would be content.

Although he rejected independence as a goal, and despite the emphasis he placed on the conditional nature of Welsh nationalist demands, it is important to note that the degree of self-government sought by Lewis was nonetheless extensive and far-reaching. He insisted that Welsh 'should be the sole medium of education from elementary school to the university'. Indeed:

> [The Welsh] language must be Wales's only official language, the language of Government in Wales, the language of every county, town and district council, of the council workers and law-courts. Every public medium that disseminates information, that teaches

or entertains the country … must also be in Welsh, and used to strengthen and elevate the Welsh concept.

In addition, he insisted that England should recognise Wales's right to be represented in the League of Nations, which Lewis referred to in Welsh as 'Seiat y Cenhedloedd' rather than the more usual 'Cynghrair y Cenhedloedd'. The Seiat was once a familiar feature of spiritual life in Nonconformist Wales – Christian fellowship meetings associated with the Methodist Revival, in particular. Lewis wanted Wales to participate in the league 'so that Wales and the Welsh can influence Europe and the world'. In this regard he appears to have imagined the league as a latter-day fellowship of nations.

It is revealing that the lecture makes no reference to any other nation or state as an example of the status Saunders Lewis wished to secure for Wales. This was because no such place existed, either then or now. International law did not (and still does not) possess the conceptual vocabulary to describe the status he desired for Wales. But for Lewis, this is the whole point. He regarded Welsh nationalism as part of a wider effort to transform the entire nature of the political, economic and social life of Wales, Europe and the world.[28] Yes, this life would incorporate some of the principles Lewis claimed were characteristic of the Middle Ages. Yet the argument made by some of Saunders Lewis's cruder critics – that he wanted to see Wales and Europe return to the condition of 'stable civilisation' he associates with the Middle Ages – is misleading.[29] Without doubt, he was guilty of romanticising that period. He knew, however, that there was no way of turning back the clock. Neither was Saunders Lewis blind to the potential of modernity – as demonstrated, for example, by his notably

[28] This is also the point made by Grahame Davies, *Sefyll yn y Bwlch: T. S. Eliot, Simone Weil, Saunders Lewis ac R. S. Thomas* (Caerdydd: Gwasg Prifysgol Cymru, 1999).

[29] Saunders Lewis, 'Dafydd Nanmor', *Y Llenor*, October 1925, 141. In his appreciation of Dafydd Nanmor, Lewis highlights the fifteenth-century poet's 'passionate love for a stable civilisation' ('cariad angerddol at wareiddiad sefydlog'). It is a phrase that very much reflects Lewis's own worldview.

progressive use of Freud's latest theories on the human psyche in his contemporaneous literary criticism.[30] Rather than turning back the clock, he sought a new way of living *in* the modern age; a means of living that would restore the most valuable elements of what he termed the 'classical tradition'.[31]

Saunders Lewis was not a reactionary, therefore, but something far more complex, paradoxical, and interesting than that. He is perhaps best described as being an 'anti-modern modernist'. He embraced some of the most challenging and even avant-garde elements of modern culture – Joyce as well as Freud – while simultaneously loathing other elements of modern life, which he compared unfavourably with his own (idealised) version of the principles, attributes and spirit of an earlier era. At that time, such a standpoint was not particularly unusual. It was embraced by many authors, poets and artists. Yeats, Eliot, Pound and Weil (towards the end of her short life, at least) are all examples of those with similar views on the right of the political spectrum. Indeed, while they certainly did not romanticise the Middle Ages, it would hardly be a disservice to such left-wing giants as Adorno, Benjamin and Bloch if we were also to regard them as 'anti-modern modernists'.

What was highly unusual (and perhaps unique) about Saunders Lewis was that he tried to turn such ideas into a programme for a political party. Doing so led to grave problems, because while the historical and social analysis he cultivated was undoubtedly capable of inspiring great art – and here one need only recall Lewis's own literary contributions – it was a weak foundation for establishing an appealing and practical political programme. Indeed, in the specific context of Wales, there were elements of Lewis's thinking view that were bound to make matters particularly difficult for the national cause for which he became the most prominent proponent. To understand why, we shall focus in turn on two important and interconnected elements of Lewis's ideas: his interpretation of Welsh history (historiography), and his attitude towards Nonconformity.

---

30 Saunders Lewis, *Williams Pantycelyn* (London: Foyle's Welsh Depot, 1927).
31 See, in this context, Lewis, *Williams Pantycelyn*, pp. 236–7.

Historiography

Although *Principles of Nationalism* presented only a brief sketch of Welsh history, there is no doubt that Saunders Lewis considered the interpretation it contained of that history and the resulting decline of civilisation in Wales to be factually correct. Even while concise, it was intended as a conventional historical narrative connecting and attempting to make sense of the relationship between various events. Yet it would be easy to amass examples, some of them Welsh and some from Europe, that demonstrate that the factual basis of Lewis's portrayal of the past is more than a little fanciful. It is certainly very difficult to support his central assertion that Wales (or Europe) enjoyed a period of freedom between Wales's conquest in the late thirteenth century and the sixteenth century.

It is kinder to consider Saunders Lewis's arguments as a form of intellectual history. In this context, his interpretation of the change in understandings of authority – or 'sovereignty' to use a term more familiar to students of politics – that occurred between the Middle Ages and modern times is more defensible. Until the Peace of Westphalia abolished any concept of a supranational authority in 1648, international law and convention did not recognise the absolute sovereignty of European leaders within their own territory. It cannot be denied, therefore, that there was an important change in the formal understanding of sovereignty at the end of the Middle Ages.

Saunders Lewis's argument, of course, was that this change had been a disastrous error. As a result, he wanted Plaid Cymru to advocate for a voice for Wales within a Europe and wider world in which interdependence rather than independence was the governing principle in international politics, with interdependence founded on respecting rather than eradicating difference. It is an attractive doctrine. Indeed, Saunders Lewis's belief in unity through pluralism may well appear enlightened, progressive and startlingly contemporary. But was that the case?

One of the fundamental problems with his analysis is Saunders Lewis's tendency to treat the history of ideas and actual history, so to speak, as synonymous. As a result, he differentiates far too categorically between the practices of sovereignty in the Middle Ages and the modern era. The (factual) truth of the matter is that, if indeed it had ever existed in the manner which Saunders Lewis contends, supranational authority had existed in name only long before it was formally abolished in Westphalia. Moreover, in practical terms, interdependence remained a fact in the age of the sovereign state; indeed, on all measures, it intensified. With the passage of time, and no doubt falteringly, this interdependence was formalised through a growing corpus of international law. That is to say, the constitutional position known as 'independence' did not prove to be a barrier to interdependence and collaboration. Neither did the recognition of a supranational authority suffice to ensure tolerance. From a historical point of view, the significant difference he claimed to exist between 'freedom' and 'independence' is a castle built on sand. In differentiating between the two – and in condemning the latter so harshly – Saunders Lewis created a significant practical problem for his party. Clearly, to successfully advocate for 'independence' would have been an extremely difficult challenge given Wales's history. But at least it would mean arguing for a condition that was familiar and meaningful in terms of international law and constitutional practice. But by accepting Saunders Lewis's assertion that there was an important moral difference between independence and freedom, it became necessary for Plaid Cymru to try to define 'freedom' in concrete political-constitutional terms. As will be seen in the rest of this study, it is hardly an exaggeration to say that every development in Plaid Cymru's constitutional thinking up until the present day can be viewed as an attempt to reconcile reality with Saunders Lewis's ideas about sovereignty as laid out in *Principles of Nationalism*.[32]

But even as an exceptionally stubborn thorn was left lodged in the party's flank because of the influence of Saunders Lewis's fanciful take on European history, the effects of another element of his historiography came close to paralysing it completely. This

[32] Plaid Cymru's eventual decision (in 2003) to begin advocating for 'independence' postdates the period under consideration in this book and is discussed in Volume Two of this study.

because Lewis's analysis of Welsh history – as outlined in *Principles of Nationalism* and expanded upon in several other works written by him around the same time – challenged conventional opinion in such a far-reaching and scandalous way that it was considered insulting by many of those that Lewis was attempting to draw into the nationalist fold. In order to fully recognise the extent of the unease (and worse) generated by Saunders Lewis's version of Welsh history, we must first understand the dominant version of that history which existed at the time. This was – for want of a better characterisation – the Cymru Fydd-style account developed at the turn of the twentieth century under the influence of O. M. Edwards.

In a discussion of the influence of O. M. Edwards's interpretation of the history of Wales, Alun Llywelyn-Williams argued that:

> the interpretation of the Welsh past that he offered his fellow countrymen was as revolutionary in content and effect on Wales as Marx's ideas had been on the world in general. We are indebted to him for much, if not most, of the myths that sustained Wales, or at least Welsh-speaking society in Wales, for half a century and more.[33]

Llywelyn-Williams was not given to hyperbole, and the fact that such an astute observer could discuss Edwards's influence in such sweeping terms underlines the latter's importance in shaping the way in which Welsh people understood their history and their place in the world.

Edwards succeeded in overhauling earlier understandings of Welsh history. Filtering out some of the more obviously problematic elements that had characterised popular historiography before the subject was professionalised in universities, he added additional elements to the mix. But most of all, he generated and popularised an overarching narrative that both encompassed

[33] Alun Llywelyn-Williams, 'Owen M. Edwards: hanesydd a llenor', in *Nes Na'r Hanesydd: Ysgrifau Llenyddol* (Dinbych: Gwasg Gee, 1968), p. 13; translation. See also, Hazel Walford Davies, *O. M. Edwards* (Cardiff: University of Wales Press, 1988); J. E. Caerwyn Williams, 'Cenedlaetholdeb haneswyr Cymru gynnar Rhydychen', in Geraint H. Jenkins (ed.), *Cof Cenedl XIII* (Llandysul: Gwasg Gomer, 1998), pp. 1–32.

and connected Wales's history from the distant past to the present day. This last point is especially important because, as R. T. Jenkins points out, Welsh historians before the days of Edwards tended to be divided in two camps. One camp focused on the history of 'old Wales' exclusively – the Age of the *Cywyddwyr*, the Age of the Princes, the Age of the Saints, and so on. The second tended to dismiss everything in Welsh history prior to the arrival of Protestantism and Nonconformity. O. M. Edwards's great achievement was to reconcile these two traditions.[34] He did so through the medium of the *Gwerin*.[35]

It was through the lens of the *Gwerin* that O. M. Edwards understood the significance of events in the history of Wales. The *Gwerin* were without compare. He spoke, as though transfixed, about the *Gwerin*'s 'faithfulness and honesty, their desire to do what was right, their love of thought, their soundness of judgement, the tenderness of their feeling and strength of their determination'.[36] He understood the history of the country as providing unmistakeable confirmation of the tenacity and dignity of its *Gwerin* in the face of every hardship and oppression. Even if O. M. Edwards, on R. T. Jenkins's account, challenged Nonconformist prejudices about the 'dark age' before Protestantism, he reserved his greatest and most extravagant praise for more recent times. Indeed, so great was his desire to champion 'Cymru'r Werin' – the Wales of the *Gwerin* – that some of his judgements can only be regarded as comically asinine. 'The glory of the Wales of Princes', he once said, 'did not come close to the glory of the Wales of the

34 R. T. Jenkins, 'Owen M. Edwards', *Y Llenor*, IX (spring 1930), 17. Puleston Jones made the same point when he claimed that Edwards's great achievement was 'keeping the old and the new in Wales's life as one' – see John Puleston Jones, *Ysgrifau*, ed. R. W. Jones (Bala: Gwasg y Bala, 1926), p. 53; translation. Jenkins may have done something of a disservice to earlier historiography by viewing it in such binary terms, cf. Dafydd Glyn Jones, 'Saith math o hanes', in Geraint H. Jenkins (ed.), *Cof Cenedl, XIV* (Llandysul: Gwasg Gomer, 1999), pp. 69–103. Nonetheless, Jenkins's discussion of Edwards remains enlightening.
35 For discussions of the idea of the *Gwerin* and its significance see Alun Llywelyn-Williams, *Y Nos, Y Niwl a'r Ynys: Agweddau ar y Profiad Rhamantaidd yng Nghymru, 1890–1914* (Caerdydd: Gwasg Prifysgol Cymru, 1960), and Prys Morgan, 'Gwerin Cymru, y ffaith a'r ddelfryd', *Transactions of the Honourable Society of Cymmrodorion*, Part 1 (1967), 117–31.
36 O. M. Edwards, 'Y nodyn lleddf', *Er Mwyn Cymru* (Wrecsam: Cyfres Gwerin Cymru, IV, 1922), p. 65; translation.

Gwerin. In the first awakening, there was no poet like Ceiriog, and the Golden Age saw no one greater than Islwyn.'[37] Figures from the past were evaluated in the context of the present and the tendency was for even the greatest to be regarded as falling short when measured against the giants of the contemporary Liberal, Nonconformist *Gwerin*. If O. M. Edwards's great achievement was to combine the two traditions, he nonetheless clung to many of the assumptions as well as the prejudices of Welsh Nonconformist historiography.[38]

Considered against this background, it becomes easier to appreciate how alien, challenging and, indeed, shocking Saunders Lewis's reading of Welsh history appeared to so many of his contemporaries. In *Principles of Nationalism* and a series of other books and essays that he produced during an astonishingly productive period between the mid-1920s and mid-1930s, he turned the O. M. Edwards-influenced understanding of Welsh history on its head. Like Edwards, Lewis's interest encompassed the entire course of Wales's history, but while the first glorified the present day, the second considered that modern Wales had fallen a very long way from its past glories.

While O. M. Edwards promoted and celebrated the *Gwerin*, in stark contrast, one of Lewis's core themes was *pendefigaeth*, which we shall translate as nobility. Edwards, it should be noted, was perhaps the principal advocate of the Welsh version of what was one of the most familiar and characteristic myths of stateless nations throughout nineteenth-century Europe, namely the myth of the class-less nation. For him, this (supposed) quality was

[37]   O. M. Edwards, *Trem ar Hanes Cymru* (Llanuwchllyn: Y Llyfrau Bach, 1893); translation. Ceiriog and Islwyn (the use of these, their bardic names, remains ubiquitous) were both celebrated poets in nineteenth-century and early twentieth-century Wales. By now, however, it is to hard conceive of any serious critic agreeing with Edwards's judgement of their (relative) merits when compared to some of their more illustrious predecessors.
[38]   O. M. Edwards's sectarianism is particularly evident in the travel writing he produced in the wake of his various overseas journeys. Emlyn Sherrington provides a scathing analysis in 'O. M. Edwards, culture and the industrial classes', *Llafur*, 6 (1) (1992), 28–41. Saunders Lewis's (mature) judgement was more restrained. As part of a wider appreciation, he suggested that contemporary readers would profit little from reading O. M. Edwards's impressions of his foreign travels. See Saunders Lewis, 'Owen M. Edwards', in *Triwyr Penllyn* (Caerdydd: Plaid Cymru, 1956), p. 34.

something to celebrate – a sign of Welsh people's moral supremacy in comparison with less fortunate peoples whose societies
were divided on class lines. For Lewis, however, a nation without
its own nobility was an incomplete nation – this because of the
indispensable leadership and educative role played by the nobility in any healthy society. For him, therefore, the decline of the
Welsh nobility was the great tragedy of Welsh history. The growth
of popular citizenship and democracy in the wake of the development of modern understandings of authority/sovereignty did
not come close to compensating for that loss.

Thus, one of the central themes in Saunders Lewis's various
critical discussions of more contemporary literatures was the
success (or lack thereof) of various authors in transcending the
inhuman and anti-artistic forces of the modern era. The point is
highlighted when we recall that 'The Artist in Philistia' was the
rather heavy-handed title he gave to the 'series' of two studies on
important figures in nineteenth-century literature, the aforementioned *Ceiriog* (1929) and *Daniel Owen* (1935).[39] But it is perhaps in
his most brilliant piece of literary criticism – *Williams Pantycelyn*
(1927) – that the boldness of Lewis's historiographical vision is
most readily apparent. In his view, Williams's greatness stemmed
from the fact that 'he and his colleagues in the Methodist Revival'
had succeeded in 'rediscovering practices and principles that
belonged to Wales and Christian Europe before the existence of
Protestantism'.[40] In other words, Lewis adopted Catholic standards from the past as a yardstick against which to measure the
work of perhaps the greatest hero of Welsh Nonconformity.
Indeed, Lewis analysed Williams's work using a conceptual
framework derived from classical Catholic mysticism. If all of this
were not enough to provoke a fit of the vapours in post-Victorian
Nonconformist Wales, his appreciation of Pantycelyn's work also

[39] As well as these, see Saunders Lewis, *Straeon Glasynys: Detholiad gyda
Rhagymadrodd* (Dinbych: Gwasg Gee, 1943). The foreword makes is made abundantly clear that this work had been originally intended as the third volume in the
series.
[40] Lewis, *Williams Pantycelyn*, p. 23; translation. Here I draw heavily on
Meredydd Evans, 'Saunders Lewis a Methodistiaeth Galfinaidd', *Y Traethodydd*,
630 (January 1994), 12–13.

repeatedly emphasised the carnality of human existence. Lewis was by no means a puritan. His claim – a deeply shocking one for many of his readers at the time – was that Pantycelyn should not be regarded as the pious, humourless puritan of Nonconformist cliché.

Nonconformism

This brings us directly to the aspect of Saunders Lewis's worldview that more than any other challenged the dominant views of his time, namely his religious attitudes and commitments. Saunders Lewis turned his back on Welsh Nonconformist beliefs and gradually came to align himself with Catholicism, before becoming a full member of the Catholic church in 1933. He did not undertake this journey of abandonment and adoption in private.[41] Famously, he debated Catholicism with W. J. Gruffydd in the pages of the literary journal *Y Llenor* in 1927. But Lewis's general opinion was by then already reasonably well known. In a speech in 1923 he had declared that 'It would be a good thing for Welsh theologians to read Pope Pius IX's syllabus on the "Principal errors of our time" so that they might observe the strength and beauty of a clear and certain mind.'[42]

His religious attitudes were also apparent – albeit implicit rather than explicit – in the outline of European history he presented in *Principles of Nationalism*. Blame for Europe's ills from the sixteenth century onwards was apportioned to Luther, as well as Machiavelli and the Tudors. While his criticism of Luther had been formulated in the way least likely to offend Welsh Nonconformist sensibilities – it was Luther the defender of the established state church rather than Luther the father of Protestantism that Lewis admonished – the point, nevertheless, was clear. It was the loss of religious unity that followed from denying the supremacy of the Church of Rome that had led Europe astray, leading directly to division, disharmony and war. Even if Nonconformism was to be

---

[41] For evidence of some of the personal dimensions of this journey see Lewis, *Letters to Margaret Gilcriest*.

[42] Quoted in John Emyr, *Dadl Grefyddol Saunders Lewis a W. J. Gruffydd* (Pen-y-bont ar Ogwr: Gwasg Efengylaidd Cymru, 1986), pp. 7–8; translation.

viewed as an improvement on the state-sponsored Protestantism of the Anglican Church, this was because its theological tenets (according to Lewis, at least) were in fact *closer* to those of Catholicism – an interpretation that ran directly counter to the view of Nonconformists themselves, of course. We shall not seek to delve further into Lewis's theological views here. Suffice to note that many aspects of them were the source of considerable vexation in Wales during his time as leader of Plaid Cymru.

Those who have come of age in an era in which Wales has become the least religiously observant country in the British Isles often find it difficult to comprehend how central Nonconformism once was to the Welsh self-image and worldview. It is also difficult to truly appreciate the extent of the passions once fired by religious sectarianism and (more politely) denominationalism. More difficult still, perhaps, is understanding and comprehending the anti-Catholic sentiment that was once umbilically linked to the militant Nonconformity of previous eras.[43] We shall return to this in the context of a separate discussion of the accusations of fascism made against Plaid Cymru.[44] For the moment we must be content with emphasising that Saunders Lewis's efforts to turn O. M. Edwards's normative order on its head and install Catholic Wales above Nonconformist Protestant Wales was not simply bold, it was nothing short of blasphemous.

The impact of this blasphemy was accentuated by Saunders Lewis's own background. Much has been made of Lewis's status as an outsider; as someone who stood on the periphery, so to speak, never 'one of us'. It is a central theme in D. Tecwyn Lloyd's biography; central too to his friend R. Williams Parry's great tribute poem.[45] There is certainly a great deal of truth in this image, and

---

43 See Trystan Owain Hughes, *Winds of Change: The Roman Catholic Church and Society in Wales, 1916–1962* (Cardiff: University of Wales Press, 1999).

44 See Wyn Jones, *The Fascist Party in Wales?*

45 These are the core lines of the poem:

> O idiot – O forsaken fool; fie for the shame
> Of a great, unloved bird winging its lonely way;
> Hatched in a different field's corner not the same
> God as ours rules over – shaped from a different clay

[Buost ffôl, O wrthodedig, ffôl; canys gwae / Aderyn heb gâr ac enaid digymar heb gefnydd; / Heb hanfod o'r un cynefin yng nghwr yr un cae – / Heb gorff o

there is no question that Saunders Lewis saw himself as a voice (and a rejected one at that) on the periphery of Welsh life.[46] Even so, this conventional picture omits one important aspect of his public impact, especially as he first came to public prominence in the early 1920s. Lewis was a product of Welsh Nonconformity; the product of a family that might be regarded as forming part of that tradition's nobility.[47] His father was a Welsh Calvinistic Methodist minister and his mother was part of a well-known family among whose members were counted 'two of the princes of the Welsh language pulpit in the nineteenth century', namely her father, Owen Thomas, and her grandfather, William Roberts.[48] His was a family that embodied the idealised image of the *Gwerin* that O. M. Edwards had done so much to promote and popularise. Before gaining respect and acclaim as ministers, Lewis's grandfather and great-grandfather had earned a living as stonemasons – both of them having worked on Telford's bridge over the Menai Strait.[49] In terms of his lineage, at least, Saunders Lewis was no outsider. Here, rather, was a man who rejected the tradition from within. Reminding ourselves of this fact is key if we wish to fully comprehend the bitterness and controversy that he aroused.

In addition, as is so often the case with those who have converted, Saunders Lewis's attitude towards the Nonconformity that he had left behind was often rather scornful. His public

gyffelyb glai na Duw o'r un defnydd]: R. Williams Parry, 'J.S.L.', in Alan Llwyd a Gwynn ap Gwilym (eds), *Blodeugerdd o Farddoniaeth Gymraeg yr Ugeinfed Ganrif* (Llandysul: Gomer, 1998), p. 53. Translation taken from *https://awenydd.cymru/ sheaves-of-awen/menu2/translation-of-jsl-by-r-williams-parry* (accessed 7 May 2024).

46   See, for example, Lewis, *Letters to Margaret Gilcriest*, p. 180, and Saunders Lewis, 'Dylanwadau: Saunders Lewis mewn ymgom ag Aneirin Talfan Davies', *Taliesin*, 2 (Christmas 1961), 13.

47   Saunders Lewis referred to the Nonconformist ministry as 'the nobility of the pulpit' ('pendefigaeth y pulpud') and saw its development as a key part of the recreation of the Welsh nation. Alas, because of the circumstances of its development, it was 'a poor and imperfect' nobility. See Saunders Lewis, 'Y deffroad mawr', in Saunders Lewis, *Meistri a'u Crefft* (Caerdydd: Gwasg Prifysgol Cymru, 1981), p. 292; translation. Also, Branwen Jarvis, 'Saunders Lewis: golwg Gatholig Gymreig ar ferched', in D. Ben Rees (ed.), *Ffydd a Gwreiddiau John Saunders Lewis* (Lerpwl: Cyhoeddiadau Modern Cymreig, 2002), p. 78.

48   R. Geraint Gruffydd, 'Portread', yn Rees (ed.), *Ffydd a Gwreiddiau John Saunders Lewis*, p. 9. See also D. Ben Rees's essay, 'Gwreiddiau J. Saunders Lewis ar Lannau Mersi', in the same volume, pp. 13–41.

49   Rees, 'Gwreiddiau J. Saunders Lewis ar Lannau Mersi', p. 23.

comments never quite matched the level of disdain found in his private letters. (Among the more memorable examples in his letters to Margaret Gilcriest is his reference to the 'black barbarism' of Nonconformity![50]) Nevertheless, what he did say in public – for example in the 1923 speech to which we have already referred – was more than enough to make clear his dim view of Nonconformist Wales. With time, he would become more appreciative of that tradition, recognising that it had value in its own right beyond its (alleged) role in steering the Welsh back to the eternal verities of Catholicism.[51] But this happened later, after the end of his time as president of Plaid Genedlaethol Cymru. During his period as party president, from the point of view of Nonconformist Wales, Saunders Lewis remained a black sheep: someone who had blasphemed against the faith, values and worldview of the fathers. Yet this was also the man who wished to become that nation's political leader.

Laying the foundations

In the year 2000, the British Labour Party celebrated its centenary, this despite the fact that the party's existence was not formalised until 1918. In Labour's case, a political party is regarded as having existed well before its constitution and standing orders were

---

[50] Lewis, *Letters to Margaret Gilcriest*, p. 441. Also pp. 468, 471.

[51] Here, I reject to some extent the interpretation put forward by Meredydd Evans in his important essay, 'Saunders Lewis a Methodistiaeth Galfinaidd'. In my view, Evans does not sufficiently acknowledge the extent to which Saunders Lewis's thinking developed and changed during the course of his long life. His attitudes to Nonconformity by the time he wrote *Merch Gwern Hywel* (1964), say, were different from his earlier attitudes, and it is rather misleading to suggest that his more mature views represented his attitude throughout. More generally, too much emphasis has been placed on Saunders Lewis's consistency and single-mindedness at the expense of appreciating the way he changed his opinion in some very significant ways over time. To give only one other example germane to the present discussion, by the time he published his essay on poet Guto'r Glyn's military career in 1976, his interpretation of the development of nationalism had changed in fundamental ways compared with the interpretation in the *Principles of Nationalism* fifty years earlier. By then, he (re)located the development of the modern nation to England and France in the first half of the fifteenth century. Luther, Machiavelli and the Tudors were not to blame after all! See Saunders Lewis, 'Gyrfa filwrol Guto'r Glyn', in *Meistri a'u Crefft*, pp. 120–1.

drafted, before membership lists were drawn up, and so on. In Plaid Cymru's case, in contrast, it is often argued that the formal framework of a party existed before an actual political party had been created to fill it. Indeed, attempting to date the point at which Plaid Cymru transformed into a 'genuine' political party has become one of the recurring tropes in the scholarly literature that focuses on its development and various trials and tribulations. One doubts whether much has been learnt from these various attempts to pinpoint the moment at which the party came of age.[52] As with so much in the social world, what is labelled a 'political party' is so fluid that, as a category, it encompasses a most extraordinary variety of forms. We need, therefore, not spend too much time worrying about when exactly the first part of the name *Plaid* Cymru (the 'party' of Wales) became a reality rather than a marker of aspiration.

Although there is no consensus among commentators on the date of this (alleged) turning point in the party's history – was it 1945, or 1958/9, or 1966, or even 1999? – there is widespread agreement about what had gone before. Before it became a true political party, it is argued, Plaid Cymru was a cultural movement or language pressure group. In other words, it was a manifestation of cultural nationalism. Only after it had matured sufficiently can it be considered to have become a political party promoting political nationalism. There is undeniably an element of truth in this. There is certainly plenty of evidence from within the party's own ranks that the cultural (and even social) aspects of its activities tended to overshadow the politics that should have been its real work. As late as 1956, for example, Tudur Jones, one of Gwynfor Evans's most loyal lieutenants, wrote to D. J. and Noëlle Davies referring to that year's party Summer School in the following terms: 'I believe it went well – but, really, we must have political lectures next year.'[53] The view that the party was at

---

52   Davies, *The Welsh Nationalist Party*, pp. 260–8, is the best of these various discussions.
53   Tudur Jones to D.J. and Noëlle Davies, 8 August 1956, Papurau Noëlle Davies, National Library of Wales; translation.

times more literary circle than political movement is certainly not without foundation.

But having acknowledged this reality, it is also important to acknowledge that this was only ever part of the story. It is certainly misleading to portray the party's nationalism during the early years of its existence as being only cultural rather than political. We saw in the previous chapter how problematic it is to attempt to posit a strict division between the political and the cultural. As with so many of the other categorisations used in discussions of nationalism, this alleged binary confuses rather than enlightens. Indeed, one of the themes that surfaces most consistently in the Plaid Cymru publications in the years before the Second World War is the inadequacy of cultural nationalism *without* political nationalism. The 'Saint David's Day Welshman' was a much-derided figure.[54] This was the quintessential cultural nationalist: a man who, on 1 March, gave forth in high emotion about the achievements of Fair Wales [Gwalia Wen], without ever feeling that there were broader political commitments that should flow from these cultural ties through the rest of the year. More than anyone else, perhaps, it was Lloyd George that was regarded as personifying this attitude. For the new generation of nationalists, only political nationalism could offer a future for Welsh culture. Cultural nationalism alone was worse than useless.

It should also be recalled that one of the things that made the establishment of the party a genuinely new development in the history of Welsh nationalism was its insistence that no Welsh nationalist should belong to any other party except Plaid Genedlaethol Cymru. Before the party's establishment, there were members in every political party in Wales who described themselves with pride as 'Welsh nationalists' (including even the occasional Tory). One of the main arguments deployed by members of the new party was that the efforts made to champion the nationalist cause through these other parties had all failed, and that there was no hope of salvation from the 'English parties'. The only hope

---

[54] See, for example, the cartoon by Gwilym R. Jones in the March 1927 issue of *Y Ddraig Goch*, 7.

for progress was to get serious, abandon other political parties and establish a nationalist party that would give priority to the national cause – create a party that would always put Wales first. This was a deeply controversial position in the party's early years. Plaid periodicals acknowledged that many more people could have been drawn into its ranks if it was prepared to slacken the rule that meant members of the nationalist party were not allowed to be members of any other political party.[55] Yet it held fast to that rule precisely because both the leadership and wider membership believed that it was only a political party that could offer salvation for Wales. It is completely insufficient, therefore, to regard the Welsh Nationalist Party – even in its first years of existence – as simply a cultural movement or language pressure group.

There is, without doubt, considerable discussion of the condition, status and future of the Welsh language in Plaid Cymru's periodicals during the period of Saunders Lewis's leadership. But this goes hand in hand with engagement with a much broader range of issues. Indeed, such an astonishingly extensive range of subjects is discussed that it may well be more appropriate to highlight a lack of focus rather than an overemphasis on the language. Consider, for example, the contents of the editorial column of *Y Ddraig Goch* – 'Nodiadau'r mis' ('Notes for the month') – a column through which Saunders Lewis expressed his own views and opinions between September 1926 and January 1937.[56] Each column tended to focus if only briefly on four or five different matters, and the variety within each individual column – let alone between one month's column and the next – is striking.

---

55 See, for example, *Y Ddraig Goch*, June 1926, 2; *Y Ddraig Goch*, July 1929, 1.
56 Ambrose Bebb was *Y Ddraig Goch*'s first editor. He held the post for a short period between the first issue in June 1926 and September 1926. He was then succeeded by an editorial committee of three – Saunders Lewis, Iorwerth Peate and Prosser Rhys. Peate gave up his role in January 1927. It is not clear (to me, at least) precisely when Rhys's role came to an end, but his biographer suggests that during his time as a member of the committee he was involved only with the business side of the paper (Rhisiart Hincks, *E. Prosser Rhys 1901–45* (Llandysul: Gomer, 1980), p. 132). By the April 1928 issue, there is a reference on the first page to Saunders Lewis as editor. He continued to act as editor until his imprisonment in January 1937 for his role in the burning of a hut at the site of the proposed bombing school in Pen Llŷn.

To note just one representative example, in October 1926 the main focus was on the recent meeting of the League of Nations at Geneva (described as 'last month's main event') which provided an opportunity to note, in turn, the inadequacy of the press in England and Wales. The conclusion of the analysis was that 'One of the requirements for the Welsh press today is a European education in politics.' Lewis also took the opportunity to champion rugby at the expense of football in Welsh schools because football in Wales was so anglicised in outlook ('Away with football from Wales!'). He also emphasised the need to care for Welsh cemeteries and supported calls to protect the old bridge at Carmarthen. But of course, the most important event by far in Wales during the summer and autumn of 1926 was the miners' strike, an exceptionally bitter strike that had a devastating effect on a quarter of a million Welsh miners and their families. The editor gives some attention to the strikes in passing. After condemning both sides his conclusion was that an economic policy must be devised for Wales based on the party's principles, 'namely, to put spiritual things first, and for every member of society to cooperate for the benefit of the whole of society'.

It would be unfair to describe the contents of these editorial notes as unpolitical – all of these various matters related to politics in one way or another. It would also be unfair to accuse Saunders Lewis and his colleagues of lacking seriousness. It is no small matter to take on the task of establishing a political party, writing and publishing associated periodicals, organising and addressing numerous party and public meetings, and undertaking the hard work required to maintain and try to expand a new organisation. Nonetheless, *Y Ddraig Goch* retains a dilettanteish feel in this period. There was a marked tendency to leap from one topic to another: the influence of Hegelianism on Welsh theology was one of the topics scrutinised in the February 1927 issue, for example, while developments in China were given priority in April. And although Saunders Lewis was a man of uncommonly wide learning, he could hardly claim specialist knowledge about everything he was so confidently and boldly pronouncing upon in his editorial notes. One might almost say that he was playing at politics.

However, from the point of view of the party's prospects, perhaps the most damaging aspect of the tone adopted on the pages of *Y Ddraig Goch* was the feeling of distance – accompanied, perhaps, by a certain insouciance – which characterised its engagement with events in contemporary Wales. The attitude of the president and his party to the miners' strike provides the best example. *Y Ddraig Goch*'s 'Notes for the month' castigated both sides to the dispute. Following the coal owners' sweeping victory at the end of 1926, it argued that it was the inadequacies of the miners' leaders that had brought about their defeat.[57] The miners may indeed have been badly led, and the disdainful treatment of miners' leader A. J. Cook in the pages of *Y Ddraig Goch* may well have been merited. Even so, there is a palpable lack of empathy with the hardship and suffering of the miners and their families.[58] A tragedy was afoot in the coalfields of south Wales; a tragedy that would have a disastrous impact on a substantial proportion of Lewis's fellow nationals. Yet Saunders Lewis's attitude towards the whole affair verged on the unfeeling. Given the importance he placed on acting honourably, it is also striking that he did not show more admiration for the solidarity and determination demonstrated by south Wales miners in such desperate circumstances. But so it was. In reading his various comments, one is left with the distinct impression that Saunders Lewis did not regard their struggle as relevant to his own. Is it any wonder therefore that so many of his countrymen and women responded to such attitudes by deciding that Saunders Lewis's cause was not their cause?

The tone of the party's publications changed over time: the dilettantism of the early years dissipated. As D. Hywel Davies shows in his masterly study of the early years of the Welsh Nationalist Party, in response to its failure to make any impression on local government politics, and especially in the wake of

---

[57]   *Y Ddraig Goch*, January 1927, 1–2.
[58]   This also contrasts with what we know from his private letters about Saunders Lewis's attitude at the time of an earlier strike in 1921. See Lewis, *Letters to Margaret Gilcriest*, p. 449: 'it is amazing that with so much provocation to riot in the display of soldiers in south Wales, the strikers have yet behaved like angels of peace'.

its disappointing result in the Caernarfon constituency in the 1929 general election, it evolved into a more 'conventional' political party.[59] It developed and adopted more detailed policy proposals in place of the generalised abstractions of earlier years. As part of this process, other figures within the party became influential – D. J. Davies being one of the most prominent. Nevertheless, neither the extent nor the speed of change should be overstated. It was a gradual transformation rather than a revolution. Furthermore, Saunders Lewis's influence continued to far outshine that of the movement's other leaders. By means of his complete control of the party in its early years, he established a set of attitudes and attributes that would continue to be associated with Welsh political nationalism for many years to come. Lewis opened a furrow – some may prefer rut – that determined the party's direction for an extended period and from which it found it difficult to escape.

What, then, were the general attitudes and attributes established by Saunders Lewis in the party's formative years? Three are all-important.

Nationalism as a crusade for civilisation. Wales needed to be 'saved', not for its own sake, but because of its small yet precious share in and contribution to Western civilisation. This was the core of Saunders Lewis's commitment to Welsh nationalism. He saw the Welsh national movement as part of a wider crusade to sustain civilisation in the face of those forces – 'materialistic' forces, above all – that threatened its annihilation. As we have already noted, there is an element of the crusade to every national movement that seeks to free a 'captive' nation. All contain important cultural dimensions as well as more narrowly defined political elements; all challenge the fundamental institutions of state and society and the varying myths and fables that sustain them. In this sense, at least, their intentions are inevitably far-reaching and, indeed, revolutionary. To view them in terms of a crusade is therefore entirely appropriate. But Saunders Lewis's vision went a step further. For him, nationalism was no less than a part of a general battle to maintain what was truly valuable in human

---

[59] See in particular Davies, *The Welsh Nationalist Party*, pp. 71–151.

society. By any measure, his was a panoramic, vastly ambitious conception of politics. At the time, of course, such an approach to 'the political' was far from exceptional. What was communism, for example, if not a crusade to transform society? By the final decades of the twentieth century, and in the West in particular, it has become rather anachronistic to conceive of politics in such a way: our vision of the purpose and indeed possibilities of politics has become more miserly and truncated. In so far as the under-standing of 'nationalism as a crusade' was adopted by successors like Gwynfor Evans, Plaid Cymru was a party that stood against the tide of contemporary politics.

The central role of the Welsh language in Welsh civilisation. Saunders Lewis considered the Welsh language and associated culture to be a central part of Welsh civilisation and, therefore, central to Wales's contribution to civilisation more generally. For this reason, he believed that the main duty of Welsh politicians was to maintain the Welshness of Wales. If this were not done successfully, then the people of Wales would be responsible for damaging and undermining civilisation as a whole.

One of the consequences of this belief, at least as it was inter-preted by Saunders Lewis, was the presence of a fundamental ambiguity in his attitude towards those in Wales who did not speak Welsh. If the language was the basis of Welsh civilisation, to what extent could those Welsh people who did not speak Welsh be considered participants in that civilisation? But to what extent could one hope to save Wales's civilisation without the support of those who did not speak the language? Then again, would it ever be possible to gain that support without destroying the very thing Welsh nationalism was trying to save? Saunders Lewis's attitude to such questions was deeply ambiguous, as indeed was his gen-eral attitude towards those in Wales who do not speak Welsh. For the avoidance of doubt, it must be stressed it was ambivalence and not animosity, hatred or indifference that characterised his attitude. For each statement by Saunders Lewis that is scornful of some aspect of Anglo-Welsh culture, we find another statement – or act – that is far more positive. Yet from a political point of view, there is little to choose between ambivalence and a more consistently hostile attitude, because the ambiguity was sufficient in itself to make it even more difficult for Plaid Genedlaethol Cymru to secure the support of its co-nationals.

There is a striking paradox here: both the most attractive and the least attractive elements of Saunders Lewis's political vision stem from the same source. It is his concern with civilisation that leads him to adopt a qualified and conditional version of nationalism which claims that the only justification for nationalism is the fact that it contributes to the maintenance of civilisation in the broadest sense. However, it is that same concern for civilisation that is responsible for the ambiguity that characterises his attitude towards a substantial proportion of the Welsh population.

Although some certainly agreed with Saunders Lewis on this matter, not everyone in the ranks of the party shared the same ambiguity. Even in the earliest days of Plaid Cymru, a number of prominent figures including D. J. Davies argued strongly that its most important mission was to evangelise amongst those in Wales who did not speak Welsh. In doing so, however, Davies nonetheless agreed with Saunders Lewis's fundamental belief that the Welsh language is central to what is now known as Welsh 'identity' and that the death of the language would signify a huge blow to civilisation in general. Indeed, it is a view shared by the vast majority of the party's supporters – both then and now.

Nationalism as a complete political ideology. One of the most striking elements of Saunders Lewis's political thinking – and the ideological legacy he bequeathed his party – was his attempt to argue that nationalism was a complete political ideology in and of itself. That is, he claimed that nationalism not only supplies the requisite intellectual tools with which to determine the boundaries of the political community, but he also argued that nationalism supplied the principles and values with which to establish the form and content of public policy within those boundaries once established.

Saunders Lewis was by no means the first nationalist to argue that nationalism offered a guide for engaging with every aspect of political life. As we will see, neither was he the last Welsh nationalist to believe this. Although the intellectual case for regarding nationalism as an ideology which exists in a symbiotic relationship with other ideologies appears overwhelming (as discussed in the previous chapter), some nationalists have denied and continue to deny that their worldview has been sullied by the influence of other political ideologies as that term is conventionally understood – liberalism or socialism, etc. Similarly, many of those who consider themselves socialists, liberals and so on, would deny that their political ideas have been tainted by nationalist assumptions.

The fact that Saunders Lewis regarded nationalism as a complete, all-encompassing ideology might be considered a matter of only academic interest. But what makes it a matter of the greatest import for those seeking to understand the development of the political thought of Plaid Cymru is the way in which Lewis tried to define nationalism in contrast with – and in opposition to – socialism.[60] For Lewis, socialism and nationalism were fundamentally opposed. Welsh nationalists had not always thought this. There were, for example, obvious elements of socialism in the thinking of Michael D. Jones, the father of Welsh nationalism. Similarly, the programme of Cymru Fydd contained elements that can only be regarded as socialist. Many members of Plaid Genedlaethol Cymru were former members of the Labour Party or the Independent Labour Party, and continued to embrace left-wing values even after changing their party allegiance. Yet, Lewis insisted that these views were inconsistent with the fundamental ideas of the party they were now members of. The assertion that nationalism was a complete, anti-socialist ideology became a means by which Saunders Lewis – and his successors – rebuffed calls to reshape the party's programme in a way that made it more consistent with the views of most of the membership and the bulk of the Welsh electorate.

60 At various points, Saunders Lewis tempered his condemnation of 'socialism' by noting that his target was 'state socialism' – a combination of Labourism and Marxism (he saw the latter as the logical endpoint of the former). But as can be seen from reading the columns of Y Ddraig Goch, he did not do so consistently. Rather, his condemnation of 'socialism' tends to be remarkably general.

If every form of nationalism exists in symbiotic relationship with other ideologies, how then should we characterise the ideas and values that Saunders Lewis combined with nationalist themes to create his political worldview? Conservative is probably the best unadorned description of his position – provided, that is, we recall that the British Conservative Party's version of conservatism does not exhaust the possibilities of that ideology. The great, historical achievement of the Tories has been to adapt to changes in society while keeping its grasp on power to safeguard the interests of the most powerful within it. In contrast, Lewis's conservatism was a romantic conservatism: one that resisted rather than embraced the principal trends of the modern age such as the growth of the centralised state and the development of capitalism. Except for Ireland, this kind of conservatism has had relatively little influence in the British Isles since the late nineteenth century. One can hardly imagine any part of these islands where it had less chance of being taken up than in twentieth-century Wales. This was, after all, a country that became deeply reliant on the central state when its marginal economic status led – ultimately – to economic and social disaster in the interwar period. Nonetheless, this was the ideology that Saunders Lewis sought to promote under the cloak of his assertion that nationalism was a complete ideology.

Here, then, were some of the main features of the kind of nationalism that Saunders Lewis promoted through his control of Plaid Genedlaethol Cymru's agenda. As will be seen in the following chapters, they continued to have a significant influence on the party long after Lewis himself had departed the political stage. There are many reasons why the party did not divest itself of them sooner than it did. One simple explanation, of course, is that those who succeeded Saunders Lewis agreed with his views. Another is that institutions of all kinds – including political parties – tend to become 'path dependent'. They follow previous patterns and behaviours, whatever their source. But in addition, Saunders Lewis fought tenaciously to maintain his grip.

Holding on

We have already seen how Saunders Lewis made his involvement in the fledgling Welsh Nationalist Party conditional on control of the policy agenda being ceded to him. He remained just as determined to retain control throughout the whole of his presidency. This can be demonstrated by tracing the early party's position on the Welsh language; its economic policy; and its policy on Wales's constitutional future.

One language or two?
A Wales with the Welsh language as its only official language was one of the core objectives of the Mudiad Cymreig. 'Ensuring that the Welsh language is Wales's only official language' was the central objective adopted by Plaid Genedlaethol Cymru at the Pwllheli meeting in 1925, and Saunders Lewis argued in favour of the same principle when he outlined his *Principles of Nationalism* in the following year. In truth, however, this was hardly a sustainable standpoint for any political movement hoping to gain mass support in twentieth-century Wales. As a result, as part of a wider effort to draw up a broader, more credible political programme in the aftermath of its disappointing result in the Caernarfon constituency in the 1929 general election, the party decided to reassess its position on the language.[61]

In the February 1930 issue of *Y Ddraig Goch*, J. E. Jones, who would succeed H. R. Jones as the party's secretary later that year, argued that the party's stance had to change. 'The Nationalist Party is concerned with the whole of Wales', he said, 'and it must win the ears and heart of the whole of Wales in order to succeed.' Imposing the Welsh language as Wales's only official language could be 'a stumbling block for many'. His suggestion was that the appropriate aim for the party was to ensure that both Welsh and English were official languages in Wales. A Welsh-language

---

[61] There is a detailed discussion in Davies, *The Welsh Nationalist Party*, pp. 73–9. I draw heavily on his analysis in the following.

Wales (*Cymru Gymraeg*) was something to be considered in the more distant future.

> Having gained Self-Government and having allowed its influence to percolate through the education and life of the country over many years, then all of the Welsh will become Welsh speakers; it would be possible at that point for the Welsh language to be confirmed as Wales's *only* official language.[62]

Saunders Lewis did not agree. He went so far as to append an editorial note to J. E. Jones's article 'explaining the party's policy' on the language. People in public posts appointed before Welsh was made the only official language of Wales would not lose their jobs. Nonetheless, the party would not be deflected from its fundamental objective as that was the 'only way in which Welsh can be safeguarded'. Whatever short-term, transitional arrangements might be required, 'it must be ensured in fairly short order that Welsh is both "the only official language", but also "the only language practised" [unig iaith ymarferol] in the public life of Wales'.[63]

The majority of the Welsh Nationalist Party's executive committee evidently sided with Jones on the matter and so, in December 1930, Lewis was asked to redraft the party's objectives which had until then referred to achieving a Wales with Welsh as its only official language. The result – revealed for the first time in the February 1931 issue of *Y Ddraig Goch* – was a clause that read as follows: 'To ensure the safeguarding of Wales's culture, language and traditions by granting them the recognition and official protection of the government.'[64]

The wording is strikingly – and surely deliberately – vague. On the one hand, the aim of creating a Welsh-language Wales was removed from the official objectives of the movement. Yet on the other hand, there was no mention of granting equal legal status to both the Welsh and English languages in Wales. Saunders Lewis

---

62   *Y Ddraig Goch*, February 1930, 3; translation.
63   *Y Ddraig Goch*, February 1930, 3; translation.
64   *Y Ddraig Goch*, February 1931, 7; translation.

and his closest allies took advantage of this ambiguity to continue to argue strongly in favour of a monolingual Welsh-language Wales. In the August 1933 issue of *Y Ddraig Goch*, for example, Saunders Lewis published an article under the title 'Un iaith i Gymru' ('One language for Wales') that chastised those within the party who wished to abandon the objective of a monolingual Wales:

> Yes, even in the Nationalist Party we fear there are some who have not yet realised that a 'bilingual Wales' is something to fear and avoid, that a reduction in the number of monolingual Welsh speakers is a tragedy, and that only a monolingual Welsh-speaking Wales is consistent with the purposes and philosophy of Welsh nationalism.

He went on to argue that 'It is a bad thing, and nothing but a bad thing, that English is a vernacular language in Wales. It must be eradicated from the land called Wales: *delenda est Carthago*.'[65] Whatever the views of the majority of the executive committee's members, and notwithstanding the exact details of the party's formal objectives, through his control over the nationalist party's publications (either directly or via his closest comrades), Saunders Lewis succeeded in ensuring that a commitment to a monolingual Welsh Wales remained a central part of the party's public image throughout his time as president.

'Three acres and a Welsh-speaking cow'

Saunders Lewis's first ever article in *Y Ddraig Goch*, 'Cenedlaetholdeb a chyfalaf' ('Nationalism and capital'), focused on economics. It was a strong condemnation of modern capitalism. Indeed, even if its author would not have appreciated the comparison, elements of his account of the evils of capitalism are reminiscent of Marx's analysis. Capitalism, he claims, alienates

---

[65] *Y Ddraig Goch*, August 1933, 1–2; translation. Saunders Lewis remained committed to this view – the piece was later to be included in a collection of his political essays, *Canlyn Arthur: Ysgrifau Gwleidyddol* (Aberystwyth: Gwasg Aberystwyth, 1938), pp. 57–63.

the worker from the fruits of their labour ('He helps create capital, but that capital escapes to further inflate the strength of the already powerful.') It also alienates man from his fellows by creating a class society ('Under capitalism, the nation is divided into two classes.') Furthermore, the tendency of capitalism is to concentrate more and more capital in the hands of an ever-smaller group of capitalists.

Such ideas will be familiar to any reader of Marx. But there were additional elements to Lewis's analysis, in particular his emphasis on the importance of the nation. He argued that it is 'the nation' that creates capital rather than an individual person or a government. Naturally, the solution he proposed in order to address the failures of contemporary capitalism was also entirely different:

> because capital is the fruit of the joint efforts of many and a renouncing by many, it should be spread amongst the multitude of members of the nation ... It is also appropriate for the majority of the workers of a nation to be capitalists. That is the only thing that befits the dignity and happiness of man. That is the only thing that ensures his freedom so that he is his own master, which is essential for his dignity, because the slave does not have an independent will. That, too, ties man to the heritage of his nation, thus giving him capital that is at the same time a sign of freedom and a symbol of debt and tradition, and therefore a way of nurturing patriotism and nobility and resilience and a stable community.

A society of 'petty capitalists' (*mân gyfalafwyr*) offers an escape from the clutches of capitalism – a society much like the one that had existed in Wales, according to Saunders Lewis, before the 'Tudors changed things'.[66]

Although he dabbled with economic analysis, neither Saunders Lewis nor, indeed, any of the party's other founders could claim expert knowledge in economics. In this sense, the party was extremely fortunate that D. J. Davies was among its early

---

66 Saunders Lewis, 'Cenedlaetholdeb a chyfalaf', *Y Ddraig Goch*, June 1926, 3–4; translation.

members. Having led an extraordinarily colourful and varied life, this former coalminer, sailor, 'hobo' [sic], US navy boxing champion, passionate trade unionist (amongst many other things) from Carmarthenshire began to study economics at the University College in Aberystwyth in 1925 (he went on to receive his doctorate for a thesis on an aspect of agricultural economics in 1931).[67] In the spring of 1927, he began contributing to *Y Ddraig Goch*, and became one of its most prolific contributors. In 1931, he published a pamphlet titled *The Economics of Welsh Self-Government* summarising and systematising the analysis he had developed in *Y Ddraig Goch*.[68] It is one of the party's first English-language publications. It remains one of the most important pieces – certainly the most original and stimulating – that it has ever published.

The pamphlet advances a credible analysis of the structural weaknesses of Wales's economy, explaining how those weaknesses had stemmed directly from its relationship with England. With Wales by then in the ruinous grip of the Great Depression, Davies also set out his proposed solution for the country's economic ills. He argued for the establishment of a Welsh state that would promote the development of cooperative ventures as part of a modern mixed economy. Denmark was clearly the country that he sought to emulate in developing an alternative economic path for Wales. Indeed, the economic plan he recommended was similar to those adopted throughout Scandinavia in the 1930s, setting the foundations of the prosperous welfare societies that developed there in the post-war era.

---

[67] There is a short biography in Ceinwen H. Thomas, 'D. J. Davies', in Derec Llwyd Morgan (ed.), *Adnabod Deg* (Dinbych: Gwasg Gee, 1977), pp. 140–53. See also Emyr Wynn Williams's important essay, 'D. J. Davies – a working class intellectual within Plaid Genedlaethol Cymru 1927– 32', *Llafur*, 4 (4), 46–57.

[68] By the time *The Economics of Welsh Self-Government* (Caernarfon: Welsh Nationalist Party) was published in 1931, he had published a number of important articles in *Y Ddraig Goch*, including 'Agwedd economig ymreolaeth i Gymru', April 1927, 5; *continued*, May 1927, 5; *continued*, July 1927, 5; 'Cyfansoddiad Ulster a'r dalaith rydd', September 1927, 3, 7; 'Diffyndollaeth a diwydiannau Cymru', February 1929, 5; *continued*, March 1929, 5, 7; 'Y Blaid Genedlaethol a diffyg gwaith', 4–5, 8; 'Canlyniadau llywodraeth estron', April 1930, 5–6; 'Glo caled dehau Cymru', September 1930, 5–8; *continued*, October 1930, 5–6; *continued*, December 1930, 5, 8; 'Llywodraeth Gymreig: paham y mae yn rheidrwydd', February 1931, 4–5; *continued*, March 1931, 4, 8.

It is a measure of Davies's achievement – as well as of the failure of economic policy in Wales over the intervening three-quarters of a century and more – that the ideas presented in this pamphlet even today appear startlingly contemporary and relevant. Of course, there is no way of knowing what might have happened if attempts had been made to put them into practice at the time. But it cannot be denied that the pamphlet, as well as other related work produced by D. J. Davies and his wife Noëlle Davies, set out the foundations of a credible economic policy for Plaid Cymru.[69] With the traditional political parties apparently paralysed in the face of the economic and social calamity of the Great Depression, D. J. Davies had offered Plaid the possibility of presenting itself as a progressive, forward-thinking force in Welsh life rather an echo of times past. In the party's Summer School in 1932, the party's members voted to commit the movement to establishing a Welsh state on cooperative foundations, strongly suggesting that they were prepared to follow the lead offered by Davies. But what of the party president?

Saunders Lewis wrote a review of *The Economics of Welsh Self-Government* in the September 1931 issue of *Y Ddraig Goch*. He was full of praise for D. J. and Noëlle Davies and considered them both to be 'amongst the most important influences' on the national movement: he even claimed 'that there is no other couple in Wales today whose company of an evening is more of an awakening and inspiration to service and consecration [ymgysegriad] than these two'. Coming from Saunders Lewis, such language – with its obvious religious undertones – was clearly a sign of genuine respect. But it also serves as an indication of the way that he would subsequently repurpose their economic and social analysis to his own ends.

Although he agreed with the emphasis placed by D. J. and Noëlle Davies on cooperation, Lewis claimed that it was 'the fire of religious sympathy and spirituality' that formed the basis

---

69 Noëlle Davies is another woman in the history of Plaid Cymru who has not had a fraction of the attention she deserves: a particularly remarkable state-of-affairs given both her intellectual range and extraordinary life. Briefly on the latter: the daughter of a wealthy Anglo-Irish family, she met her husband in Denmark before returning with him to Wales and devoting herself to the national cause. After D.J.'s untimely death in 1956, she returned to Ireland.

of the pamphlet's arguments – this despite the fact that, at the time at least, D. J. Davies's attitude towards religion was distinctly agnostic. Furthermore, towards the review's conclusion, he claims that:

> The objective of the Nationalist Party is to de-proletarianise the Welsh people, to make Wales as it used to be, a country of independent men who were of strong character because they owned property, were their own masters, and not merely hired servants. This is not the aim of Socialism at all, but that is the aim of national cooperation [cydweithrediad cenedlaethol], and Dr. Davies's pamphlet will be a motivation to that end.[70]

By theologising D. J. and Noëlle Davies's economic vision, Saunders Lewis distorted it. The two understood their economic doctrine as an extension of ethics rather than of theology, and this is a fundamental difference. But more importantly still from the point of view of the political prospects of the national movement, by linking the essentially progressive socio-economic vision of the two Davieses to his vision of a country of small-scale capitalists 'as it used to be', Saunders Lewis began a process that would for many years undermine the credibility of any of the party's commentary on economics.

If we are to pinpoint the moment at which the political potential of D. J. and Noëlle Davies's economic ideas was squandered, then it is the March 1934 issue of *Y Ddraig Goch*, and the publication of Saunders Lewis's 'Deg pwynt polisi' ('Ten policy points'). These 'ten points', together with the wider the doctrine of *perchentyaeth* with which they became associated, shaped perceptions of the party's economic and social ideas for many years to come.

---

[70] Saunders Lewis, 'Economeg hunan-lywodraeth: pamffled pwysig Dr. D. J. Davies', *Y Ddraig Goch*, September 1930, 2–3; translation. It is only fair to point out that Saunders Lewis pays tribute to both D.J. and Noëlle Davies, this even though, until this point, the various economic analyses had appeared under D. J. Davies's name only. Can this be taken as confirmation of the widespread impression that these early articles – while attributed to D. J. Davies – were in fact the joint work of both? Later, both names were credited together on many articles and pamphlets. For D. J. Davies's religious beliefs, see Thomas's short treatment, 'D. J. Davies', pp. 152–3.

(Note that *perchentyaeth* translates literally as 'homeownership-ism' but is used to imply the wider distribution of both property and capital across society.) This was clearly the intention. In that respect, therefore, the publication – and republication – of the ten points can be considered a success.[71] But in terms of persuading anyone beyond a small circle of party supporters that it had solutions that might help alleviate Wales's contemporary misery, it was all deeply counter-productive.

Even if they were only intended as a summary, the ten points are strikingly abstract and lacking in nuance. Indeed, given that they appeared for the first time almost three years after the publication of *The Economics of Welsh Self-Government*, it is clear that the party was in a position to offer far more substantial fare should its president have desired it. Indeed, the great irony that the president *himself* was in a position to offer a great deal more. In one of his pamphlets published a year earlier, Lewis had argued *The Case for a Welsh National Development Council*, proposing the creation of a body very like the future Welsh Development Agency. In this respect, his ideas were more than thirty years ahead of their time.[72] But rather than offering specific solutions for Wales's ills by drawing on various proposals already outlined in party's publications, Saunders Lewis instead offered up a general narrative that can only be regarded as bordering on the crankish.

The first sentence of the eighth point is by far the best-known part of the ten. Indeed, it is perhaps the best-known (and notorious) sentence in Saunders Lewis's voluminous political writings. The oddness – and, politically speaking, foolishness – of the ten points as a whole are underlined when we also recall the sentence that follows:

---

71 See *Y Ddraig Goch*, March 1937. They were also reprinted again as the first essay in Lewis's collection, *Canlyn Arthur*, pp. 11–13. Emyr Wynn Williams suspects that Saunders Lewis's decision to concern himself with economic ideas from 1932 onwards was part of a deliberate attempt on his part to lessen the influence of progressive ideas – such as those of D. J. Davies – within the party; see Williams, 'D. J. Davies', p. 56. For an English-language version of the ten points see Davies, *The Welsh Nationalist Party*, pp. 100–1.
72 For more of his constructive economic ideas, see Saunders Lewis, *The Local Authorities and Welsh Industries* (Caernarfon: Welsh Nationalist Party, 1934).

> For the sake of Wales's moral health and for the moral and physical welfare of its population, South Wales must be de-industrialised. All of Wales's natural resources are riches to be managed with care for the benefit of the Welsh nation and to help its neighbours in other parts of the world.

Without further qualification or explanations, it is very difficult to interpret the first sentence as anything other than an attack on a very substantial part of Wales's population, who were at this time experiencing enormous distress. The fundamental ambiguity of Saunders Lewis's attitude towards those Welsh people who did not speak Welsh has been mentioned already. On this occasion, however, there is little indication of ambiguity; nothing to mitigate the obvious disdain inherent in 'For the sake of Wales's moral health.' And then we have frankly mind-boggling demand that south Wales be 'de-industrialised'. This is not the message in *The Economics of Welsh Self-Government* nor, indeed, is it the message in Saunders Lewis's own economic pamphlets. Why, then, did he use this form of words in a declaration that he intended to become widely publicised and read as a foundational statement of his party's core beliefs?

Alas, rather than explain or elaborate on the explosive words in that first sentence, the second sentence proceeds in an entirely different direction. Indeed, it is so ambiguous and vague in terms of its practical implications that one can easily imagine any vaguely enlightened nationalist of any nationality – from Masaryk to Blair – saying something broadly analogous. But of course, few people ever notice this sentence. What precedes it has always been enough to ensure that the remainder of the point – and other nine points, for that matter – have been completely eclipsed. The Labour Party's manifesto for the 1983 general election was described as 'the longest suicide note in history'; the opening sentence of point eight of Saunders Lewis's ten policy points may be among the shortest.

As a result of Saunders Lewis's intervention, the doctrine of *perchentyaeth* came to define Plaid Cymru's economic and social objectives: a Welsh-speaking rural society, based on small-scale landownership and agriculture, 'as it used to be'. It was a doctrine once summarised as 'three acres and a Welsh-speaking cow'.[73] Satire, of course. Nonetheless, it contained a kernel of truth. It is no surprise that the party's economic and social policy were not taken seriously.

Dominion status

We have already noted that several of those involved in the establishment of Plaid Genedlaethol Cymru believed that it should seek independence for Wales. It should come as no surprise, therefore, that Saunders Lewis caused some discontent when he insisted on opposing independence in the name of 'freedom'. H. R. Jones's dissatisfaction was so great that he wrote to Saunders Lewis to say that he was considering resigning his role in the party in protest. Saunders Lewis wrote back outlining his reasons 'for not fighting for independence':

1. it has never been a Welsh principle in politics: neither Hywel Dda nor Llywelyn Fawr nor Owain Glyndŵr attempted it; It is childish folly to be led by Ireland's *Republicans*. The great Welsh politicians of the past and the Welsh tradition should be our leaders and our motivation;
2. the principle of independence, as I demonstrated in the Machynlleth pamphlet [i.e. 'Principles of nationalism'], is anti-Christian, and I cannot accept it for that reason;
3. it is totally impractical, and shows a lack of ability to think and to face the facts as they are.[74]

Both the content and tone of the first two arguments will now be familiar. The third is a little different, and suggestive. Unfortunately, however, there is no further elaboration.

H. R. Jones might be forgiven for having been less than impressed on hearing Saunders Lewis – of all people – accuse him of impracticality and of being unwilling to 'face facts as they

---

73 See the *Western Mail* editorial article, 4 December 1942 (I am grateful to Rhys Evans for the reference). The characterisation was later adopted by Harri Webb when he castigated advocates of *perchentyaeth* in the ranks of Plaid Cymru.

74 Saunders Lewis to H. R. Jones, n.d. [but January 1926?] (APC, B5); translation.

are'! But in truth, we don't know how he reacted. As far as is known, the matter seems to have gone no further. Jones remained in post. Neither did he challenge Saunders Lewis's ideas in public. Nevertheless, it seems unlikely that he was satisfied. His true attitude may well have been revealed in an article he wrote (under a pseudonym) in *Y Darian* in 1930. In it, he sympathises with what he regarded as the discontent among ordinary Irishmen at the continuing links between the Free State and the British Crown: 'they cannot for the life of them understand why they have to accept England's king as their king'.[75] Their aim was complete independence from the British state; it was an aim shared by the man who did the spade work in the process that led to the foundation of Plaid Genedlaethol Cymru.

Because of the contradiction between Saunders Lewis's view and the aspirations of the wider membership, the party's attitude towards the constitutional question became characterised by an element of schizophrenia. On the one hand, Saunders Lewis had insisted on omitting any reference to self-government from the list of objectives agreed at the Pwllheli meeting. Furthermore, despite self-government not being the central focus of *Principles of Nationalism*, that lecture had nevertheless committed the party to opposing independence for Wales in the name of 'freedom' – even if it was unclear what, concretely, was meant by the latter. Nevertheless, self-government remained a matter of the greatest importance for many of the party's members, and a central part of the message it propounded in the numerous public meetings organised to evangelise on its behalf; in particular, it seems, those organised by H. R. Jones.

Here then was a party that placed self-government at the centre of its public message yet – for many years – omitted self-government from its formal list of party objectives. Lewis Valentine's letter to the Caernarfon electorate ahead of the 1929 election, for example, claimed that he was 'the first parliamentary candidate in Welsh history to make freedom and self-government for Wales the sole basis of the appeal for votes'. The

[75] Quoted by Gwilym R. Jones, 'H. R. Jones', in Morgan (ed.), *Adnabod Deg*, p. 43; translation.

special issue of *Y Ddraig Goch*, published in May 1929 in support of Valentine's campaign, was full of references to self-government. 'Sut i gael ymreolaeth' ('How to achieve home rule') was the title of one article. 'Ymreolaeth i Gymru: paham?' ('Home rule for Wales: why?') the title of another. Even the subtitle of Saunders Lewis's editorial article was 'Mynd ati i gael ymreolaeth' ('Setting out to achieve home rule') (although there was no mention self-government in the body of the article itself!)[76] But what did Plaid Cymru mean by self-government or 'home rule'? It would be five years from the 'founding' meeting in Pwllheli before it could provide a formal answer to this most basic of questions.

In its early years, *Y Ddraig Goch* featured a series of articles discussing possible constitutional models for Wales, including forms of devolution, federalism and dominion status. Amongst them was D. J. Davies's influential comparison of the devolved powers of Northern Ireland's Stormont parliament and the dominion status of the southern Free State. His conclusion was that only dominion status would provide sufficient power to enable a Welsh government to alleviate the country's economic problems.[77] But in addition, we find acknowledgement that the party's lack of clarity on the central matter of home rule was a stumbling block. The situation was explained in the following terms in the editorial notes of the February 1927 edition: 'It is true that the Party has not yet decided on the form of a Home Rule Bill for Wales. That is not something to be undertaken lightly, and a thorough study is required.' By January 1930, however, it appears that some in the party's ranks were beginning to suspect that 'thorough study' was synonymous with foot dragging. In a pointed letter to *Y Ddraig Goch*, J. E. Jones noted: 'There has been frequent mention in the ranks of the Nationalist Party that a home rule measure for Wales would be drawn up by its experienced men (gŵyr cyfarwydd) … As far as I can gather, this has not

76 *Ymreolaeth* was the familiar Welsh-language term for 'home rule' in the context of various constitutional debates of the late nineteenth and early twentieth centuries. Hence the use of home rule in what follows.

77 *Y Ddraig Goch*, April 1927, 5. See also Davies, 'Cyfansoddiad Ulster a'r dalaith rydd', 3, 7.

happened.'[78] It was time for the executive committee to match words with action.

Saunders Lewis returned to the matter in his editorial notes for the March 1930 issue of the party newspaper. The tone of his remarks was noticeably different from those that characterised his 1926 Machynlleth lecture and is testimony to the development of his political thinking in the intervening period. In them he criticises the Liberals' support for devolution: 'The Nationalist Party and its policy were not formed for such trifling purposes.' Indeed, 'We vomit it from our mouths.' Why? Ironically enough, it appears that sovereignty was at the heart of the matter after all!

> The objective of the Nationalist Party is not to give Wales 'home rule on local matters' [i.e. devolution], but to give it a 'Constitution'. What that means is that Wales will have a parliament and government that England's parliament can neither change nor dissolve nor interfere with. The moral independence and freedom of the Welsh constitution would be secured through ensuring that Wales has complete control of all its taxes including, above all, income tax. Indeed, if someone were to ask us for a brief definition of the Nationalist Party's objective, we could not give a better answer than the following: 'A Dominion Constitution for Wales and financial independence'.[79]

Saunders Lewis was speaking somewhat prematurely, since dominion status had not yet been formally adopted as party policy. Yet given his grip on the party, it is no surprise that this soon changed. February 1931 saw the publication of an updated list of formal objectives for Plaid Genedlaethol Cymru:

Objectives
1. to gain for Wales the same position and constitution within the system of nations called the British Empire as are now possessed by the Dominions of Newfoundland, Canada,

---

[78] *Y Ddraig Goch*, January 1930, 7; translation. In his later years, J. E. Jones seems to have completely forgotten his youthful frustration. Rather, he boasted of Plaid Cymru's measured approach to policy-making in these, its formative years; see *Tros Gymru: J. E. Jones a'r Blaid* (Abertawe: Gwasg John Penry, 1970), p. 72.

[79] 'Nodiadau'r mis', *Y Ddraig Goch*, March 1930, 1, 2; translation.

and Australia and South Africa and the Free State of Ireland etc.;

To gain for Wales a PARLIAMENT with full authority to legislate for the benefit and advantage of Wales, together with a GOVERNMENT answerable to that parliament.
2. to safeguard Wales's culture, language and traditions by granting them the recognition and protection of the government;
3. to gain Wales the right to become a member of the LEAGUE of NATIONS.[80]

This was the point, then, that attaining dominion status for Wales became the party's central constitutional objective.

Despite Lewis's having suggested to H. R. Jones that it would be childish to seek to follow Ireland's example, following the Irish precedent (as things stood at the time, at least) is exactly what the party ended up doing when formulating its constitutional policy. The great advantage of dominion status was that it could bridge the different viewpoints within Plaid Cymru. On the one hand, it satisfied those who wanted to see Wales enjoying the largest measure of self-government – a group that seems to have included the vast majority of Plaid Cymru members. For them, 'dominion status' was synonymous for all practical purposes with independence. Indeed, after the signing of the Statute of Westminster in 1931, this became the common understanding. On the other hand, the supranational element that was retained through the maintaining of the link to the British Empire was consistent with Saunders Lewis's condemnation of the modern concept of sovereignty in *Principles of Nationalism*.[81] Thus, from his point of view, insisting on dominion status was perfectly consistent with the principled argument in favour of 'freedom' rather than 'independence'. 'Dominion status' could therefore permit different interpretations. The consequence of

80 *Y Ddraig Goch*, February 1931, 7; translation, with emphasis in the original.
81 D. Hywel Davies notes, also, that dominion status was consistent with Saunders Lewis's support for the monarchy. There is a critical discussion of Lewis's attitudes towards the monarchy in Lloyd, *John Saunders Lewis*, pp. 329–33, but cf. the more measured commentary in Pennar Davies, 'His criticism', in Jones and Thomas (eds), *Presenting Saunders Lewis*, pp. 100–1.

this, however, was that the doctrine of *Principles of Nationalism* was not directly challenged: as will be seen in the following chapters, the lecture retained its status as the fundamental declaration of the party's constitutional thinking.

It would be incorrect to give the impression that Saunders Lewis always succeeded in having his own way with regards to party policy. For example, he fought for a long time to retain the nationalist party's policy of refusing to take seats in the House of Commons. But in this case his efforts were in vain. This was, however, one of few exceptions. The fact of the matter is that he succeeded to a remarkable degree in maintaining his grip on the party's policy agenda. There is also no doubt that it was he who was primarily responsible for shaping public perceptions of that agenda. Given that so many of his ideas ran counter to the broadly progressive, left-leaning instincts of most of Plaid Cymru's members, the fact that he managed to retain control for so long speaks volumes not only about his political skills but also the respect in which he was held among them. But, as we shall see, there were nonetheless limits to their loyalty and ideological flexibility.

A flash in the pan

The *Tân yn Llŷn* – the 'Fire in Llŷn' – has become a central part of Welsh nationalist folklore. Most nationalists' knowledge of what happened before, during and after the actions of 'The Three' (*Y Tri*) at Penyberth is, more than likely, rather vague.[82] Such is the case with important symbolic events that colour the history of political movements. It was not the precise circum-stances of the 'Martyrs of 1868' that were important to the Welsh Liberals of a previous era. Indeed, one suspects that the more respectable members of the current Welsh Labour movement

[82] The history is recounted in Davies, *The Welsh Nationalist Party*, pp. 154–66, 207–10. See also, Karl Davies's fascinating, *Beth am gynnau tân… Hanes llosgi'r Ysgol Fomio* (Llanrwst: Gwasg Carreg Gwalch, 1986) as well as the eyewitness accounts in O. M. Roberts, *Oddeutu'r Tân* (Caernarfon: Gwasg Gwynedd, 1994).

would prefer not to know too much about the Tonypandy Riots! It is not the detail – or even the facts – that count in such cases: myths are too powerful to be constrained by such trivial considerations. And what we might term the myth of Penyberth 1936 certainly continues to resonate, especially among Welsh-speaking nationalists.[83]

Yet measured against the intentions of perpetrators and those that assisted them, the Fire in Llŷn was little more than a flash in the pan. Yes, light and heat were generated, but the political impact of their actions proved very short-lived. While 'The Three' received much praise in nationalist circles, they inspired little by way of political activity. D. Tecwyn Lloyd evaluates the response to their actions in the following terms:

> it failed to do more than ensure that the party members placed The Three on a pedestal after their release, singing their praises and inviting them hither and thither to give interesting and amusing lectures on their experiences in Wormwood Scrubs prison; to allow those who listened to them to shut their eyes to their sacrifice and its wider significance by chatting in wonderment about daily life in prison and other such trivia.[84]

Too cynical? Maybe so. But it also hard to argue with his verdict. Even though 'The Three' were in prison at the time, only nine candidates were prepared to fight the March 1937 county council elections in party colours. After an increase in 1936 and 1937, financial contributions to the 1938 and 1939 iterations of the party's annual fundraising drive (its St David's Day Fund) were bitterly disappointing. Indeed, as D. Hywel Davies makes clear, by 1939 there were doubts about Plaid Cymru's future.[85] Given that this was the situation among party members, is it really a surprise that so few of the 12,000-strong crowd that gathered in Caernarfon in August 1937 to welcome Saunders Lewis, Lewis

---

83 Another Welsh-language song plays an important contemporary role in sustaining the myth, namely 'Y Tân yn Llŷn' written by Ann Fychan and popularised by the folk group Plethyn.

84 D. Tecwyn Lloyd, 'Dwy wedd ar bethau', Y Traethodydd, January 1989, 30.

85 Davies, The Welsh Nationalist Party, pp. 208–9, 164, 210.

Valentine and D. J. Williams on their release from prison decided to make a longer term commitment to their cause?

Saunders Lewis was well aware of their failure. Given that he was dismissed from his university post in Swansea – and exiled from academia – in further punishment for his actions, his now extremely challenging personal circumstances made it difficult for him to continue as president. He attempted to resign at a meeting of the executive committee at Easter 1938. Yet even though (according to Ambrose Bebb's testimony) he did not enjoy the unanimous support of even that small group, Lewis was nonetheless persuaded not to resign immediately. But he made it clear that he was determined not to accept renomination for the presidency when his latest four-year term came to an end in 1939.[86] Explaining his decision, he referred, not primarily to his personal circumstances, but rather to the lack of action follow-ing the Fire and to a lack of loyalty from party members at a time of criticism. In a speech before the party's Summer School in Swansea later in 1938, Lewis made clear that 'the greatest dis-appointment he ever experienced' was the failure of party mem-bers to reap the benefits of the seeds sown at Penyberth.[87] He confirmed several times subsequently that this disappointment was a central factor in his decision to give up the presidency. In a letter to Kate Roberts ten years later, for example, he noted that:

> One of the reasons why I decided to get out of Plaid's public life was because it was clear that the Penyberth policy would not be fol-lowed up; but that is not the only reason, I was too weak financially by then to be able to remain leader.

In another letter to the same friend a year later, he returned to the same theme: 'Seeing that there was no hope that the party would follow the example set by the Fire in Llŷn persuaded me to leave

---

86 See Chapman, *W. Ambrose Bebb*, pp. 111–12 and Davies, *The Welsh Nationalist Party*, pp. 196, 215 n.

87 *Baner ac Amserau Cymru*, 16 August 1938, 1; translation. In an abridged ver-sion of his presidential speech in the September 1938 issue of *Y Ddraig Goch* he makes clear his view that 'a great opportunity was missed'; translation.

public life completely – as well as the fact that I could no longer afford to stay in the presidency.'[88]

Why did the Fire not take hold? J. E. Jones pondered the question in his autobiography: 'The enthusiasm of the crowd at the huge Welcome Meeting in Caernarfon suggested there would be an enormous, fast-paced expansion. It did not happen. There has been much wondering why; I have not seen nor heard a satisfactory explanation.'[89] Yet is this really the case? If we scrutinise the party's activities around this time – that is, only a few months after 'The Three' were released from prison – we find plentiful evidence that a substantial gap had opened between the president and his fellow members, this even though personal loyalty to Lewis meant that he was subject to little direct criticism.

As well as the pathetically small number of electoral candidates and the lack of financial support referred to above, Ambrose Bebb highlights the membership's lukewarm response to Lewis's lecture at a conference organised by the party in Caernarfon in February 1939. His topic was 'The Nationalist Party and Marxism' – a somewhat unlikely subject given the party president's strictures on the need to reap the benefits of Penyberth.[90] Lewis was challenged more directly at the party's Swansea Summer School. In his 'official' report on proceedings for the readers of Y Ddraig Goch, the party's treasurer, Francis Jones, claimed that there 'was very little disagreement', 'this probably because such a level of unanimity had been arrived with regards the party policy programme that there is no longer any need to spend much time arguing over it'.[91] It is indeed true that the student members of Bangor's Mudiad Gwerin received very little support when they tried to challenge the

88 Dafydd Ifans (ed.), *Annwyl Kate, Annwyl Saunders* (Aberystwyth: Llyfrgell Genedlaethol Cymru, 1992), pp. 145, 152; translation.
89 Jones, *Tros Gymru*, p. 188; translation.
90 See Chapman, *W. Ambrose Bebb*, p. 110. The speech was published over three issues of *Y Ddraig Goch*, Saunders Lewis, 'Y Blaid Genedlaethol a Marxiaeth', March 1938, 12, 14; *continued*, April 1938, 9, 10; *continued*, May 1938, 12, 14.
91 'Argraffiadau o'r Ysgol Haf', *Y Ddraig Goch*, September 1938, 4; translation.

party's policies from an uncompromisingly socialist standpoint. Instead, the conference passed a motion declaring that the party's economic and social policies were based on the principles of 'cooperation and *perchentyaeth*' – the first time *perchentyaeth* had received the imprimatur of the membership in this way.[92] Yet even if the challenge of Mudiad Gwerin made little impression, other developments at the Summer School served to rile Saunders Lewis.

D. J. Davies delivered a lecture insisting that the party's resources and attention must be concentrated in the south, the home of the overwhelming majority of Welsh people, including most Welsh speakers.[93] This meant moving the party's central office to the area as well as making more use of the English language in both the internal organisation and wider work of the movement. Davies's position on all this was already well known. Even so, the fact that a person who was so loyal to Saunders Lewis on a personal level was willing to express opinions that directly contradicted those of the party president – this at a time when the press was already drawing attention to internal divisions within its ranks – was significant.

Furthermore, with another world war fast approaching, the party had become solidly pacifist in outlook. Lewis was, of course, not a pacifist – a fact known well known to Plaid Cymru members at the time, and the source of considerable discomfort for many a pious Nonconformist nationalist ever since. Nonetheless, he had no reason to oppose a motion put forward by Gwynfor Evans, which passed unanimously, committing the party to using peaceful means to attain self-government. After all, he had already made it clear that he saw no justification for using violence against people in the battle for Wales's freedom. But for Lewis, this was a matter of policy or tactics rather than dogma. He certainly did not want to see the party embrace pacifism as a fundamental principle. He was also concerned that a commitment to

---

[92]   There is a list of the motion passed at the Summer School in *Y Ddraig Goch*, September 1938, 10.
[93]   There is a summary of the comments in *Y Ddraig Goch*, August 1938, 5.

peaceful means might be equated with quiescence. In his presidential address, he emphasised time and again that a commitment to peaceful means did not mean a commitment to the use
of only constitutional means. The path to freedom, he said, lay
through English prisons.[94]

What was the reason for the increasing distance between the
party's leader and its members? It was, quite simply, a difference
of political ideologies. Despite Saunders Lewis's assertions to the
contrary, nationalism is not in itself a complete political ideology.
Rather, as discussed in the previous chapter, it is an ideology that
exists in a symbiotic relationship with other political ideologies.
While Saunders Lewis's 'nationalism' stemmed from a blend of
nationalist themes and romantic conservatism, the nationalism
of the overwhelming majority of the party membership blended
nationalist themes with economic and social ideas that were
broadly progressive in nature. As the rush towards war in the
Europe of the 1930s served to increase polarisation between left
and right, not even the enormous respect in which Saunders
Lewis was held across the party – as a person, as a literary figure
and as a man who (in their view) had put Wales first in a way
that had not been seen for generations – was sufficient to bridge
the ideological gulf that separated members from leader. This
was the fundamental reason why not even Plaid Cymru members, let alone the people of Wales more generally, were prepared
to accept Saunders Lewis's political leadership. Above all else,
that is the reason why the Fire in Llŷn proved to be nothing but
a flash in the pan.

To be clear, this is not a case of being wise in retrospect. Prosser
Rhys, the editor of *Baner ac Amserau Cymru* and a member of the
party even before the Pwllheli meeting, made precisely the same
point in March 1938:

> For the majority of party members – people of *gwerinol* and rad-
> ical tendencies, Leftists if you will. Many of them came to the
> Nationalist Party from the Labour Party, many came from the

94   *Y Ddraig Goch*, September 1938, 5.

Liberal Party, and the majority of the remainder people who were not members of any party, but who were certainly of Radical tendencies. No one came to the party from among the followers of Lord Rothermere and the 'Daily Mail', yet it is the 'Daily Mail' approach that is adopted by the party's papers on many issues except Wales's domestic problems. This is entirely contrary to the inclinations of the majority of party members … Many party members are uneasy on this account, but too loyal, particularly so loyal on a personal level to Mr Saunders Lewis, to say or write anything on the matter.[95]

Party members were too loyal to Saunders Lewis to oppose him directly yet were also unwilling to follow the path he tried to lay down for them. It is little wonder that he was frustrated and disappointed.

Saunders Lewis succeeded to a quite astonishing degree in capturing and shaping the Welsh Nationalist Party's intellectual agenda. But while his fellow members shared his zeal for Wales, Lewis's grip on the movement was not sufficient to persuade the majority to reject their progressive political values. In the febrile atmosphere that characterised the months and years before the outbreak of the Second World War – a period when it became increasingly clear that the future of civilisation far beyond Wales was in the balance – it became impossible to conceal or ignore the differences between them. From 1938 onwards, therefore, a process of distancing began that would see Saunders Lewis becoming increasingly estranged from the party which he had almost completely dominated since the first months of 1925. For the majority in Wales, none of this much mattered. Given the strength of the forces promoting British nationalism, the prospects for any effort to establish a political party advocating for Welsh nationalism in the Wales of the 1920s would always have been bleak. But by allowing Saunders Lewis to dominate its political thinking to the extent that it did, Plaid Cymru ensured that very few would regard it as anything more

---

95   *Baner ac Amserau Cymru*, 8 Mawrth 1938, 5; translation.

than a marginal voice on the periphery of politics. Saunders Lewis clearly took Wales seriously – the story of his life is eloquent testimony to that. But while Plaid Cymru was led by a man of his political inclinations, there was no prospect that the people of Wales would take his party seriously.

3

'A Reconciliation with her Fair Past':
The Gwynfor Evans Era

A reasonable man, Bernard Shaw once said, adapts himself to the world, while an unreasonable man tries to adapt the world to himself. Yet we rely on unreasonable men for development and growth. Assuming that Shaw was right then we must regard the two most important men in Plaid Cymru's history as quite exceptionally unreasonable. We have already encountered the unreasonableness of Saunders Lewis: the way that he rejected the dominant mood and mores of his times, demanding instead an acknowledgement that another kind of Wales and Welsh worldview was possible. Gwynfor Evans was cut from the same cloth. He dedicated his life to becoming the chief advocate of a cause that was painfully unfashionable for the larger part of his political career; a cause that was not only rejected but branded as abhorrent much more often than is now recalled. To a degree, it was because of his perseverance and stubbornness – because of his very unreasonableness – that the course of Welsh history eventually shifted.

Gwynfor Evans was president of Plaid Cymru between 1945 and 1981, a period of thirty-six years. That bare statistic alone is astonishing. The Labour Party had five different leaders during the same period. Of those leaders, Harold Wilson, the man who reminded us that even a week is a long time in politics, spent the longest time in the job, leading his party for thirteen years. Churchill was the leader of the Conservatives when Gwynfor Evans took over the presidency of Plaid Cymru; Thatcher was prime minister when he passed the reins to Dafydd Wigley. Thirty-six years! But this fact alone, astonishing enough though it is, scarcely begins to indicate the extent of his commitment and contribution to Plaid Cymru. Recall, for example, that Abi Williams was (to all intents and purposes) president in name only between 1943 and 1945, and that it was Gwynfor Evans as vice-president who took on much of the executive burden of the presidency during that time.[1] He played a central role in Plaid Cymru's annual conferences for a period of sixty years. He proposed a motion at the Bala Conference in 1937 calling for official status for the Welsh language; in 1997, following the Yes vote in the second devolution referendum, he was led to the platform in Aberystwyth to greet, and to be greeted by, a hall crammed with emotional delegates.

It is also worth bearing in mind just how fragile Plaid Cymru organisational structures were during much of his presidency, with the party short of both members and resources.[2] For an extended period it appeared as if Gwynfor Evans was doing much more than leading the party: he, 'Gwynfor', essentially *was* Plaid Cymru. He travelled tirelessly the length and breadth of Wales addressing thousands of public meetings and attending countless committees. He estimated that he 'regularly clock[ed] up between thirty and thirty-five thousand miles a year, mainly on Party business'.[3] If true, this means that he drove about a million and a quarter miles 'for the sake of Wales'. For some perspective: the moon is slightly less than a quarter of a million miles away from the earth. The journeys themselves were onerous. The roads of Wales in the 1950s and the 1960s were (even) worse than they are now and cars far less reliable.[4] In addition,

1   Abi Williams seems to have taken over the presidency in 1943 as a stopgap because Gwynfor Evans did not feel that he could take up the post while his father's shop in Barry was suffering attacks in the wake of his son's public stand against the war as both a nationalist and a pacifist.
2   The years immediately after he took on the presidency were particularly bleak as acknowledged in his autobiography, *Bywyd Cymro* (Caernarfon: Gwasg Gwynedd, 1982). In the following I will cite the relevant passages in the translated version: Gwynfor Evans, *For the Sake of Wales: The Memoirs of Gwynfor Evans*, trans. Meic Stephens with a preface by Dafydd Elis-Thomas (Caernarfon: Welsh Academic Press, 1996). See in this case, pp. 96–7.
3   Evans, *For the Sake of Wales*, p. 61.
4   He shares several of his misadventures during those journeys in *For the Sake of Wales*; see, for example, pp. 61 and 143–4.

Gwynfor Evans's preferred practice was to return home to his family – and his greenhouses – after evening meetings. The greenhouses themselves were a further sign of his commitment to the cause. He used them for his tomato growing business – not the obvious career choice for a law graduate, but one he selected to facilitate the work that he considered to be far more important than any other. That is, his unwavering work on behalf of Plaid Cymru.

If any further confirmation is required of a perseverance bordering on the preternatural, consider also Gwynfor Evans's contribution in promoting the case of Welsh nationalism through his various publications. The English translation of his autobiography contains a bibliography of his writings including sixteen books, each evangelising for the cause.[5] More were to appear after that bibliography was published. The same source lists as many as fifty pamphlets. Thus far, no attempt seems to have been made to record his other publications – it will be a challenging task for anyone who seeks to do so. He contributed chapters to various edited volumes, along with countless articles to papers, magazines and periodicals large and small. Although it is fair to say that these various publications feature a substantial amount of recycling, they nonetheless represent an enormous amount of work by their author. A great deal has been made of Gwynfor Evans's charisma, but his stamina may be a better starting point for any attempt to assess his contribution to the national movement.

Gwynfor Evans's unreasonable efforts to try to compel the world – or one small part of it – to conform to his vision were to be rewarded with a measure of success; more obvious success than ever achieved by Saunders Lewis. During Gwynfor Evans's time as president, his party grew, and its leader's success in the Carmarthen by-election on 14 July 1966 was clearly a transformative moment for the party. It is difficult to imagine how any other candidate could possibly have brought that seat into the nationalist fold: it was a happy (and fortunate) combination of an exceptional person in a unique context that created the shock result.

---

[5] The bibliography was compiled by Meic Stephens and Beti Jones.

Certainly, that was the feeling within Plaid Cymru. In the party's annual report for 1966, the secretary, Elwyn Roberts, celebrated the Carmarthen result as a personal victory for Gwynfor Evans:

> More than anyone else, this was the president's victory. His strength of personality, his ability and sincerity, his clear vision, his tireless service, his brave leadership, his perseverance over many years in his own county and throughout Wales, these things above all carried the day.[6]

This feeling was shared even amongst the relatively large group of nationalists who, by the mid-1960s, had begun to doubt Gwynfor Evans's strategy for the party and were suspicious of the influence of the small circle of close advisors that surrounded him (a group referred to as 'Llys Llangadog' – the Court of Llangadog – in reference to the president's home in the village of Llangadog).[7]

For a period after 'Carmarthen' it seemed that anything was possible for Welsh nationalism – to the great joy of its followers and to the dismay of its political enemies. In the words of Alan Butt Philip: 'In a day, the political complexion of Wales was radically altered, its new face revealed. *Plaid Cymru* had established its credibility as an alternative party, and all the other political parties began seriously to assess its challenge and its objectives.'[8]

The Carmarthen victory was followed by impressive results in a series of by-elections in Rhondda West, Caerphilly and Merthyr

---

6 *Adroddiad Blynyddol Plaid Cymru 1966*, p. 1c (section 6).
7 There is a discussion of the tensions within Plaid Cymru before the Carmarthen victory by Alan Butt Philip, *The Welsh Question: Nationalism in Welsh Politics 1945–1970* (Cardiff: University of Wales Press, 1975). The subtitle of the chapter that discusses Plaid Cymru's trials and tribulations in the period between 1959 and 1966 is 'Drift and Fragmentation' (pp. 85–104). It should be noted, however, that Phil Williams interprets the same period in a very different way in his chapter 'Plaid Cymru a'r dyfodol', in John Davies (ed.), *Cymru'n Deffro* (Talybont: Y Lolfa, 1981), pp. 121–46. Nevertheless, even he acknowledges that the Carmarthen victory was preceded by 'a difficult and frustrating period' (p. 123). The members of the Llys Llangadog were J. E. Jones, Elwyn Roberts, D. J. Williams, Tudur Jones, Pennar Davies, Wynne Samuel and Gwynfor Evans's father-in-law, Dan Thomas. Gwynfor Evans paid them a very personal tribute in *A National Future for Wales* (Plaid Cymru, 1975), pp. 68–79.
8 Philip, *The Welsh Question*, p. 109.

Tydfil. In the 1970 general election, Plaid Cymru secured 175,016 votes, a number that it would not match until the establishment of the National Assembly for Wales. Gwynfor Evans himself was fond of recalling that the French celebrated Bastille Day on 14 July. Echoing Wordsworth's celebrated greeting for the French Revolution, he considered Bastille Day 1966 to be the equivalent of a new dawn for Welsh nationalism. Having struggled so long in such apparently hopeless circumstances, he can perhaps be forgiven the hyperbole. Moreover, even if that original confidence waned, and although there were many more dark nights to follow in the history of Plaid Cymru and the wider national movement, Carmarthen served as promissory note that perseverance was not in vain. In that respect, it is no overstatement to claim that the result had a permanent impact on the collective psyche of Welsh nationalists: after Carmarthen they *knew* that victory was at least a possibility.

But as Alan Butt Philip's words suggest, it was not only Plaid Cymru itself that felt the impact of Gwynfor Evans's triumph. It is, of course, impossible to know definitively how the subsequent history of Wales – let alone that of Scotland and the United Kingdom as a whole – might have differed without this result. 'Carmarthen' was certainly not enough in itself to trigger those initial steps towards establishing a Welsh proto-state from the mid-1960s onwards. It is not a case of 'because of Carmarthen we now have the Senedd'. The Welsh Office had already been established before the by-election took place, underlining the fact that there were other important influences at work – something that Plaid Cymru supporters are wont to forget! Nonetheless, Gwynfor Evans's victory was a critical step on that journey. Which is to say, were it not for Gwynfor Evans's victory and its impact, it seems highly unlikely that Wales would have the degree of autonomy that it now enjoys – which is something that Plaid Cymru's opponents in the Labour Party and the Liberal Democrats also tend to forget.

Before the publication of Rhys Evans's outstanding biography, *Gwynfor: Rhag Pob Brad*, in 2005, it is fair to say that Gwynfor Evans had remained a somewhat enigmatic figure.[9] Yes, he was

---

9   Rhys Evans, *Gwynfor: Rhag Pob Brad* (Talybont: Y Lolfa, 2005). Subsequently published in English as *Gwynfor Evans: A Portrait of a Patriot* (Talybont: Y Lolfa, 2008).

a prolific author and, in the words of Kenneth O. Morgan, a 'lucid expositor of his own credo'.[10] But despite his prominence, our knowledge of him was in fact quite superficial.[11] What possessed him to fight with such conviction over such an extended period of time for a cause that often appeared so hopeless? Now we know how his double conversion – to the Almighty and to Wales – intertwined to create an ideal of a 'Christian Wales' that Gwynfor Evans was called to serve throughout his life. We also know how the obviously romantic elements in Evans's personality were yoked to a harder-edged and more stubborn side: it is, after all, impossible to lead any political party without a well-developed ego and at least some share of those political skills praised by Machiavelli. In addition, the biography gave readers an insight into the impact that his decision to dedicate his life to the cause of Wales (as he saw it) had on his family. Thanks to Rhys Evans's efforts, therefore, our understanding of Gwynfor Evans is much more complete than it was. This chapter will seek to avoid treading that same ground and will rather focus its attention on Gwynfor Evans's political thought. We shall begin by considering the relationship between his ideas and those of Saunders Lewis, before discussing Gwynfor Evans's own distinctive contribution to Plaid Cymru's intellectual heritage.

I was rejected …?

The most important intellectual question facing anyone who wants to understand the development of Plaid Cymru's political thought is the relationship between the thinking of Saunders

10   Kenneth O. Morgan, 'From eulogy to elegy: Welsh political biography', in *Modern Wales: Politics, Places and People* (Cardiff: University of Wales Press, 1995), p. 472.
11   His fame and prominence continued into his final years. If I may be forgiven for sharing a personal anecdote in illustration: in the early years of devolution, I organised a lecture at Aberystwyth University by a then prominent figure in the Labour Party – a man, at that, who would not be regarded as a particularly enthusiastic supporter of devolution. Nonetheless, when he was asked who should be invited as part of the audience for the lecture, the very first name on his list was Gwynfor Evans. Even then, Evans's aura continued to cast its spell.

Lewis and the ideas propounded by Gwynfor Evans. After all, if one considers that the 'Saunders era' lasted from 1925 to 1943 and that the 'Gwynfor era' extended from 1943 to 1981, then, between them, the two dominated the party for most of its existence. The degree and nature of the ideological continuation between one era and the next, as well as what precisely served to distinguish these periods, are, therefore, crucial considerations. To what extent did Gwynfor Evans's elevation to the presidency represent a turning point in the political thinking of Plaid Cymru? Or is 'turning point' too dramatic a term to use in the context of a more organic and gradual process of change? Or indeed, is continuation rather than change the most obvious feature of this story?

The first point to note is that delving into the true nature of the ideological (and personal) relationship between these two giants in the history of the national movement is no simple matter. Various pieces of evidence tend to contradict each other, suggesting very different interpretations. Indeed, perhaps only a playwright of Saunders Lewis's stature could do full justice to their complex, multi-layered relationship? Nonetheless, focusing on their intellectual relationship, the argument advanced in the following pages can be crudely summarised as follows: Gwynfor Evans's ideological debt to Saunders Lewis was much greater than either of them was willing to acknowledge. In ideological terms, therefore, there was much more continuation between these two 'eras' in the party's history than both of the main dramatis personae were prepared to admit – or that most observers have appreciated.

Gwynfor Evans was promoted to the presidency of Plaid Cymru with Saunders Lewis's enthusiastic seal of approval. In October 1944, Saunders remarked how 'Gwynfor Evans should have his opportunity to become president and stay in the post as long as I did to build authority in the country.' Pennar Davies reported that, three years later, Lewis even referred to the new president as a 'saint' during a private conversation.[12] With time, however, he was to become profoundly disillusioned. We shall

12   Quoted by Pennar Davies, *Gwynfor Evans* (Abertawe: Tŷ John Penry, 1976), pp. 9, 34; translation.

not pursue the story of that process here. Suffice it to note that, by the early years of the 1960s, Saunders Lewis made little effort to conceal his disappointment in how Gwynfor Evans and Plaid Cymru had strayed from the path that he had sought to establish. His bitterness at this turn of events was crystallised in his well-known comments during an interview with Aneirin Talfan Davies in 1961: 'I was rejected by everybody. I was rejected in every election in which I tried to be a candidate; every one of my ideas – those I developed in social policy and in the social policy of nationalism – have been cast aside.'[13] As mentioned in the previous chapter, he did not just complain just from the sidelines. Rather, Saunders Lewis worked determinedly to encourage Gwynfor Evans's opponents within Plaid Cymru. He did so publicly by such actions as delivering his lecture on 'Tynged yr Iaith' ('The Fate of the Language'), but he was also active behind the scenes, meeting, cajoling and giving succour. As John Davies makes clear, 'Saunders Lewis ... did more than anyone, at the beginning of the sixties, to undermine the faith of Plaid Cymru members in Gwynfor Evans's leadership.'[14]

It is no secret, therefore, that Saunders Lewis felt that both he and his ideological inheritance had been rejected by this successor. What is less known is the way in which Gwynfor Evans also set out to distance himself from Saunders Lewis. This process can be traced by comparing how Saunders Lewis was treated in Gwynfor Evans's early writings with his treatment of him in later works. During Gwynfor Evans's early years as president, he was very happy to acknowledge Saunders Lewis's central role in Plaid Cymru's first two decades and to defend him from his numerous critics. Thus, in an essay published in 1950, Gwynfor Evans discussed his predecessor in the following terms:

> Mr Saunders Lewis was president of the party from 1926 until 1939, and an abundance of work fell to him, not only in terms of leading

13 Saunders Lewis, 'Dylanwadau: Saunders Lewis mewn ymgom ag Aneirin Talfan Davies', *Taliesin*, 2 (Christmas 1961), 13; translation.
14 John Davies, *Plaid Cymru oddi ar 1960* (Aberystwyth: Llyfrgell Genedlaethol Cymru, 1996), p. 2; translation.

day-to-day, but also explaining Plaid's policy as it developed. If his articles in *Y Ddraig Goch* and *Y Faner* [i.e. the weekly, *Baner ac Amserau Cymru*] frequently sparked inevitable disagreement, they also demanded the attention of the party's enemies as well as its friends. There is no doubt that his political writings during these years will be regarded amongst the greatest contributions ever made to political thought in Wales, on the basis of their knowledge, consistency and depth. And of the great patriots of the last two centuries, in the opinion of many, he is the greatest.[15]

This remained the essence of Gwynfor Evans's position (in public, at least) long into the 1970s.

In a discussion on Plaid Cymru in *Wales Can Win*, published in 1973, there is a reference to Saunders Lewis as the party's 'true founder' and 'outstanding figure', as well as an extensive quote from his celebrated speech before the court in Caernarfon in the aftermath of the Fire in Llŷn.[16] He returned to the party's history in *A National Future for Wales* (1975) – in fact, this became an increasingly important theme in his writings from around the middle of the 1970s onwards. Once again, Saunders Lewis ('generally thought to be the greatest Welshman of the century') received suitably deferential treatment.[17] Here, however, we see a tendency that becomes increasingly obvious in Evans's later writings, namely his tendency to overestimate D. J. Davies's role in the early years of the party, this at the expense of Saunders Lewis. Davies was a relatively minor character in *Wales Can Win*. Although he was acknowledged as the principal inspiration for the party's commitment to cooperatives and the wider principle of cooperation, most attention was focused on his extraordinarily colourful life.[18] By the time *A National Future for Wales* was published, Gwynfor Evans had come to consider D. J. Davies as the

15 Gwynfor Evans, 'Yr ugeinfed ganrif a Phlaid Cymru', in D. Tecwyn Lloyd (ed.), *Seiliau Hanesyddol Cenedlaetholdeb Cymru* (Caerdydd: Plaid Cymru, 1950), pp. 139–40; translation.
16 Gwynfor Evans, *Wales Can Win* (Llandybïe: Christopher Davies, 1973), pp. 52–86 and in particular pp. 55–9.
17 Evans, *A National Future for Wales*, p. 71.
18 Evans, *Wales Can Win*, in particular pp. 55–6.

person that, together with Saunders Lewis, had made 'the greatest contribution to developing party policy'.[19] When he returned
to the history of the Plaid Cymru in the mid-1990s, in an essay
in the series *Cof Cenedl*, the pendulum had swung even further
towards Davies.[20] Although he notes Saunders Lewis as 'the main
leader from the start', Davies had now become the main hero of
the story as 'the principal author of the young party's economic
policies as well as the most important influence on its constitutional policy'.[21] Now it may well have been wiser for the party to
follow Davies's lead, but as we have already seen, the historical
evidence suggests that this is not what occurred. But that proved
no obstacle for Gwynfor Evans. In a final assessment of the party's history, Gwynfor Evans exaggerated D. J. Davies's role even
further: he now considered Davies not only to be the author of
the party's economic and constitutional policies, but also claimed
that he had a significant influence on the party's policies towards
the Welsh language.[22]

In this respect, Gwynfor Evans's later discussions of Plaid
Cymru's history follow a pattern established in his autobiogra-
phy, *Bywyd Cymro*. One of the more striking features of that book
is its generosity. Evans is quick to acknowledge the influence of D.
J. Davies, George M. Ll. Davies, G. D. H. Cole, Giuseppe Mazzini,
Tomáš Masaryk, and many others on his thinking. Indeed, his
treatment of some political enemies is remarkably magnanimous.
Take George Thomas, for example, a man who was often distinctly unpleasant towards Gwynfor Evans and his fellow Plaid
Cymru Members of Parliament, but who is commended for being
so 'wonderfully generous' towards the party president when he
was speaker of the House during Gwynfor Evans's second spell
at Westminster between 1974 and 1979.[23]

---

19   Evans, *A National Future for Wales*, p. 76.
20   Gwynfor Evans, 'Hanes twf Plaid Cymru 1925–95', in Geraint H. Jenkins
(ed.), *Cof Cenedl, X* (Llandysul: Gomer, 1995), pp. 153–83; translation.
21   Evans, 'Hanes twf Plaid Cymru 1925–95', p. 156.
22   Gwynfor Evans, *The Fight for Welsh Freedom* (Talybont: Y Lolfa, 2000), pp.
141–2; 'Saunders Lewis ... was influenced by him [D. J. Davies] even on the language issue' (p. 142).
23   Evans, *For the Sake of Wales*, p. 216. Some of George Thomas's unpleasant
behaviour during Gwynfor Evans's first period in Parliament is related on pp.

Seen in this context, it is striking how little Gwynfor Evans has to say about the influence that Saunders Lewis had on his thinking. He mentions the matter twice in *Bywyd Cymro*. Both references are suggestive but brief to the point of curtness. In the first, with reference to D. J. Davies's two volumes – *Can Wales Afford Self-Government?* and *Towards an Economic Democracy* – Evans makes clear the 'powerful influence' that D.J and Noëlle Davies had on him, before adding 'second only to Saunders Lewis'.[24] Separately, he describes himself as an enthusiastic European, adding, 'no one who has been so greatly influenced by Saunders Lewis could do otherwise'.[25] Taken out of context these statements may appear to be a generous acknowledgement of Lewis's influence. But the fact of the matter is that a fine toothcombed search through 344 pages is required to unearth these two half sentences. Neither are the comments particularly illuminating. In which ways did Lewis influence Evans? What, specifically, amongst Lewis's various ideas and standpoints – apart from Europeanism – appealed to him? Despite his acknowledgement that Saunders Lewis had the greatest influence on his thinking, Gwynfor Evans is uncharacteristically taciturn on such matters. Neither do his references to Lewis exhibit the same warmth and generosity of spirit as the rest of the book.[26]

In fact, the only substantial reference in the autobiography to Saunders Lewis's opposition to Gwynfor Evans's leadership seems designed to reflect his predecessor in the worst possible light. Referring to the court case against members of the Free Wales Army in 1969, Gwynfor Evans claims that his refusal to

182–3. The truth of the matter, however, is that George Thomas used his position as speaker to damage the devolution plans of James Callaghan's Labour government during their long and tortuous journey through Parliament. If sincerely meant, Evans's suggestion to the effect that Thomas had risen above such dirty tricks after being promoted to the post of speaker is not just generous, but credulous.

24   Evans, *For the Sake of Wales*, p. 78.

25   Evans, *For the Sake of Wales*, p. 187.

26   For the avoidance of misunderstanding, I note once again that the claim here is that Gwynfor Evans distanced himself from Saunders Lewis over the course of his presidency. He was eloquent in his acknowledgement of Saunders Lewis's influence on both him and the party in his earlier writings: for one example amongst many, see Gwynfor Evans, *Plaid Cymru and Wales* (Llandybïe: Silurian Books, n.d. [but 1950]), p. 3.

comply with Saunders Lewis's request that he attend the court to support the defendants 'contributed to the coolness between us for some years thereafter'.[27] Saunders Lewis's request was preposterous. Had Gwynfor Evans agreed, then it could easily have put at risk the whole future of the party. But also note the deliberate ambiguity in the quote about when precisely – as well as how – the gap between the two had begun to open. In truth, the relationship between Gwynfor Evans and Saunders Lewis had deteriorated long before the FWA had even been established.[28] And while disagreement about the methods that the party should adopt was an important part of the rift between them, Saunders Lewis never seriously believed that Plaid Cymru should devote itself to fomenting or supporting armed struggle against the British state. Despite the impression created in *Bywyd Cymro*, the FWA court case was a symptom and not a cause of division: theirs was a relationship that had long since been become embittered.

Why did Gwynfor Evans seek to distance himself from Saunders Lewis and minimise his central role in Plaid Cymru's first two decades – at least to the extent that the latter was possible? A number of factors might readily be suggested: a desire to take revenge for Saunders Lewis's lack of loyalty, and the personal unpleasantness of some of the former leader's most loyal supporters; a pragmatic desire to try to protect Plaid Cymru from impact of the wildest accusations thrown at it because of Saunders Lewis's (alleged) fascist sympathies; a desire to present a picture of Plaid Cymru's past that was consistent with its present position, that is to say as a movement of the liberal left. Or is the key to be found in Shakespeare? 'Two stars', he said, 'keep not their motion in one sphere.' In the (constricted) firmament of Welsh nationalism, was there perhaps only sufficient space for one star? Hence, one could shine only if the light of the other was obscured?

27 Evans, *For the Sake of Wales*, p. 193.
28 There is some acknowledgement of this from Gwynfor Evans in his joint contribution with 'Ioan Rhys' [Ioan Bowen Rees] to *Celtic Nationalism* (London: Routledge and Kegan Paul, 1968), a peculiar composite volume that includes two other contributions, one from the eminent Irish historian, Owen Dudley Edwards, and the other by poet and Stalinist-Scottish nationalist, Hugh MacDiarmid.

Ultimately, of course, we cannot know for certain whether it was one of these factors, or a combination of them – or indeed a combination of entirely different factors – that were chiefly responsible for the way that Gwynfor Evans chose to present the history of his party or acknowledge his personal debt to his most significant predecessor as party leader. What seems more certain is that Gwynfor Evans spent most if not all his long political life (metaphorically) looking over his shoulder in the direction of Penarth. For there, in Saunders Lewis's home, stood the person against whom he measured himself. It is also demonstrably the case that Saunders Lewis had more of an influence on Gwynfor Evans than he, Saunders, was prepared to acknowledge. Indeed, as we shall see in the next section, so great was this influence that one must take what little Gwynfor Evans had to say about their intellectual relationship completely literally: Saunders Lewis was the biggest influence on his political ideas. As a result, Saunders Lewis continued to have an enormous (indirect) influence on Plaid Cymru far beyond the point at which he claimed that he had been rejected by the party.

The inheritance: the core ideas of 'Saunders' and 'Gwynfor'

There are very clearly identifiable similarities between some of the main elements in the political thinking of Saunders Lewis and Gwynfor Evans. These similarities manifest themselves in the context of those features that are central to the worldview and moral framework of any political nationalist, namely their beliefs about the nature of the nation and the importance of the national community. Their ideas about the specific characteristics of the Welsh nation and the aims of the Welsh national movement are also very closely aligned. Of course, demonstrating similarity does not equate to proving the influence of one over the other. There are several ways by which any two individuals can come to share the same views. Most obviously, they may be part of the same general ideological milieu, or they might both be influenced by a third thinker or intellectual influence. When, as in this case, the two individuals are members of different generations, it is possible that the younger may have been influenced by the elder more subconsciously – through their wider, more generally disseminated influence. That said, Gwynfor Evans's own autobiographical comments, even if brief, are surely an invitation to interpret the similarity between his ideas and those of Saunders Lewis as an example direct influencing. Even if that were not the case, the similarity between the ways in which their views are expressed provides undeniable evidence that Lewis influenced his successor's thinking. This can be demonstrated by distilling Lewis's core ideas to their essence and showing how they were echoed by Evans step by step, clause by clause, and often word for word.

Saunders Lewis's core ideas

Saunders Lewis defined the nation as a 'community of communities' or as 'a society of societies'.[29] He has quite a lot to say about a number of these different 'communities', for example the trade unions. But there is no doubt that he attributes particular importance to two 'elements' within the nation, namely the family and the individual. It is to them that he attributes the highest moral value. Indeed, it is the nation's indispensable contribution to the maintenance of the family and the individual which justifies taking the nation seriously in the form of nationalism.[30]

Why is the nation important to the individual and the family, in particular, but also to the other communities which exist within it? It is important, according to Saunders Lewis, because the nation is

[29] A strikingly pluralist definition which should be sufficient in itself to cast doubt on any suggestion that he embraced fascist and totalitarian ideas.

[30] 'To us, a nation is not a society of individuals, but a society of societies ... And because a nation is a society of societies, a nation's civilisation is complex and rich, and as a result, the freedom of the individual is possible ... The freedom of the individual depends on his being a member of a number of societies and not of only one, and attacking the reasonable rights of small societies, such as the family, churches, cooperative unions and trade unions, means depriving the individual of his natural defences': Saunders Lewis, 'Undebau llafur a'r Blaid Genedlaethol', *Y Ddraig Goch*, November 1932, 1; translation.

a kind of vessel or container. Or better, perhaps, the nation is the 'glue' that ensures the various social elements within it share a sense of belonging and collective responsibility, allowing them all to develop and prosper.[31] In short, it is the feeling of nationhood that creates a single community from these different and disparate communities. The content or the substance of that 'glue' is culture. Values are conveyed through culture, not only 'horizontally' at any given point in time, but also bequeathed from one generation to the next. It is through culture that people express their humanity. Through culture, also, that they glorify their Creator. Thus, any political philosophy that disregards culture – such as, in Saunders Lewis's view, socialism/Marxism – is guilty of disregarding the very essence of civilised life.

Does all of this suggest, therefore, that Saunders Lewis regarded nations as isolated, self-sufficient communities – like 'billiard balls', to use a metaphor that will be familiar to students of international politics? Not at all. How indeed could that ever be the case for a thinker who celebrated the European influence on Welsh culture and condemned Wales's servile relationship with England precisely because it isolated Wales from these influences? Contacts and connections between the nations and national cultures of Europe were regarded as a sign of their vitality. (Like so many European thinkers of his generation – on both sides of the political spectrum – he had little interest in the world beyond Europe.) Every individual culture is a manifestation of a wider culture or 'civilisation'. But – and here we come to the key point – he considered that every such manifestation was precious and, indeed, indispensable because of its role in enriching the whole.

It seems that Lewis thought that this enrichment occurred at several different levels. Most obviously, national cultures enrich through their influence on other national cultures, as, for example, in the case of the influence of Welsh fables on European

---

[31] 'The country or the nation is the normal form of society in Europe. Through experience of generations, it has been found to be small enough to love and big enough to allow men to live a full life. The nation is the foundation of western civilization': Saunders Lewis, 'Cenedlaetholdeb a chyfalaf', *Y Ddraig Goch*, June 1926, 3; translation.

civilisation via the Arthurian cult. But there is also an all-important theological element to his argument: individual cultures enrich because nations and national diversity are, according to Saunders Lewis, part of the divine order. In the same way as he emphatically denied the right of the nation – or, more precisely, the state acting in the name of the nation – to infringe on the sanctity of the family and the individual, he considered any attempt to deprecate or destroy the nation as nothing less than blasphemy and an offence against God. In general terms, therefore, the importance of the nation lies in its mediating role – it mediates between the universal and the particular, between humanity and the divine, between the individual and the society around it. Without the nation, all that remains is a herd of disconnected, uncultured, uncivilised, and thus in the end, de-humanised individuals.

Moving from the abstract to the concrete, Welsh level, it becomes obvious why Saunders Lewis attributed so much importance to the Welsh language and its associated culture. Following the logic of his argument, the existence of Welsh-language culture – that is, the mainstream of Wales's culture, historically speaking – must be regarded as forming part of God's plan. Defending and restoring this culture to its rightful place is therefore nothing less than a sacred duty. But equally, without the bonds of nationhood there is no hope for any kind of salvation within this world or in this life. For only these bonds provide the necessary basis – the requisite feeling of joint responsibility and, therefore, willingness to work together – that allow the living of a full, dignified life.[32]

---

[32] This argument was expressed in a striking way by one of Saunders Lewis's most faithful acolytes, J. E. Daniel, in his pamphlet *Welsh Nationalism: What it Stands for* (London: Foyle's Welsh Co., n.d. [but 1937]), during the devastation of the Great Depression: 'The fatal mistake of the rootless Marxist deraciné Socialism of South Wales is the supposition that fifteen centuries count for nothing in the rehabilitation of Wales. It is in the poetry of Taliesin and Dafydd Nanmor, in the ruling conceptions of the ancient laws of Wales, far more than in the Special Areas Act of the Five Year programmes that the salvation of Wales is to be found. There is a far closer connection between his language and his bread and butter than the Welshman has yet dreamed' (p. 40).

Gwynfor Evans's core ideas

If this may be regarded as a fair summary of Saunders Lewis's core ideas vis-à-vis the nation, then, equally, it also summarises Gwynfor Evans's most fundamental beliefs with regards the same issues. He, too, referred several times to the Welsh nation as 'a community of communities' and 'a society of societies':

> It must be emphasised that the nation is a society. It is a society that is an organic communion [cyfundod] of small societies with which its people identify, and with their roots in its earth, its history and in its tradition.[33]

> He [man] is a member of many groupings, all of which contribute to the enriching of his personality ... These communities cohere in the nation, which through her language, traditions, culture and history, safeguards the values of the past and transmits them to the future. The nation is a community of communities.[34]

Within this national community, he considered the family to be the most important institution and attributed the highest moral value to the individual:

> The smallest of communities within the nation is fundamental in more ways than one. It is the family, which alone can be called a natural community. The structure of society depends more upon this than any other entity within it, and the ill-effects of weakening it are quickly visible.[35]

And for Welsh nationalists, like any other nationalists, there is great value to the nation. Why is this? In short, on account of its

---

[33] Gwynfor Evans, *Rhagom i Ryddid* (Bangor: Plaid Cymru, 1964), p. 13; translation. Note also the sentences that follow: 'It is this society that protects and transfers from generation to generation the values that civilise a man. In Wales, these values are Christian and they are shared with the countries of Europe, although the pattern varies from country to country.'

[34] Evans, *Plaid Cymru and Wales*, pp. 10–11.

[35] Gwynfor Evans, *Welsh Nationalist Aims* (Plaid Cymru, 1959), p. 9.

importance in the life of the individual. It is not the nation that has the highest value, but the human personality. It is for man that everything exists, every institution, every society. This is the reason the nation and the state exist; their function is to ensure sustenance and a richer life [bywyd helaethach] for man.[36]

The particular importance of the nation lies in the way that it – through cultural means – disseminates values throughout society and 'from generation to generation'.[37] Societal disintegration is the price we pay for losing sight of this fundamental fact: '[T]he nation is today our greatest medium for the transmission of human values from generation to generation. When it disintegrates community becomes a rootless mass, unresisting before the onrush of Hollywood.'[38]

Again, we find Gwynfor Evans claiming a role for the nation as part of the divine order. He also emphasises the importance of the individual nation and its particular culture as a manifestation of a wider cultural system. Although he was undoubtedly more drawn to 'Celticism' – the alleged 'Celtic connection' – than Saunders Lewis (as discussed further below), Evans also considered the culture of Wales and those of nations on the continent to be part of a wider European civilisation:

Wales is one of the nations of Europe, one that has maintained its distinctiveness through long centuries until now, despite being grievously wounded and weakened as a result of a lack of institutions to defend and nourish itself. We have been placed in this corner of Europe as guardians of this small part of civilisation. As the people of Wales, it is here that our responsibility lies.[39]

36 Evans, *Rhagom i Ryddid*, p. 11; translation; also, inter alia, 'The nation exists for man, not man for the nation. There is a moral law above all nations and states': Evans, *Plaid Cymru and Wales*, p. 14; 'But it [the state] is an instrument. It is not its place to dominate a nation, but to serve it, by trying to ensure an environment suitable for the individual to live and prosper in': Gwynfor Evans, *Cristnogaeth a'r Gymdeithas Gymreig* (Abertawe: Undeb yr Annibynwyr, 1954), p. 9; translation.
37 Gwynfor Evans, *Aros Mae* (Abertawe: Tŷ John Penry, 1971), p. 277; translation.
38 Evans, *Plaid Cymru and Wales*, p. 13.
39 Evans, *Rhagom i Ryddid*, p. 16; translation.

It is in the national traditions of Europe, and nowhere else, that European civilisation is to be found. When a European nation's life is destroyed, part of European civilisation is destroyed. The first duty of every nation is to remain a nation and care for its small part of the wider civilisation.[40]

Once again, then, it is clear that Gwynfor Evans did not regard his ('Christian') form of nationalism as an attempt to retreat from the world, or to avoid wider responsibilities. Rather, he saw 'healthy' nationalism as a means of mediating between the local and the global; between the individual and wider humanity.[41]

The striking resemblance between the ideas of Saunders Lewis and Gwynfor Evans – and the influence of the former on the latter – is further underlined when we consider the emphasis Gwynfor Evans placed on acting politically in order to support and restore Welsh-language culture. In his view, this was central to the party's mission. Gwynfor Evans was being orthodoxly Saundersian when he claimed that: 'Because man is interwoven so closely with his country's culture, and because his personality is so dependent on that culture for nourishment, the problem of restoring the person and of restoring his cultural society are intrinsically linked.'[42] Moreover, with the Welsh language forming 'the blood and the heart of the national tradition', it is no surprise that he also claims:

> Plaid Cymru … is more than a political party. It is a national move-
> ment and a moral crusade which has given much of its time to edu-
> cate people in nationhood, awakening them to a sense of loyalty to

---

40 Evans, *Aros Mae*, p. 223; translation.
41 We have already noted the extent to which Saunders Lewis's nationalism was a conditional one, reflecting the fact that he was a nationalist who was always very conscious of the dangers of nationalism. In the aftermath of the Second World War and the full unveiling of the horrors of the Nazi extermination camps Gwynfor Evans tended to use adjectives such as 'healthy' or 'Christian' to qualify the claims of Plaid Cymru's nationalism. For Welsh nationalists, some things are more important than the nation, but these cannot be protected without securing a healthy national life. Evans's use of these adjectives is also another example of the phenomenon discussed in the first chapter, namely the constant attempts to distinguish between acceptable and unacceptable forms of nationalism.
42 Evans, *Cristnogaeth a'r Gymdeithas Gymreig*, p. 6; translation.

their community, and cultivating the incipient will to live a national life. Faced with anglicisation it is a resistance movement, confronted by English Government a freedom movement.[43]

For Gwynfor Evans, as for Saunders Lewis, Welsh nationalism was a 'local' crusade with global motivations and implications.

Fundamental policies: the inheritance and its evolution

It should now be clear how reliant Gwynfor Evans's ideas were on those of Saunders Lewis regarding matters that are central to the credo of every political nationalist. This point was also made by John Davies in his pamphlet *The Green and the Red: Nationalism and Ideology in Twentieth-century Wales*: 'On a number of central issues Evans's views differ little from those of Lewis.'[44] But Lewis's influence on Evans's thinking went even further than John Davies allows. This becomes obvious on returning to those policy areas discussed in some detail in the previous chapter, namely the party's economic, constitutional and Welsh-language-related standpoints and policies. On doing so we find that 'Saundersian' ideas continued to dominate the party's policy agenda far beyond the point at which Saunders Lewis himself, let alone most commentators, thought that their influence had come to an end. Scrutinising these policy areas in more detail also allows us to observe how – very gradually – Gwynfor Evans adapted the ideological inheritance handed down by his predecessor.

The Welsh language
We have already seen how influential Saunders Lewis was in determining Plaid Cymru's attitude towards the Welsh language. He, and he alone, insisted that the language, and not self-government, was at the core of the movement's first declaration of fundamental objectives. Even after those objectives were revised,

43 Evans, *Aros Mae*, p. 277; translation; Evans, *Wales Can Win*, p. 140.
44 John Davies, *The Green and the Red: Nationalism and Ideology in Twentieth-century Wales* (Aberystwyth: Plaid Cymru, 1980), p. 30.

it was he who was primarily responsible for ensuring that the health of Welsh language culture was such a central part of Welsh nationalists' own understanding of the nature of their political commitment. It was also Saunders Lewis's influence, above all else, that generated a contradiction between the party's official position on the Welsh language and the perception of that position resulting from the public statements of its most prominent and eloquent spokespeople. This contradiction may be expressed in terms of a tension between the commitment to a bilingual Wales and the aspiration for a monolingual Welsh-speaking Wales. In terms of its formal policy, Plaid Cymru soon returned to the commitment to bilingualism that had characterised H. R. Jones and Evan Alwyn Owen's first incarnation of Plaid Genedlaethol Cymru. Considering the language's lack of status at that time, the implications of this commitment were far-reaching if not revolutionary – as remains the case today. But Saunders Lewis wanted to go much further than this. His aim was a Welsh-speaking Wales, a Wales with Welsh as the only language of its civic life and the principal medium of general social intercourse. A bilingual Wales could have been a step along the journey towards that objective, but it was not the desired destination.

One of the consequences of this commitment to the Welsh language as the main medium of Welsh culture was an ambiguous attitude towards non-Welsh-speaking Wales. For the avoidance of doubt, let us be clear what is meant by this claim. It does not mean that Saunders Lewis was hostile towards Welsh people who did not speak Welsh. Such an inference would be grossly unfair. Neither did he deny the Welshness of those who did not speak Welsh. But he did consider Welsh people who do not speak the Welsh language to be incomplete: as people who were missing a part, at least, of the key to a rounded, complete and contented life. One suspects that a similar ambiguity pervades the attitudes of those among us who regret the fact that the language lost so much ground during the twentieth century and who long for its decline to be reversed? After all, are not all those parents who do not speak Welsh themselves but who nonetheless insist that their children receive an education through the medium of Welsh motivated by a sense that they have missed out by not having the opportunity to embrace it themselves? In Saundersian terms, might such parents feel that they themselves are in some sense incomplete without the Welsh language? In terms of the political implications of such an attitude, much is likely to depend on the way in which this 'ambiguity' is expressed. In Saunders Lewis's case, the manner of expression was problematic. His forte as both politician and literary critic was the memorable sweeping statement; not for him the 'honeyed, vote-seeking smile'. He deployed words as one might explosives to try to detonate the dam of indifference and prejudice that was rapidly submerging Welsh language and culture. When words rendered in this deliberately provocative manner are read out of context, all nuance is lost and it is easy to lose sight of the ambiguity that was, in fact, at their heart.

Gwynfor Evans's inheritance from Saunders Lewis in respect of Plaid Cymru's attitude towards the Welsh language was, therefore, threefold:

1. a commitment to safeguarding and restoring the Welsh language as Plaid Cymru's *sine qua non*;
2. a tension between the formal commitment to bilingualism and the desire for a monolingual Welsh-speaking Wales; and, connected to this,
3. a degree of ambiguity in the party's attitude towards non-Welsh-speaking Wales.

In general terms, Evans remained faithful to the first of these (even if Lewis did not necessarily see it that way). There can also be no doubt that Gwynfor Evans shared the same desire for a monolingual Wales, but with the passage of time and further deterioration in the situation of the language, that dream became increasingly irrelevant. As a result, he redefined the meaning of 'Welsh-speaking Wales' to imply a bilingual rather than a monolingual Welsh-speaking Wales. In terms of the third element of this inheritance, there is also more than a hint of the same (inevitable?) ambiguity in Gwynfor Evans's attitude towards those who did not speak the language, though the manner in which that ambiguity was expressed was not quite as damaging politically as it was in the case of Saunders Lewis.

With this by way of introduction, let us turn to a more detailed consideration of the significance of the Welsh language's place in Gwynfor Evans's political thought and his understanding of Welsh nationalism's defining objective. We start by noting that ensuring a parliament for Wales – any kind of parliament – was an enormously important priority for Gwynfor Evans, as is discussed further below. It would also be fair to claim that this was more of a priority for him than it was for Saunders Lewis. Nonetheless, it remained the case that Gwynfor Evans regarded rescuing and restoring the language as, ultimately, an even higher priority. In this respect his attitudes were more aligned with those of Saunders Lewis's than many have realised.

The priority accorded by Evans to the language is rendered crystal clear in his voluminous writings. It is also worth underlining that his English-language books and pamphlets reflect the same attitudes as those found in his Welsh-language publications. One of the things that made it possible for Gwynfor Evans to repeat himself so extensively in his various works is the fact that he did not seek to adapt either his message or tone when switching from one language to the other! But, of course, demonstrating that safeguarding the future of the Welsh language was a priority for Gwynfor Evans is not the same as showing that he regarded the language as a more important priority than attaining self-government. In fact, one of his main arguments was that the two objectives were irrevocably bound together: the long-term future of the language could only be secured via a measure of self-government. What makes it possible to argue that Gwynfor Evans was a faithful follower of Saunders Lewis's is his attitude in the late 1960s when tension developed between the aim of securing self-government and the struggle to save the language. When choosing between them became unavoidable, Gwynfor Evans prioritised the latter.

By the middle of the 1960s, Cymdeithas yr Iaith Gymraeg (the Welsh Language Society) had developed into a very active movement which regularly engaged in non-violent direct action in the name of the Welsh language. By the end of that decade, this activism, alongside the more militant activism of peripheral groups such as Mudiad Amddiffyn Cymru and the Free Wales Army, together with the decision to hold an ostentatious ceremony in Caernarfon to mark Charles's investiture as prince of Wales – the first step in 'Diana-fication' of the Windsors – had all combined to create a sense of crisis. Plaid Cymru co-existed (if sometimes unwillingly) in a symbiotic relationship with the language movement. There is no doubt that it was substantially strengthened by the zeal and dedication of the new generation of nationalists. But by the same token, it became increasingly clear that the backlash triggered by language campaigners' actions was threatening the momentum that had built in the wake of the party's success in Carmarthen and its subsequent by-election results. Unsurprisingly, therefore, the party's leadership came under pressure to disassociate itself from the language campaigners and, indeed, to condemn them.

Gwynfor Evans was clearly in a particularly difficult personal situation given that his own children – in particular, his daughter Meinir – were prominent campaigners. Nonetheless, Gwynfor Evans's various contemporaneous publications were uncompromising in their support for the (mainly young) women and men of Cymdeithas yr Iaith. Time and again, he went out of his way to express his admiration for their courage, continuing to do so even after their actions had contributed – at least in the view of many party members – to his loss of his Carmarthen seat in the 1970 general election. His attitude cannot be explained simply in terms of family loyalty – even if such feelings should not be disregarded as a factor. He would offer the following explanation for his behaviour in *A National Future for Wales*, published in 1975:

> There is no doubt that Plaid Cymru would have grown more quickly, perhaps very much more quickly, but for its adherence to the language. If it had been prepared to drop its struggle for the language, until Wales has her own parliament, as some of its foremost members have urged it to do, perhaps it would today at least be comparable in

parliamentary strength to the SNP which does not have this problem [after the October 1974 General Election, the SNP had eleven members of parliament]. Constantly we have evidence of the way the language is holding us back; and of course our opponents exploit, sometimes quite unscrupulously, the resentment and prejudices of some non-Welsh speaking people. But the Welsh language goes to the heart of what Plaid Cymru is trying to do. In the first place its struggle is for the civilisation of Wales, of which the language is the main medium. That is its *raison d'être*. If it abandoned the ancient tongue, even temporarily, it would be betraying its most fundamental purpose.[45]

Because of the fundamental and formative nature of the commitment to the Welsh language, nationalists had to prioritise the campaign for its survival even at risk of damaging the popularity and success of their party. To pursue any other path would be to betray the soul of the movement.

Of course, a general commitment to the Welsh language may be associated with many different views about the rightful position the language in public life. Saunders Lewis dreamt of a 'Welsh-speaking Wales', a monolingual Wales. This was hardly a practical aspiration at any point during the twentieth century, but the continuing decline in the number of Welsh speakers during the course of the century meant that a 'monolingual Wales' could not be regarded as a credible objective for any political party that wished to be taken seriously. Even so, there is no doubt that Gwynfor Evans shared the same aspirations as Lewis on this matter. This is perhaps most clearly apparent in his pamphlet *Eu Hiaith a Gadwant* (1949), which was – significantly – the first he published under the party's imprimatur. In it, he argues that Welsh should become 'the principal language [prif iaith] in every part of life in Wales, in trade and entertainment as well as in education and worship'. Why? 'Because it is the only possible medium through which the Welsh mind can thrive; it alone could be an organic part of Welsh life.'[46]

---

[45] Evans, *A National Future for Wales*, p. 84.
[46] Gwynfor Evans, *Eu Hiaith a Gadwant* (Caerdydd: Plaid Cymru, 1949), p. 4; translation.

Welsh as the principal language of Wales. Did Gwynfor Evans ever change his mind about this? Not a bit of it. His fundamental ideas remained remarkably consistent throughout his political career. Here's what he said, for example, in *Diwedd Prydeindod* (The End of Britishness), published towards the end of his political career in 1981: 'However great the difficulties, Plaid Cymru must hold fast to its vision of a Wales that speaks Welsh [Cymru Gymraeg] and feels Welsh, as well as a Wales that is free and just. Wales's future must grow out of the wealth of her traditions.'[47] As we see, he also continued to use the phrase 'Cymru Gymraeg' – 'Welsh-speaking Wales' – to describe the party's objective throughout. But underlining the combination of stubbornness and pragmatism that characterised Gwynfor Evans, it is important to note that the linguistic condition regarded as embodying this state of grace changed gradually over the course of his presidency. It shifted from referencing a monolingual Welsh-speaking Wales to denoting, instead, a thoroughly bilingual Wales. In a chapter bearing the title 'Cymru Gymraeg' in his volume *Rhagom i Ryddid* (1964), Evans argued that 'striving for an official and equal status to English for Welsh … had been part of Plaid Cymru's policy' from the outset.[48] This may have been more or less true in literal terms, but omitted to mention that, in the first decades of the party's existence, this was considered to be a stepping stone towards the attainment of a monolingual Wales. By the 1960s, however, a bilingual Wales had come to be regarded as an objective in its own right, rather than simply a way point on the journey to a 'higher' goal. This, though, was a commitment to a bilingualism that went far beyond today's comfortable and rather stodgy consensus. In *Wales Can Win* (1973), Gwynfor Evans argued that 'The aim in Wales must be to give the people the opportunity to become bilingual within a generation.'[49] If this were taken seriously – and there can be no doubt that he was absolutely serious on this score – then it was and remains an objective with wholly

---

47 Gwynfor Evans, *Diwedd Prydeindod* (Talybont: Y Lolfa, 1981), pp. 139–40; translation.
48 Evans, *Rhagom i Ryddid*, p. 114; translation.
49 Evans, *Wales Can Win*, p. 122.

revolutionary implications. Although he had been forced (out of necessity) to set aside the objective of a monolingual Wales, that did not affect the priority Evans accorded to the Welsh language.

It should come as no surprise to learn that this priority was also accompanied by ambiguity in his attitudes to those who did not speak Welsh. This surfaces time and again in Gwynfor Evans's writings. On the one hand, his definition of Welshness and Welsh identity was strikingly 'inclusive' long before that word would become a part of the Welsh political lexicon. He regarded Welshness not as a linguistic condition – let alone a matter of race and lineage – but rather a completely subjective sense of belonging. The Welsh, he said in 1963, were 'all those people of whatever race, creed, religion or colour, who live in Wales and regard it as their home'.[50] He emphasised the ability of Welshness to transcend social differences of every kind:

> We shall move forward united, a family of Welsh people in our varied callings and various circles, be our language English or Welsh, for we are one nation and we can all take pride in the same past, all work in the same present, all with the same future to hope for.[51]

He took particular pride in the way that immigrants to Wales as well as their children – of both earlier periods and in the present time – came to consider themselves to be Welsh.[52] It is therefore no surprise that he later became one of the founders of PONT (which translates as 'bridge'), a voluntary organisation that tried to assist with this process.

That being said, however, it is also the case that he believed that Welsh speakers in Wales tended to live richer lives compared

[50] Gwynfor Evans, *Plan for a New Wales* (Plaid Cymru, 1963), p. 11.
[51] Gwynfor Evans, 'Yr ugeinfed ganrif a Phlaid Cymru', p. 143; translation.
[52] Gwynfor Evans's discussion on the descendants of those immigrants who flocked Wales at the time of the Industrial Revolution makes the argument in the following terms: 'Today, the majority of these immigrants, or their descendants, are proud to call themselves Welshmen; and since common membership of the Welsh community rather than language or descent is the test of nationality in Wales, nationalists are proud to know them as fellow-Welshmen': Evans, *Plaid Cymru and Wales*, p. 17.

with non-Welsh speakers, and this because they possessed the ability to speak the language. 'When Welshness recedes,' he claimed, 'the life of the individual Welshman is made poorer and he is not able to realise as much of his potential; he is less of a man than he might be.'[53] He compared and contrasted those areas where Welsh continued to be the primary language of communication with those where it had been replaced by English, adjudging the Welsh areas as more civilised:

> Despite all the damage of the last three generations, there remains much life and wealth in Wales's language and culture, it is still sufficiently strong to lift the ordinary people who partake in them to a higher level of life, as we see clearly on comparing those parts of Wales where they flourish with those from which they have been lost.[54]

One comparison he returned to more than once to confirm this view was between Meirionnydd and Radnorshire:

> Here are two rural counties not too dissimilar from each other geographically, but while the Welsh-speaking county has produced a host of cultural, educational and religious leaders, the anglicised county is much poorer: nobody in Welsh life has emerged from this area since the days of Vavasor Powell.[55]

Evans's Nonconformist prejudices also surface when he praises Welsh-speaking areas at the expense of those areas where English had become the main language of social association: 'in whole anglicised areas the dominance of cultural and religious institutions is replaced to a great extent by club, pub and bingo'.[56]

One of the most fascinating aspects of Gwynfor Evans's tendency to equate Welshness with moral superiority (and it is no exaggeration to describe his views in those terms) is its potential

53   Evans, *Rhagom i Ryddid*, p. 15; translation.
54   Evans, *Cristnogaeth a'r Gymdeithas Gymreig*, pp. 13–14; translation.
55   Evans, *Rhagom i Ryddid*, p. 14; translation.
56   Evans, *A National Future for Wales*, p. 22.

impact on the internal politics of Plaid Cymru. The matter will not be discussed in detail here, nonetheless, it is worth noting the extent to which Gwynfor Evans's assessments of his fellow party members seemed to centre on their grasp of the language. This is seen most clearly, perhaps, in *A National Future for Wales*, which includes a series of pen portraits of prominent Plaid members. Almost without fail, portraits of those from a non-Welsh-speaking background focus on their success in mastering the language.[57] Indeed, such is the extent of his emphasis that one might be forgiven for thinking that Gwynfor Evans placed a higher value on their fluency than on any particular talent they may have had as politicians! Given that the concept of 'Welsh learner' was a much less familiar one in the 1970s than it has subsequently become, Gwynfor Evans's words may be interpreted as an attempt to urge others to learn the language by drawing attention to exemplary success stories. But equally, it would be easy to forgive those party members who did not succeed in mastering the language – or those who felt no compunction to try – if they felt that Gwynfor Evans's attitude meant that they were destined never to enter the inner sanctum of the 'redeemed'. Reading Gwynfor Evans's assessments of his fellow members certainly highlights the significance of something I was once told by the late, deliciously mischievous Phil Williams. Such were the advantages that accrued within Plaid Cymru from learning Welsh that he wished to be known as a 'permanent learner'. The fact that he was learning the language gave him an enormous cachet in the eyes of Gwynfor Evans and his ilk. Yet, the fact that he did not count as a completely fluent Welsh speaker meant that those within the party who were suspicious of the influence of 'the bogs and the gogs' (to use Harri Webb's memorable phrase) would not feel that he was a completely lost cause!

If the ambiguity of Gwynfor Evans's attitude towards those who did not speak Welsh generated tensions within the party, it is difficult to evaluate its precise impact on wider public perceptions of its president. As has already been noted, it is almost

---

57 Evans, *A National Future for Wales*, for example, p. 75.

certainly the way that any such ambiguity is communicated that matters. In Evans's case, there is certainly no suggestion that he 'blamed' those who did not speak Welsh for their situation. He rather reserved his disdain for the British educational system – a system that he described time and again, using Pádraig Pearse's famous phrase, as 'the murder machine'.[58] The products of this machine could not be blamed for their condition; rather, they had to be helped to regain their lost heritage. But the context of the listening is as important as the manner of telling. Although Éamon de Valera referred to Irish speakers in remarkably similar terms to the ways in which Gwynfor Evans referred to Welsh speakers – this while continuing to stand head and shoulders (both literally and metaphorically) over everyone else on Ireland's political stage – the situation in Wales was different.[59] Here, it is likely that Gwynfor Evans's ambivalence contributed to a process which saw his party becoming a hegemonic force amongst fluent Welsh speakers while remaining marginal amongst those who did not speak the language. While the conversion of Welsh speakers to Welsh nationalism has likely contributed to strengthening the language's overall position, the grip of British nationalism on the majority of their co-nationals was not seriously challenged.

Perhaps the last word on this matter should be left to Dafydd, one of Gwynfor Evans's sons. In a diary entry written on 22 August 1966, a few days after the Carmarthen victory, he shares the following, highly suggestive tale:

> On Friday and Saturday, Plaid Cymru made their way through the villages of the county to thank the people. Dad spoke only in Welsh, and I believe that this was a mistake. I saw many ordinary people, non-Welsh speakers, coming joyfully to listen and leaving in low-spirits. I hope the victory will not be thrown away.[60]

Deliberate or not, the insult was pointed.

58 See, inter alia, Evans, *Diwedd Prydeindod*, pp. 19–22.
59 Tim Pat Coogan, *De Valera: Long Fellow, Long Shadow* (London: Arrow, 1995).
60 Dafydd Evans, *Y Blew a Buddugoliaeth Gwynfor* (Talybont: Y Lolfa, 2003), p. 154; translation.

Economic policy

Remarkably, Gwynfor Evans's publications continued to cite *perchentyaeth* as one of the cornerstones of Plaid Cymru's economic policy twenty years into his presidency. In *Rhagom i Ryddid* (1964), readers were reminded that the party had always believed that 'it was beneficial to share property and responsibility widely, and unhealthy for them to be concentrated in the hands of a few. It believes that to be owner of your own home is a good thing and called this part of its policy *perchentyaeth*.[61] In a version of the pamphlet *Welsh Nationalist Aims* reprinted sometime after the Carmarthen victory, the policy was linked to that old shibboleth about the nature of ownership patterns in Wales during the (pre-conquest) era of the Laws of Hywel Dda:

> from its inception the party has been what can be called anti-capitalist. But it has believed that the abolition of property would lead to evils far greater even than those to which it has given rise in the past. Not abolition but thoroughgoing distribution is its remedy, and it has applied this to land as to all other forms of property. It has kept to the spirit of Welsh law, which knew nothing of primogeniture.[62]

Even a quarter of a century and more after Saunders Lewis conceded the presidency, the three acres and its Welsh-speaking cow were still alive and well![63]

---

61 Evans, *Rhagom i Ryddid*, p. 111; translation.

62 This specific pamphlet seems to have been republished several times – having been first published as an essay in the July 1957 issue of a journal published in Hyderabad, India, titled *Mankind*. Here, however, the quotation comes from Gwynfor Evans, *Welsh Nationalist Aims* (Cardiff: Plaid Cymru, n.d. but the name of the author is given as Gwynfor Evans MP), p. 14. It should be noted that the pamphlet acknowledged that the term *perchentyaeth* itself had not entered general usage. The reason? '[P]robably because the form of property to which it refers is too limited' (p. 14).

63 Indeed, Gwynfor Evans continued to wax lyrical on the central role of agriculture. Thus, in *Plaid Cymru and Wales* (1950) we find various 'Saundersian' flourishes including: 'Welsh agriculture, which must always be the foundation of Welsh economic life' (p. 53) and '[T]he development of Welsh agriculture is imperative for reasons of social, economic and physical health' (p. 54). By this point, less than 10 per cent of the Welsh workforce was employed in the industry.

The fact that *perchentyaeth* had continued to play such a central role in Plaid Cymru's political thought for so long is itself
further evidence of Saunders Lewis's long-standing influence.
But it may also be taken as a sign of Gwynfor Evans's own particular shortcomings as an economic thinker, this at a time when
the party's weakness was such that he was expected to be a
spokesman on everything, including the economy. His writings
demonstrate time and again how heavily he relied on the help
of others in his various attempts to discuss economic matters. In
the early years of his presidency, he was to all intents and purposes completely reliant on the knowledge and expertise of D.
J. and Noëlle Davies. After D.J.'s untimely death in 1956 and the
departure to Ireland of his partner in the wake of her bereave-
ment, Evans and the party turned to the ideas and analyses of
Edward Nevin.

Paradoxically enough, because of Evans's lack of knowledge
– and lack of interest? – in economic matters, on occasion his various declarations on the subject became a medium for disseminat-
ing pioneering and notably progressive analyses of the state of the
Welsh economy. Thus, in *Plaid Cymru and Wales* (1950), 'Gwynfor
Evans' offered a notably insightful analysis of the economic situation in Wales after the Second World War. It contained a discussion on Britain's economic development (and the implications for
Wales) that previewed much of the discussion of British 'decline'
heard so insistently from the 1960s (as discussed in Chapter 1,
above).[64] The economic themes raised – such as the lack of balance in Wales's economy and the urgent need for divergence, the
price paid for Britain's imperial pretensions, the economic need
for self-government – were already very familiar to those who
read the work of D. J. and Noëlle Davies. Indeed, the book's preface contains the following testimonial:

> I owe a heavy debt to Dr Noëlle Davies and Dr D.J. Davies, whose
> books and pamphlets I have used without burdening the text with

---

[64] Evans, *Plaid Cymru and Wales*, pp. 28–36, and particularly in the present context, pp. 32–3.

acknowledgements in footnotes, and who generously placed at my disposal their valuable notes on the economic situation in Wales.[65]

It was an appropriately generous comment given Gwynfor Evans's reliance on the two, particularly in the field of economics. The enthusiastic response in party circles to Edward Nevin's pioneering work and, in particular, to the publication of his *The Social Accounts of the Welsh Economy*, suggests that at least some were hopeful that Nevin might step into D. J. Davies's shoes and become 'Plaid's economist'.[66] The importance of finding someone prepared to undertake this role is underlined when we consider that, at the time, official economic statistics on the Welsh economy were hard to come by and academic research into the state of the modern Welsh economy practically non-existent. As a result, the party had to rely on its own members and supporters to undertake basic research themselves. Considerable attention was paid to the research undertaken by Nevin, a lecturer in the Department of Economics and Politics at the University of Wales, Aberystwyth, in *Welsh Nation* in 1957.[67] In 1960 and 1961 a long essay by Nevin drawing on his experiences working as a consultant to the government of Jamaica as that country moved towards independence was published over two issues of *Triban*.[68] Regrettably from Plaid Cymru's perspective, despite the fact that the party offered an appreciative audience for his work, Nevin was a Liberal supporter. In addition, Wales's economy was only one of a number of his intellectual interests and he eventually shifted his attentions elsewhere.[69] Consequently, as

65   Evans, *Plaid Cymru and Wales*, p. 3.
66   Edward Nevin (ed.), *The Social Accounts of the Welsh Economy, 1948 to 1956* (Cardiff: University of Wales Press for University College of Wales, Aberystwyth, 1957).
67   There was a series of three essays by E. M. Alexander and G. Richards in the pages of *Welsh Nation*: 'Why Social Accounts?', March 1957, 6–7; 'Some implications for policy', April 1957, 3–5; 'Income, profits and the balance of payments', May 1957, 7. See also, 'Y lleidr penffordd yn nacáu gwaith i Gymru', *Y Ddraig Goch*, November 1957, 4.
68   Edward Nevin, 'The monetary aspects of independence', *Triban*, 2 (1) (April 1960), 3–19; Edward Nevin, 'The problem of independence', *Triban*, 2 (3) (December 1961), 1–20.
69   See Esmond Cleary, 'Edward Nevin MA (Wales), PhD (Cantab)', in Jeffery Round (ed.), *The European Economy in Perspective: Essays in Honour of Edward Nevin*

he prepared *Rhagom i Ryddid*, published in 1964, Gwynfor Evans
was still having to rely on data gathered by Nevin for the years
1948 to 1956 as he examined the financial relationship between
Wales and the British state.[70] These were, in fact, the most recent
economic statistics on the economic performance of the country
that he could offer to his readers. By the mid-1960s it is hard to
imagine anyone beyond the most loyal of the party stalwarts
taking what Gwynfor Evans and his party had to say about the
economy seriously. It was only with the formation of the Plaid
Cymru Research Group under the leadership of Dafydd Wigley
and Phil Williams, and in particular after the publication of the
fruits of its efforts in the *Economic Plan for Wales* (1970), that
some element of intellectual respectability was restored to the
party's arguments in this all-important field.[71] Apart from ask-
ing countless parliamentary questions, ensuring that the House
of Commons research staff acted as proxy researchers for the
party's research group, Gwynfor Evans's direct role in the process of forming economic ideas was very minor from that point
onwards.[72] One senses that he was relieved to able to hand over
the reins.

Until that point, though, there was – as has already been
pointed out – an extended period when Gwynfor Evans was
the party's main spokesman on economic matters as on all else.
As his party's best-known and most high-profile figure, Evans's

(Cardiff: University of Wales Press, 1994), pp. 1–5.

70 Evans, *Rhagom i Ryddid*, pp. 82–5. Note also that Gwynfor Evans uses a footnote in the same volume to thank Noëlle Davies, who had by then returned to
Ireland, for drawing to his attention statistics detailing that country's military expenditure in 1963 (see p. 85). These are the most recent data in the whole chapter.

71 Establishing such a research group or section had been a long-standing ambition. See, for example, Wynne Samuel, 'Adran Ymchwil i Blaid Cymru', *Triban*,
1 (2) (October 1957), 56–9. The need for such an arrangement is here connected
directly to the gap created by the death of D. J. Davies and Nöelle's decision to
return to Ireland (p. 56).

72 Gwynfor Evans made very effective use of the opportunity given to every
Member of Parliament to ask questions, in doing so revealing a mass of informa-
tion that had not previously been collated. Plaid Cymru published a number of
pamphlets in order to try to disseminate this knowledge as well as convince the
electors of Carmarthen and the rest of Wales of the perseverance and energy of
Plaid Cymru's Member of Parliament. See, inter alia, *Black Paper on Wales 1967*
(Plaid Cymru, 1967); *Black Paper on Wales 1967 Second Series* (Plaid Cymru, 1967);
Black Paper on Wales Book 3 (Plaid Cymru, 1968).

statements on the subject continued to be important in forming wider public perceptions of Plaid Cymru's programme until his retirement. As such, it is worth scrutinising some of the central themes in his comments on economics in a little more detail.

In the years following the Second World War, as the Labour government pursued its policy of nationalisation, Plaid Cymru was vocal in demanding that these newly nationalised industries be organised on a territorial basis that acknowledged the existence of Wales. These demands fell on deaf ears. But it had more success in influencing the development of regional policy in Wales. The party had long advocated the need for an energetic regional policy that treated Wales as a unit. As we have seen, it appears that Saunders Lewis was among the first to call for the establishment of an economic development authority for Wales in a 1933 pamphlet titled *The Case for a Welsh National Development Council* (a fact that is so subversive of the conventional view – of both the Welsh Development Agency (WDA) and of Saunders Lewis himself – that it is hardly surprising that it has been long since forgotten!) Later, towards the mid-1940s, Plaid Cymru published a series of enlightened and indeed visionary pamphlets recommending the establishment of a development authority for Wales based on the model of the Tennessee Valley Authority (TVA) – a body established as part of President Roosevelt's attempts to alleviate the effects of the Great Depression in the southern states of the United States.[73] The demand for a 'TVA for Wales' came to be repeated almost ad nauseum in the party's publications during the 1950s.

When attempts began during the 1960s to institutionalise Wales's economy by creating a series of bodies dealing with Wales as a single economic entity, it is no surprise that Gwynfor Evans interpreted this as a victory for Plaid Cymru. In truth, it is difficult to know how much influence the party had on that process. After all, one can hardly expect its political enemies to have been eager to acknowledge any contribution it might have made.

---

[73] *Plan Electricity for Wales* (The London Branch of the Welsh Nationalist Party, 1944); *TVA for Wales* (Caernarfon: Welsh Party Offices, 1945); *TVA Points the Way* (Caernarfon: Welsh Party Offices, 1946).

It should also be recalled that others were arguing in favour of similar steps – if for different reasons than those motivating Plaid Cymru. For example, the idea of establishing some sort of development authority for Wales was part of an unofficial manifesto published by Labour party candidates in north-west Wales ahead of the 1945 general election (and completely disowned by the central Labour Party machine).[74] But, naturally, Gwynfor Evans himself had no doubts. He went so far as to argue that the party's 'greatest achievement' was forcing the government to treat Wales as an economic unit through measures such as the establishment of the WDA. 'As a result, there are tens of thousands of people in work in our country today who can thank the party for that.'[75] There is no evidence that they ever did. Nevertheless, no other body or movement was as fervent or as consistent in its demands that Wales be treated as an economic unit as Plaid Cymru, and it surely deserves at least a measure of any credit due when this did finally happen.

Another recurring theme in Gwynfor Evans's economic commentary also stems directly from the influence of Saunders Lewis, and that was the need for an economy where the ownership of property and capital was distributed widely throughout society: 'mân-gyfalafiaeth' (petty capitalism) was the term used by Lewis. This was manifested in Plaid Cymru's sharply critical attitude towards Labour's nationalisation programme. Instead of state ownership and management, Plaid Cymru favoured cooperatively owned ventures in which workers took over control and responsibility for their own enterprises. The party insisted that cooperative schemes were not only better in principle but offered practical advantages as well. Certainly, the serious problems that later came to characterise nationalised industries came as no surprise to Plaid Cymru. Even as early as 1950, Gwynfor Evans felt that his doubts and those of the party were already being confirmed:

---

74   There is a strong case that Plaid Cymru's ideas were influential on the thinking of these candidates. After all, a number had previous connections or, at least, interactions with the party, most obviously Goronwy Roberts (a former member of Mudiad Gwerin which had tried to forge links between left-wing Plaid members and socialists who were also Welsh nationalists).

75   Evans, *Diwedd Prydeindod*, p. 67.

The government had expected much from the nationalised industries and services, but the bureaucratic form of nationalisation adopted has done nothing to increase the sense of responsibility among the workers concerned, because they have in fact no greater share of responsibility and ownership than they had under the old order.[76]

Moving ownership from capitalist enterprises to the state had not led to any fundamental change in the situation of the workers. Only the feeling of responsibility and indeed dignity that arises through direct ownership and control could achieve that.

In retrospect, Plaid Cymru's attitude towards nationalisation appears to have been both clear-eyed and far-sighted. At the time, however, few were prepared to listen to such views. The strength of the cross-party consensus in Britain in the post-war period – extending even to nationalisation (in some sectors, at least) – was such that Plaid Cymru's doubts appeared irrelevant and frankly eccentric. Thus, even as the party attempted time and again to use the labour movement's dogmatic opposition to attempts to establish Cwmllynfell Colliery as a cooperative enterprise as a means to chastise the Labour Party, it made little impression.[77] By the time that nationalised industries had lost their credibility, the opportunity to implement Plaid Cymru's alternative ideas had also been missed. From the mid-1970s onwards, only right-wing solutions (the introduction of 'market discipline', privatisation and so on) were seen as credible.

Another recurring theme in Gwynfor Evans's various economic commentaries was the argument – first made (credibly, at least) by D. J. Davies – that Wales's subservience to England had had a disastrous effect on Welsh economic development.[78] Of course, even if we accept that the relationship with England has had a disastrous effect in the past, it does not necessarily

---

76 Evans, *Plaid Cymru and Wales*, p. 34.
77 There are numerous references to the Cwmllynfell episode in Gwynfor Evans's writings – up to and including *Diwedd Prydeindod* (1981), p. 78.
78 See D. J. Davies, *The Economics of Welsh Self-government* (Caernarfon: Swyddfa'r Blaid Genedlaethol, 1931), pp. 3–12; D. J. and N. Davies, *Can Wales Afford Self-government?* (Caernarfon: Welsh Nationalist Party, 1939), pp. 22–52.

follow that breaking off that relationship – or changing its nature by attaining home rule – will necessarily lead to economic improvement. One might rather seek to argue that the 'patient' – perhaps because of past mistreatment – is now so enfeebled and weak that it has no hope of making a full recovery. The best that can now be hoped for is better and more loving care than that received in the past. (Is this in fact not a very common attitude in Wales towards our economic relationship with England and the British state?) But of course, D. J. and Noëlle Davies's central argument was that 'self-government is a vital necessity for the restoration of prosperity to Wales.'[79] In the most striking expression of their view, they claim: 'The vital question is not, "Can Wales afford self-government?" but "Can Wales afford to be without self-government any longer, and survive?"'[80]

This argument was echoed by Gwynfor Evans. 'There is little doubt', he once said, 'that no other country has faced the prospect of self-government with greater certainty of economic prosperity than we in Wales.'[81] His work is full of this type of confident declaration. In the mid-1970s, he argued that this new prosperity would be built on the firm foundations of the oil he believed was about to start flowing from the seas off the coast of Wales.[82] Neither did his confidence wane when it was proven that these hopes were nothing more than a fantasy.[83] In the early 1980s, with the recession of Thatcher's monetarist experiment biting, Evans hoped that '[t]he people in due course will be forced to see that a Welsh government is the one most likely to develop an economy that will provide them

---

79 Davies, *The Economics of Welsh Self-government*, p. 12.
80 Davies and Davies, *Can Wales Afford Self-government?*, p. 52.
81 Evans, *Plan for a New Wales*, p. 5.
82 Evans, *Wales Can Win*, pp. 85, 114–15.
83 When hopes of discovering oil began to fade, he succeeded in putting a positive spin on the development: 'One is glad that the serious exploration for Celtic Sea Oil is likely to be postponed for a decade, by when one hopes that Wales will have a Parliament strong enough to control the development of the Welsh sector in the best interests of the Welsh people': Evans, *A National Future for Wales*, p. 112. Gwynfor Evans had a remarkable facility for finding a silver lining to every cloud.

with work'.[84] Freedom was the key to the door of economic prosperity.

It should be noted, however, that Gwynfor Evans oscillated between this argument and another: one to the effect that it was of no great importance whether or not freedom gave rise to economic prosperity.[85] Freedom would lead to other blessings – 'spiritual blessings' seems an apposite characterisation – that would more than make up for any material losses. After all, freedom bestows dignity while lack of freedom is experienced as an affliction, regardless of the degree of economic prosperity with which it is associated.[86] This argument took on several different forms. One version has obvious echoes of Saunders Lewis. Thus, in 1959, Gwynfor Evans argued that:

> A great social heresy of the last 50 years has been to make the Economic the end of life. Throughout Europe society has been sacrificed to the imagined demands of economic factors. Society has been run as an adjunct of the market ... This perversion of the right ordering of society sprang from a failure to apprehend man as a whole ... For man is an essentially social creature whose humanity and dignity require a place in a fitting cultural environment at least as much as they require proper economic provision.[87]

[84]   Evans, *Diwedd Prydeindod*, p. 67; translation.
[85]   Gwynfor Evans expressed this argument in the following way in his pamphlet *Plan for a New Wales*: 'what sort of sissy would he be who, because he wasn't certain what the future held, because he was afraid that his wife's sponges might not be quite as good as his mother's, because he preferred red curtains to his wife's choice of yellow, decided to call it all off and remain tied to his mother's apron strings?' (p. 8) In fairness, it should be emphasised that this style of expression is entirely uncharacteristic of his work.
[86]   Evans's argument was that refusing freedom for Wales on economic grounds would mean that one would see 'at best, a peninsula of well-fed, well-housed people perhaps, but no longer a community bound by the ties of two thousand years of history, and no longer stimulated by the traditions and thought-ways handed down through those centuries. At worst, it could be a peninsula of people to whom the word "society" would not be applicable at all, the community atomized, the people a rootless mass, a proletariat': Gwynfor Evans, 'Wales as an economic entity', *Wales* (September 1959), 38. This essay was published as a pamphlet by Plaid Cymru the following year under the same title. Note the 'Saundersian' use of 'proletariat' as an insult.
[87]   Evans, 'Wales as an economic entity', 37. Note that ideas of this kind are shared widely throughout the Party during the period of Saunders Lewis's

Later, as he (quite characteristically) sought to align his core messages with more current ideas to ensure a more contemporary impact, we find the same broad ideas being reframed. In *Wales Can Win* (1973) he sought to link the party's ideas to those of the New Left: both rejected the worldview that elevated consumerism above those things that make us truly human. In *A National Future for Wales* (1975) he appealed to the values of green movement: 'Plaid Cymru's aims and values put it in line with those who see that the conditions of our day compel changes from an expansionist to a stable society.'[88] The central message of these two books, and many of his other works, was that there were much more important things than economic prosperity, and that one of the most important was national freedom.

We can see, therefore, that there was an element of ambiguity in Gwynfor Evans's messaging regarding the economic consequences of self-government (as had been the case with Saunders Lewis before him). On the one hand, he insisted that self-government was bound to lead to economic prosperity; on the other, he also argued that economic success was not the most important concern – and that even if Wales prospered economically without its freedom, it would remain impoverished in other, more significant ways. These two views are not necessarily contradictory. It is possible to envisage an argument to the effect that whether or not Wales would gain from becoming a free country is not the most important consideration; but as it happens, freedom would presage prosperity.[89] But in terms of political communication – propaganda – this is a weak, unclear message. One can hardly expect electors to ignore their own material prospects – especially in a country that had been scarred so deeply by the traumas of

presidency. Thus, according to D. J. Davies, 'we recognize spiritual rather than material factors as being of ultimate importance in the development of the life of the individual and the nation': 'Economic nationalism', *Triban*, 5 (summer 1939), 39. (The foreword to this issue notes that the essay had been written four years previously.)

88 Evans, *A National Future for Wales*, p. 99.
89 This argument is made in Dafydd Wigley and Phil Williams's Foreword in *Economic Plan for Wales* (Plaid Cymru, 1970).

the Great Depression and which had subsequently experienced a period of relative post-war affluence.

Why then did Plaid Cymru fail to articulate a clearer message – a message that would be much more appealing so long as the putative audience could be persuaded of it – namely that the Welsh people stood to benefit in material terms if their country became a state? There are several potential explanations. Was it perhaps the fact that the party's leaders and most ardent supporters had such zeal for their nation that they were prepared to suffer materially for it and were thus insensible to the need to communicate effectively to those with different priorities? Be that as it may, at this point it is worth recalling Hroch's study of nationalist movements in nineteenth-century Europe discussed in Chapter 1. His key finding was that nationalist movements among the small nations of Europe were successful to the extent that they managed to link their national cause to material improvements in the lot of the 'target' national group. Viewed in this context, it seems clear that Plaid Cymru missed an opportunity by not attempting to more consistently link the struggle for self-government with an argument showing how self-government would improve the material quality for life of people in Wales – as well, of course, as improving life in other ways. It might of course be argued that Plaid Cymru was part of a new wave of 'post-material' politics in which a higher value is placed on other non-material considerations. We have already seen that arguments of this kind emanated from within the party's own ranks and it is a framing that has also been adopted by external analysts.[90] But it remains the case that no nationalist movement has ever succeeded in a developed country on post-materialist terms. For better or worse, material considerations remain key.

---

[90] The starting point of the (extensive) academic discussion on post-materialism is to be found in Ronald Inglehart, *The Silent Revolution: Changing Values and Political Styles Among Western Publics* (Princeton: Princeton University Press, 1977). There is evidence from the Welsh context in Sydney A. Van Atta, 'Regional nationalist party activism and the new politics of Europe: the Bloque Nacionalista Galego and Plaid Cymru', *Regional and Federal Studies*, 13 (2) (summer 2003), 30–56.

Constitutional objectives

Plaid Cymru's constitutional policy during Gwynfor Evans's presidency provides yet further evidence of the enormous influence of Saunders Lewis on the ideas of his successor. Indeed, Plaid Cymru stuck so rigidly to Lewis's idiosyncratic constitutional views that it found itself in deep and difficult waters as a result. By the time Gwynfor Evans handed over the presidency to his successor, the long-term constitutional objectives of his party were incoherent to the point of being nonsensical. Given that these objectives formed one of the most important cornerstones of the party's policy programme and wider mission, it is likely that this did nothing but damage its credibility and prospects.

The previous chapter discussed the way in which Saunders Lewis insisted on framing Plaid Cymru's constitutional aims in terms of 'freedom not independence', and how this rhetorical stance was successfully reconciled with the more 'militant' beliefs of other party members by means of a policy that sought 'dominion status' for Wales. It might well be objected that this policy ignored the fact that some of the less loyal dominions considered that the constitutional discussions of the 1920s and the 1930s – including those that led to the passing of the Statute of Westminster in 1931 – had opened the door to something that was (in political terms) akin to 'independence'. Nonetheless, Plaid Cymru's position retained a certain intellectual respectability. The connection of the empire remained strong, especially in places like New Zealand where there was a general reluctance to see the loosening of imperial ties. Nor was this connection merely abstract or sentimental in character. Consider the emphasis that Churchill put on the (difficult) task of maintaining contact and coordinating with the dominions during the United Kingdom's darkest hours in the early years of the Second World War. Consider also the determination of Irish republicans to sever those remaining ties even after they themselves had played an important role in rendering them less constrictive through the Statute of Westminster and other negotiations.

All of this is to say that during Saunders Lewis's presidency, it was credible to argue that dominion status was not synonymous

with independence. There was therefore no great inconsistency
when Plaid Cymru called for dominion status for Wales while,
at the same time, rejecting 'independence' in the name of 'freedom'. Nor was there any inconsistency between insisting on
both dominion status and membership of the League of Nations,
since the other dominions were already members. Furthermore,
dominion status meant something in concrete, constitutional
terms. Whatever people in Wales might have felt about it as a
proposed remedy for their country's ills, there was no doubt
about what dominion status would entail in real terms. During
Gwynfor Evans's presidency, however, as the world and the
British state's international position within it continued to
change, Plaid Cymru's constitutional arguments lost their intellectual respectability. Relatedly, they also lost all connection to
actually existing reality. Rather, the party's position with regards
Wales's long-term constitutional future became contradictory
and inconsistent. It found itself advocating a position that was
utopian in the negative sense: that is, the party's long-term constitutional aims lost their mooring in any possible form of constitutional reality. Theirs was no longer a position that could sustain
any serious scrutiny. All this becomes particularly ironic when
we recall Saunders Lewis's doleful assertion that his own party
had 'rejected' him. It was in fact Gwynfor Evans's unwavering
commitment to Saunders Lewis's exact words on the party's constitutional objectives in his lecture at the party Summer School in
1926 that led Plaid Cymru into this mire.

Gwynfor Evans repeated Saunders Lewis's rhetoric about
the constitutional question with gusto and evident conviction.
Time and again, he would declare that his party rejected absolute or unconditional sovereignty, that is 'independence', but
rather sought national freedom for Wales. It is no coincidence
that his 1964 book was titled *Rhagom i Ryddid* (Towards Freedom).
Observant readers will have noticed how the discussion of constitutional aims contained with it – and indeed, in all of Evans's
other attempts to tackle the subject – was heavily influenced
and shaped by Lewis's *Principles of Nationalism*. 'What is needed
is sufficient freedom for Wales to live its own life', said Evans;

Lewis wanted 'Not independence. Not even unconditional freedom. But just as much enough freedom as may be necessary to
establish and safeguard civilisation in Wales.'[91] But while the
argument was the same, the political circumstances facing Evans
were by now very different.

In the years following the Second World War, the empire transformed into the British Commonwealth. Ties continued to loosen
as the Commonwealth itself approximated more to an occasional
coming together of old acquaintances than the gathering of close
'family' members fondly imagined by imperial nostalgia. There
could hardly have been a surer sign of the process that was afoot
than the decision, in 1949, to allow independent India to join the
Commonwealth, despite it being a republic. The holder of the
Crown continued as head of the Commonwealth in name, but in
truth that was the extent of the constitutional relationship with the
'Great White Mother' for an increasing number of member states.[92]
The Commonwealth was a collection of independent countries –
no more and no less. Despite his and his party's honourable record
in opposing British imperialism, Gwynfor Evans was strangely
reluctant to acknowledge the implications of this development.
'Commonwealth status' was Plaid Cymru's constitutional objective for Wales throughout the 1950s and the 1960s, which the president attempted to portray as no more than a rebadging of 'dominion status'. Witness the following passage in *Welsh Nationalist Aims*:

> Setting its face against the concept of absolute sovereignty, the Party
> demanded the measure of freedom necessary to the full develop-
> ment of the nation's life, which implied control over both domestic
> and external relations. Within the Commonwealth there is only one
> status of freedom for nations, that which is called dominion or com-
> monwealth status. That is the Party's aim for Wales.[93]

---

91 Evans, *Rhagom i Ryddid*, p. 61; translation; Lewis, *Principles of Nationalism*, p.
15.
92 Hywel Teifi Edwards and E. G. Millward, *Jiwbilî y Fam Wen Fawr* (Llandysul:
Gomer, 2002).
93 Evans, *Welsh Nationalist Aims* (1959 version), p. 6. See also Gwynfor Evans,
Commonwealth Status for Wales (Plaid Cymru, n.d. [but 1965]).

The first sentence signifies a significant change in Gwynfor Evans's constitutional ideas which was to become increasingly evident throughout the 1960s and 1970s. While rejecting absolute sovereignty, Gwynfor Evans nevertheless insists on 'control over both domestic and external relations'. That is, while opposing sovereignty on principled grounds, he insists on the substance of sovereignty – that is on 'control'. By the time he published *Rhagom i Ryddid*, this inconsistency had become even more obvious. In a discussion of the Commonwealth, Gwynfor Evans acknowledges – indeed celebrates – how loose the ties within it had become. 'In everything', he said, 'each country makes its own decision on each matter; we see differences of opinion even in foreign policy.'[94] Once again, the substance of sovereignty is celebrated even while the label for this constitutional condition as used in international law, political discourse and everyday language is rejected.

By the early 1970s, Gwynfor Evans had even cast off the (admittedly feeble) historical foundations that Saunders Lewis had used to try to establish a principled distinction between independence and freedom. Recall that Lewis had argued that despite losing its independence with the death of Llywelyn the Last, Wales had nonetheless retained its freedom. This has only been lost with the passing of the so-called Acts of Union in the sixteenth century. In contrast, in a discussion on the significance of 1282 for Wales in *Aros Mae* (1971), Evans argued that 'What [Wales] lost was its freedom. From now on it would be a nation without a state: that is, a nation that failed to form the conditions of its own life; a nation at the mercy of external events.'[95] Which is to say that any semblance of the substance that underpinned Saunders Lewis's distinction between freedom and independence was completely obliterated by Gwynfor Evans's treatment of freedom and independence as if synonymous. Unfortunately, he seems to have been incapable of acknowledging this. The ensuing intellectual

94 Evans, *Rhagom i Ryddid*, p. 61; translation.
95 When citing passages from the *Aros Mae* in the following I will draw on the translated text, namely Gwynfor Evans, *Land of my fathers: 2,000 years of Welsh history* (Swansea: John Penry Press, 1974). In this case, p. 237.

confusion is nicely illustrated in the following passage from *Wales Can Win* (1973):

> The Welsh state would be endowed with all the powers of modern statehood; but they would not exceed the powers recognised as being generally necessary for the well-being of any nation. There will be no old-fashioned insistence on 'sovereignty' and 'independence'. Nevertheless, the whole range of government, together with the assets, liabilities and functions of state enterprises in Wales, must be transferred to the Welsh State and its appropriate authorities.[96]

The first and third sentences constitute a description of independence and sovereignty, even as the second tries to deny this!

This quotation serves to highlight another important development in the way that Gwynfor Evans framed his party's constitutional objectives compared with Saunders Lewis. For Lewis, the problem with independence was its connection to the dawn of the modern world; to the growth of large, centralised states, and their abominable, un-Christian practice of seeking uniformity within their own boundaries. In contrast, Gwynfor Evans frames independence as 'old-fashioned'. This reflects a significant difference in the worldviews and mentality of both men. We shall return to this matter in due course. In the interim, however, it is fair to acknowledge that the very different tone adopted by Evans in justifying the party's long-term constitutional objectives may well have worked in the party's favour in the context of the self-consciously radical political culture that characterised twentieth-century Wales. In this context, it was easy to portray Saunders Lewis as the Welsh manifestation of Reaction. But Gwynfor Evans was determined to present his constitutional objectives in a way that echoed the international rhetoric (if not actions) of the liberal left. He would frame his party's constitutional aspirations, not in terms of the alleged experiences of the European past, but rather in terms of positive aspirations for the global future. This, in turn, may have helped shield the detailed

---

96 Evans, *Wales Can Win*, p. 133.

policies concerned from critical attention.[97] Another explanation, of course, is that Plaid Cymru was so insignificant in electoral terms that there was no reason for anyone outside the movement to take much notice of constitutional objectives that quite literally had no chance of ever being enacted. Whatever the explanation, the party in general, and Gwynfor Evans in particular, were fortunate to escape closer scrutiny of this dimension of Plaid Cymru's policy programme.

From around the mid-1950s, Gwynfor Evans's writings would return on a regular basis to another of his constitutional preoccupations, namely his desire to establish a different constitutional framework for the UK – indeed, for the British Isles as whole. In 1956, it seems that Plaid Cymru took the lead role in a process that led to the publication of a booklet in collaboration with the SNP and a now long-since forgotten political party, Common Wealth. The argument of *Our Three Nations* was that a 'Cofraternity' should be established between England, Scotland and Wales. Although the name given to this new political formation varied – by 1960 the party's annual conference supported the formation of a 'Common Market' among the nations of the British Isles, while the term 'Britannic Confederation' was being used by the beginning of the 1970s – and although there is little evidence that others took the idea seriously, Gwynfor Evans's enthusiasm remained characteristically undimmed.[98] Even as late as 1981, he continued to wax lyrical about the possibility of 'creating a community of free and equal nations in these islands, with no single nation being inferior to the others in any way or in any aspect of their internal lives or external relations, but working closely together in confederation'.[99]

[97] One exception was the Welsh Republican Movement's discussion of Plaid Cymru's constitutional aims. But even then, the republicans were more riled by the party's moderation and (in their view) general quiescence, as well as the fact that so many of its members were pacifists ('a filthy and pharisaical doctrine as far as it is comprehensible at all', according to Harri Webb); see Harry Webb, *No Half Way House: Selected Political Journalism 1950–1977* (Talybont: Y Lolfa, 1997), p. 34, and Republican, *The Young Republican: A Record of the Welsh Republican Movement-Mudiad Gweriniaethol Cymru* (Llanrwst: Gwasg Carreg Gwalch, 1996).

[98] See, for example, Gwynfor Evans, *Self-government for Wales and a Common Market for the Nations of Britain* (Plaid Cymru, n.d. [but 1963]), p. 9; Evans, *Land of my fathers*, p. 450.

[99] Evans, *Diwedd Prydeindod*, p. 142; translation.

But what would such a 'confederal' relationship look like in practice? It seems that Gwynfor Evans desired a kind of 'inside-out' federalism. To generalise, federal systems are characterised by internal variety – for example, in terms of economic, social and cultural policies – but external unity with regards to foreign and defence policy. In contrast, the Britannic Confederation's members would vary policy in those areas where unity prevails in federal arrangements, while maintaining unity (or something very similar to that) in those policy areas in which we see most variety in federal states. In Gwynfor Evans's opinion, the consequence of this would be to unite 'the countries of Britain where union makes sense – at the economic level, while preserving sovereignty [*sic*] where national freedom makes sense – at the social, cultural and political levels'.[100] But note the degree of internal unity he considered necessary as underlined in one of his other essays: 'inside the partnership it would be necessary to co-ordinate trade and budgeting policy and social services, and to ensure uniform levels of taxation, customs duties and social security benefits'.[101]

The idea that a governing system could be constructed that would allow for so much variation in defence and international policies while at the same time maintaining near total unity in other policy areas ('uniform levels of taxation') reveals Gwynfor Evans's naivety. Such a system would be completely impractical – and given that he criticised supporters of a federal Britain on the grounds of 'impracticality' of their proposals, it is surely right to hold him to the same standard.[102] But perhaps the most striking marker of Gwynfor Evans's lack of realism as he pondered the future of these islands is the fact that he believed that the Republic of Ireland could be drawn into the fold of a Britannic

[100] Evans, *Self-government for Wales and a Common Market for the Nations of Britain*, p. 11.

[101] Evans, *Wales Can Win*, p. 132.

[102] Among his discussions of the problems relating to the creation of a British federation see *Plaid Cymru and Wales*, pp. 45–9; *Rhagom i Ryddid*, pp. 65–7; *Wales Can Win*, pp. 130–2. Also, Gwynfor Evans et al., *Our Three Nations: Wales, Scotland and England* (Cardiff: Plaid Cymru, 1956), pp. 24, 49–50. It should be emphasised that there was real substance to his arguments. This does not negate the fact that Gwynfor Evans's own proposals for a Britannic Confederation were more problematic still.

Confederation. References to Ireland were notably absent in *Our Three Nations*. The country was certainly not mentioned as a prospective member of the 'Cofraternity'. Yet only a year after its appearance Gwynfor Evans was claiming that:

> The facts of geography and history dictate close cooperation with England, Scotland and Ireland, and it [Plaid Cymru] has therefore put forward, in conjunction with the Commonwealth Party of England and the National Party of Scotland [*sic*], a plan for a Cofraternity of the nations living in these islands.[103]

Some years later, he claimed that Éire would find the idea of joining the 'British Common Market' attractive.[104] Indeed, Gwynfor Evans claims to have been invited to give a lecture on the subject to a Fianna Fáil meeting in Dublin.[105] One can only imagine what the members of that party would have made of the suggestion that they should renounce independence in order to join a new state form with the English Crown as its symbolic head! Nevertheless, in 1973, with the Republic in the process of becoming a member of the European Common Market, and the north in a state of civil war, Gwynfor Evans continued to hope for the establishment of a 'Britannic Confederation' that accepted 'the Crown as a symbolic link' and would include 'both Ireland and the Six County State' as members.[106] It was delusional stuff.

There is a marked contrast between Gwynfor Evans's enthusiasm for the fantasy that was the Britannic Confederation and his apparent indifference in the face of the hugely significant constitutional developments underway on the European continent, namely the evolution of what is now called the European Union. Of course, he was aware that this development was taking place. He regarded it as the model for the British Common Market and it

103 Evans, *Welsh Nationalist Aims*, p. 7.
104 Evans, *Self-government for Wales and a Common Market for the Nations of Britain*, p. 18.
105 Evans, *For the Sake of Wales*, p. 66. Given the pacifism and gradualism of Gwynfor's nationalism, it may be regarded as somewhat ironic that in his discussion of the republic's politics in the same book he makes clear that 'My sympathies were with Fianna Fáil.'
106 Evans, *Wales Can Win*, p. 132.

formed part of the general political context referred to in his various writings. But there is no evidence to suggest that he had any particular interest in the development of the European Common Market, nor any great enthusiasm for it. He was far from alone in this, of course. Even though he considered himself an enthusiastic European and deprecated the arrogant self-regard of the British state, Plaid Cymru's president shared much the same disregard for developments in western Europe as the majority of Britain's political class. He therefore does not seem to have grasped their significance.[107] This should perhaps not surprise us. Evans did not have access to the same alternative sources of information on developments in continental Europe as Saunders Lewis, for example. While the latter took great pleasure in reading French newspapers, Evans focused on the Welsh and British press.[108] It is not surprising, therefore, that his was a variant of a British world-view rather than an entirely different perspective.

Gwynfor Evans's views about European integration are first set out in any detail in a speech he delivered to the House of Commons in May 1967 during a debate on British membership of the Common Market. He claimed that the impact on Wales 'would be deleterious and they could be damning' if the UK were to join the Common Market. As a result, it would be 'an act of criminal folly' to join under the present circumstances. Why these prophecies of doom? Because becoming a member of the Common Market would mean that the 'economic centre of gravity is bound to move further to the east', meaning the 'development of new industries in Wales will be still more difficult. Even so, he acknowledges that 'if Wales had her own Government, if she were in the Common Market as a separate political entity',

107 The literature on attitudes in Britain towards the development of a Common Market is vast. For a reliable introduction see Stephen George, *An Awkward Partner: Britain in the European Community* (Oxford: Oxford University Press, 1998).
108 In a diary entry dated 17 September 1964, Dafydd Evans lists 'the newspapers Dad reads regularly', which were the *Western Mail, Y Cymro, Manchester Guardian, Y Tyst, The Economist, Y Faner, The Spectator, The New Statesman, Peace News, Tribune* and *Carmarthen Journal*. He further notes: 'He has stopped reading the *Liverpool Daily Post* after some disagreement. He worries that Saunders Lewis says that he's a product of the *New Statesman*': Evans, *Y Blew a Buddugoliaeth Gwynfor*, p. 99; translation.

then there would be 'room for debate about the economic effects'. Towards the end of the speech, he offers an alternative vision that deserves to be quoted in full:

> I do not want to give the impression that I am against the idea of the Common Market. I am saying that if we go in in our present position the effect on Wales could be devastating. I think that the Common Market idea can be a very effective device for ensuring the perpetuation and development of the lives of smaller nations in Europe by safeguarding their political freedom and ensuring for them the advantages of the economies of scale. It opens up a vista in which European civilisation will be the richer for giving its national communities the conditions for developing their full potential. It will be a Europe of the nations, rather than a Europe of the states. Wales, Scotland, and Brittany, among others, would be the gainers from a Europe of this kind, and they would have a great contribution to make to such a Europe.[109]

In the penultimate sentence we find the first shoots of what later became a central part of Plaid Cymru's constitutional rhetoric after Gwynfor Evans had handed over the party presidency: 'a Europe of nations, rather than a Europe of states'. It is a suggestive but deeply ambiguous remark. What, after all, does it mean in concrete constitutional terms? How institutionally, legally and politically would a 'Europe of the nations' differ from a 'Europe of the states'? Gwynfor Evans did not provide any answers at the time. When he returned to his vision for the future of Europe towards the end of his long period as party leader, it transpired that it looked remarkably like a Europe of the states after all. Displaying yet again the fundamental inconsistency of his constitutional thinking, what concerned him most was the need to safeguard national sovereignty against more extensive integration.

When a referendum was called in 1975 to determine whether the UK should remain part of the Common Market, Plaid Cymru

---

[109] HC Deb Hansard 9 May 1967, vol. 746. This speech was among those included, in translation, in Gwynfor Evans, *Gwynfor yn y Senedd* (Plaid Cymru, n.d. [but 1967]).

recommended a No vote. A series of arguments was presented as an intellectual basis for this stance in a weighty Plaid Cymru Research Group publication entitled *Wales and the Common Market*.[110] Amongst the contributions to the collection is an essay by Robert Griffiths – later a prominent Welsh Socialist Republican and more latterly general secretary of the Communist Party of Britain – which argued that

> The fundamental objective of the Treaty of Rome is to create the international political and economic atmosphere in which monopoly capitalism can flourish. There is no evidence to suggest that Wales's economy will likewise prosper in a wider community governed by the economic dictates of the market place.[111]

Phil Williams's conclusion was that political union would bound to mean 'a common foreign policy and a common defence policy, based on nuclear arms'.[112] Although Griffiths and Williams were both considered to be part of Plaid Cymru's left wing, their concerns regarding the consequences of larger economic units and nuclear armaments were fully shared by Gwynfor Evans. Another concern he shared with the left was that European integration could constrain the freedom of member states to develop their own distinctive policy agendas.

After Wales and the rest of Britain voted in favour of membership, Gwynfor Evans and his party wasted no time in accepting the verdict. Nonetheless, the president continued to worry about the path 'Europe' was following. 'The Common Market cost Wales dearly', he said in the early 1980s. 'But since it is in, it should be a full member, with representatives on the Commission, the Council

110 Plaid Cymru Research Group, *Wales and the Common Market: Referendum Study Papers* (Cardiff: Plaid Cymru, 1975). See also E. Gwynn Matthews, *Wales and the European Common Market* (Cardiff: Plaid Cymru, 1970), and in particular pp. 26–9 for a summary of Plaid Cymru's official policy.
111 Robert Griffiths, 'Industry and Capital in the E.E.C.', Plaid Cymru Research Group, *Wales and the Common Market: Referendum Study Papers* (Cardiff: Plaid Cymru, 1975); no page numbers.
112 Phil Williams, 'Defence Policy and the European Economic Community', in Plaid Cymru Research Group, *Wales and the Common Market: Referendum Study Papers* (Cardiff: Plaid Cymru, 1975); no page numbers.

and the important committees.' On being a full member, Wales would then be able to raise its voice 'against the strong view that exists in favour of creating a federal European state': 'We require a loose European confederation that will defend and nurture the life of all the European nations including those small nations that today are state-less, as well as those historic regions that were once self-governing.'[113] Once again, the reference to a European confederation is more rhetorical pose than positive constitutional proposal. Indeed, his vision in this regard is even more ambiguous and vague than his plans for a Britannic Confederation. What we can be certain of, however, is that Gwynfor Evans remained doubtful about what we now call the European project precisely because of the way it encroached on state sovereignty.

Gwynfor Evans portrayed the development of Plaid Cymru's constitutional policy during his time as president as a natural and logical development of the party's views during the interwar period:

> The Empire was transformed into, first, the British Commonwealth and then the plain Commonwealth of Nations. Dominion status was re-baptised Commonwealth status, which remained Plaid Cymru's constitutional objective. As the Commonwealth fades, especially with Britain's entry into the EEC, Plaid Cymru still seeks for Wales the status of freedom; our aim continues to be full national status.[114]

The Saunders Lewis-derived rhetoric certainly remains as a connecting link throughout this period. That said, the argument that Commonwealth status in, say, the mid-1950s was equivalent to dominion status in the mid-1930s is simply unsustainable. Rather, at some point during the developments captured in the first sentence of the quotation, Commonwealth status became synonymous with being an independent state. Of course, it was also the case that only independent countries could – and can – be full members of the European Union. In constitutional terms, freedom or 'full national status' is synonymous with independence,

---

113 Evans, *Diwedd Prydeindod*, pp. 82–3.
114 Evans, *A National Future for Wales*, p. 97.

and regardless of his commitment to the rhetoric of 'freedom not independence', this is precisely what Gwynfor Evans desired on behalf of Wales. If further confirmation were required, we need only recall his consistent rejection of any kind of federal arrangement – whether at British or European level – that might constrain Wales's sovereignty, especially in the fields of defence and foreign policy. Thus, even as he embraced such esoteric notions as 'cofraternity' and a 'Europe of the nations', his constitutional ideas remained at heart rather conventional. Put simply, he wanted to see Wales becoming a 'normal' nation state playing its part in the life of Europe and the broader international system. What remained unconventional about all of this was his unwillingness to refer to this condition by its proper constitutional name.

The political question that arises in the wake of this discussion is whether the inconsistency and incoherence that characterised Gwynfor Evans and his party's constitutional views mattered in any meaningful way. Is there perhaps a danger that we are merely splitting hairs or making mountains out of molehills by paying so much attention to the matter? Or did Plaid Cymru miss an important opportunity during Gwynfor Evans's presidency to reassess its long-term constitutional objectives and render them meaningful and intellectually credible? I suggest that the second interpretation is most likely to be correct. To understand why, let us return to the comparison with Saunders Lewis.

As we have seen, Lewis was part of a cohort that was, simultaneously, deeply sceptical of those political, social and economic institutions and processes that historians and social scientists regard as constitutive of modernity, while also embracing the themes and modes of cultural expression that students of the humanities associate with modernism. It was a relatively small but nonetheless highly influential group in the world of culture. It was a much smaller cohort in the field of politics, and one that enjoyed minimal influence – the latter being wholly unsurprising given the strength of the historical tides against it.[115] What makes

[115] Some might argue that fascism is an influential example of anti-modern hyper-modernism, or, at least, that anti-modern hyper-modernism is one of the characteristics of fascist political thinking. The allegations of 'fascism' against

Lewis such a fascinating figure is that he made a serious attempt to promote this complex intellectual stance in *both* the cultural and political realms. It is fair to say that his efforts were more successful in the former than in the latter. The reason for this, above all else perhaps, was because he sought a language and conceptual vocabulary for politics that negated much of what had been taken for granted across the political spectrum since the nineteenth century, promoting ideas and values most regarded irrelevant. Given that there was so little connection between his core positions and what electors considered relevant or credible, his efforts were almost guaranteed to fail. Of course, from the point of view of those interested in political ideology, this does nothing to diminish the interest of his ideas. Indeed, their failure to strike a chord is part of their intellectual fascination. But from the point of view of the prospects for Plaid Cymru, Lewis's grip on his party's ideological agenda was deeply unfortunate. This becomes very apparent when we consider Plaid Cymru's constitutional aims.

Saunders Lewis was sceptical of the modern state and all its works. Relatedly, he was indifferent towards – or considered largely worthless – those progressive developments that we associate with its evolution. In particular, he had practically nothing to say about those ideas and political practices what were popularised by the revolutions of the seventeenth century and institutionalised by those of the eighteenth and nineteenth century, namely *popular sovereignty* (which is to say, democracy) and its twin, *citizenship*. These concepts proved to be an essential part of the intellectual armoury of nationalist movements worldwide (as discussed in Chapter 1). By comparison, Plaid Cymru made few attempts to mobilise them in the cause of Wales. It was especially uncomfortable with the rhetoric of 'sovereignty' – and arguably remains so today. Neither did it seek to develop the political potential of a rhetoric emphasising Welsh citizenship. Much of the

Saunders Lewis and Plaid Cymru have now been discussed in detail elsewhere. Suffice it to note here that those allegations are without foundation. The fact that they were repeated for so long tells us much more about the nature of Welsh political culture than they do about the political thinking of Welsh nationalists.

responsibility for this failure can be attributed to Saunders Lewis's influence on the constitutional thinking and rhetoric of Gwynfor Evans. By arguing that there was a difference of principle between freedom and independence, and by making a straw man out of 'unconditional sovereignty' (because where outside the ideas of various nineteenth-century thinkers has such a state ever existed?), the party found itself in a situation in which it could not hope to develop a mature debate on constitutional matters even within its own ranks, let alone across the whole of the country. After all, a party that rejects 'independence' while at the same time calling for the establishment of a political system that every international lawyer, every statesman and indeed everyone else outside the higher echelons of the movement itself would describe as independence, is bound to lack credibility. Indeed, the danger of such intellectual contortions is that the party's constitutional objectives come to be regarded as in some way devious or dishonest.

Attaining Plaid Cymru's constitutional objectives was always going to represent an enormous challenge, given not only the long history of Wales's unequal relationship with England, but also the way that the British political system has succeeded for most of the twentieth century in burying constitutional questions under layers of quasi-mystical mumbo jumbo. Yet Plaid Cymru managed to make that task even more difficult by failing to articulate its constitutional aims in a more credible and coherent manner. The longevity of Saunders Lewis's influence is one of the main reasons why this did not occur. What is particularly ironic is that the problems created by the intellectual legacy that he bequeathed his party only became obvious after he had handed over the presidency. During his leadership, the negative effects of 'freedom not independence' were mitigated by the existence of dominion status – which helped smooth the contradictions – as well as the absence of a wider public debate about Wales's constitutional status. But during the era of Gwynfor Evans the inadequacy of Plaid Cymru's position became an altogether more pressing matter – this in large part precisely because of the party's success in dragging the subject of Wales's constitutional future back onto the political agenda.

One of Plaid Cymru's most important campaigns in the imme-
diate post Second World War period was the Parliament for Wales
campaign. Gwynfor Evans provides an insight into the decision
to devote so much of the party's scarce resources to this effort in
a letter to D. J. and Noëlle Davies in July 1949:

> You will have seen that we intend to press for a Parliament within
> a short number of years. This is an attempt to bring things down to
> earth. Since our situation is so wretched, and our prospects so poor,
> I feel strongly that we must be prepared to accept any kind of par-
> liament as a first step, as long as it is democratic … It may be that its
> greatest value would be spiritual or 'psychological'.[116]

Given the weakness of both Wales and Plaid Cymru, something
would be better than nothing, and by accepting that 'something'
the Welsh people could become accustomed to standing on their
own feet and so develop the necessary confidence to allow them
to press ahead further in due course. This is the reasoning that
has informed Plaid Cymru's willingness to dedicate itself so determinedly to various 'multi-party' campaigns in favour of some
measure of Welsh devolution: twice during Gwynfor Evans's
presidency (in the early 1950s and towards the end of the 1970s)
and twice after that (1997 and 2011).[117] Indeed, Plaid Cymru
supporters have made up the largest – and most active – group
amongst the grassroots supporters of these various campaigns,
even if their public faces were dominated by prominent figures
from other parties. There is little evidence, however, that the party had much influence on what was being demanded by these
various campaigns. To use a military analogy (at which the dedicated pacifist that was Gwynfor Evans would doubtless have
baulked) the party supplied most of the foot soldiers and a great
deal of the logistical resources. In addition, Plaid Cymru played a
central role in planning the strategy for the various campaigns: in

---

116 Noëlle Davies's papers, National Library of Wales.
117 On the 2011 referendum see Richard Wyn Jones and Roger Scully, *Wales says
Yes: Devolution and the 2011 Welsh referendum* (Cardiff: University of Wales Press,
2012).

deciding who would do what, how and when. But the campaign objectives were, in the main, decided by others.

There was, of course, an obvious political logic to the view that it was the party's duty to extend its unconditional and unwavering support for any campaign that could bring Wales closer to the threshold of its own elected parliament. Relatedly, it is interesting and revealing to note the extent to which Gwynfor Evans and his party appreciated the significance of securing a body brought into being by the results of a Welsh election. Even if the party was always uneasy with the rhetoric of popular sovereignty and citizenship, it nonetheless recognised their substantive importance. Furthermore, it is impossible to know what might have happened if the party had adopted a different, more assertive attitude than the one it did. Having said that, Wales has always been more follower than leader on constitutional matters. Back in the era of E. T. John, it was the Irish who provided a model for emulation. Later, the Scots stepped into the breach: or in Kenneth O. Morgan's play on the infamous *Encyclopaedia Britannica* entry, 'For Wales – see Scotland'.[118]

In addition, the intellectual standard of Welsh constitutional debate has been low. The Wales Act 1978, for example, was an abomination, and from a narrow constitutional perspective, wholly deserving of its undignified fate at the 1979 referendum. There are a number of factors that help explain why we have not succeeded in fostering a more sophisticated discussion about the constitutional future of Wales, the pathologies of the Welsh Labour Party foremost among them. But the nationalist party's failure to provide an intellectual lead has been another contributary factor. By clinging to such incoherent long-term constitutional objectives – and by contributing next-to-nothing to debates on political-constitutional structures that might offer a first step towards self-government (in its desire to support *anything* that might be an improvement on the status quo) – Plaid Cymru has

[118] Kenneth O. Morgan, 'Welsh devolution: the past and the future', in Bridget Taylor and Katarina Thomson (eds), *Scotland and Wales: Nations Again?* (Cardiff: University of Wales Press, 1999), p. 200.

allowed discussions on Wales's constitutional future to languish in a morass of insubstantial wishful thinking.

It may well be objected that Plaid Cymru should not be criticised too harshly on this account. Given its relative weakness, simply persevering was itself an achievement. And was this persever-ance not essential to keeping alight the flame of self-government, this no matter how dim its light at times? Perhaps so, but nei-ther can the party entirely escape responsibility. After all, would persevering have been made more difficult if Plaid Cymru's con-stitutional discourse had been more coherent? Hardly. Indeed, although we are speculating at this point, is it not unreasonable to assume that had the party been clearer and more persuasive about its constitutional aspirations it would have been easier to gain the support of those electors (non-Welsh speakers, in the main) who supported self-government but who were doubtful of Plaid Cymru's cultural agenda. Be that as it may, we do not need to speculate in order to ascertain why Plaid Cymru failed to give a clearer lead on the constitutional matters. This is due above all to Gwynfor Evans's failure to cast off the influence of Saunders Lewis on his own and his own party's thinking.

* * *

By examining Gwynfor Evans's attitude towards the place of the Welsh language, the economy and Plaid Cymru's constitution-al objectives, it becomes abundantly clear that Saunders Lewis's ideas had a far-reaching influence on those of his successor. Evans not only adopted Lewis's ideas on the importance of the national community and the particular characteristics of the Welsh nation, but also his ideas and much of his rhetoric on those policy are-as that the party regarded as most important. These ideas and rhetoric did evolve, but only very gradually. Saunders Lewis's assertion that his ideological legacy had been 'cast aside' was utter nonsense. Indeed, given the peculiarity of so much of that legacy, the surprise is that it was not cast aside much sooner and much more systematically than it was. Despite Gwynfor Evans's increasing reluctance to fully acknowledge Lewis's influence on him – and Lewis's bitterness towards his successor – the fact of the matter is that Evans's political ideas where very largely those of Saunders Lewis.

This is not the whole story, however. Despite the continuity between the views of Saunders Lewis and those of Gwynfor Evans – and the continuity in the policy positions developed by Plaid Cymru during its first two decades of existence and its positions in subsequent decades – there were also some significant differences; ones which we will now examine.

One of the few authors to have acknowledged the extent of Lewis's influence on Evans is R. M. (Bobi) Jones. In his view, future generations will come to consider Gwynfor Evans as Saunders Lewis's 'pupil on many counts'.[119] This is a most apposite metaphor. A good pupil is not content with simply repeating the work of the teacher but rather builds on the foundations that she or he established, usually by incorporating additional influences. The good pupil will also reframe and find their own ways of expressing knowledge and opinions. A changing world (and did any century experience more dramatic change than the twentieth?) will also inevitably shift perspectives as well as context. In short, the relationship between a teacher and an able pupil is never static. Neither is it necessarily one of friendship. All of which suggests that it is useful to conceive of the relationship between Saunders Lewis and Gwynfor Evans as a relationship between teacher and pupil. Thus far we have focused on the lesson learnt from the teacher. But what of the pupil's own contribution? In what way did he build on these foundations? What other influences did he embrace? How did he integrate these with the 'Saundersian' legacy?

Aros Mae[120]

To compare the political essays and speeches of Saunders Lewis and Gwynfor Evans is to be struck immediately by a difference

119 R. M. Jones, *Ysbryd y Cwlwm: Delwedd y Genedl yn ein Llenyddiaeth* (Caerdydd: Gwasg Prifysgol Cymru, 1998), p. 331.
120 Which translates as 'It Endures'.

in tone and expression. Evans is far less abstract and focused on issues of high principle and is substantially more concrete and direct. In short, he is much more conventionally political. It is, for example, impossible to imagine Gwynfor Evans emulating Saunders Lewis's decision to dedicate his main contribution to the 1938 party conference to a lecture on Marxism. It seems that even the most ardent members found that difficult to digest. Evans was certainly aware that it was highly unlikely that a popular political party could ever be built on a foundation of rather dry political philosophy lectures. His sensibilities were more popular and even, occasionally, populist.

This difference in style was in turn a manifestation of a much more fundamental difference between them. Lewis's politics were an aspect of a broader worldview that, as we have seen, rejected many of the political and social characteristics of modernity. It is no surprise, therefore, that his ideas tended to be the source of considerable unease even among those who were willing to listen to them. Here was a man who spoke a political language that was completely alien. In contrast, even if Evans's political agenda was very far-reaching compared with the agendas propounded by most unionist politicians, it was nevertheless distinctly more limited than Saunders Lewis's. His political nationalism was also part of a worldview that intersected with one held by at least some of his co-nationals. Gwynfor Evans transplanted Saunders Lewis's political ideas from the barren soil in which they had originally been planted into new ground; that of Nonconformist, left-liberal, Welsh-speaking Wales. To the extent that the ground remained fertile, then Gwynfor Evans and his party succeeded in setting down roots.

Locating Saunders Lewis's place on the political spectrum is not straightforward. His emphasis on nobility, tradition and duty, and of course his hostility towards Marxism and socialism, locate him on the right. Yet his opposition to capitalism and his almost pathological suspicion of state authority of any kind, turn conventional expectations of the right on their head. In contrast, locating Gwynfor Evans on the left-right spectrum is a relatively straightforward task: he falls neatly into the mainstream of left-liberal

opinion in Wales. His emphasis on international peace and reconciliation, his enthusiasm for Scandinavia welfare state societies,
and above all, perhaps, his eagerness to claim a place for Plaid
Cymru in the much-vaunted radical tradition in Welsh politics,
sit comfortably with the views and aspirations of the political
'mainstream' in the Wales of his time. Evans consistently strove
to frame his message in ways that would resonate with the more
progressive elements within that mainstream. This was, moreover, entirely sincerely meant and consistent with the party president's personal instincts and political inclinations.

Some may well ask how this argument – that Evans shared the
left-liberal outlook of the majority in Wales while Lewis was a
right-wing thinker (albeit a rather unusual kind) – can be reconciled with the argument presented thus far in this chapter, namely
that Saunders Lewis had an enormous influence on Gwynfor
Evans's political thought. The answer lies in the fact that nationalism exists in a symbiotic relationship with other political ideologies (as discussed in Chapter 1). Contra the views of many
nationalists, nationalism is not a complete ideology in itself. It is
an argument about the boundaries of the demos rather than an
argument about how to govern within them. Equally – and again
contra to the views of many on the left of the political spectrum,
in particular – adherents of 'conventional' political ideologies rely
on nationalistic assumptions to establish the boundaries of their
political community. Bearing this in mind, any apparent inconsistency falls away. One may, for example, agree with Saunders
Lewis's ideas regarding the nature and importance of national
community or the significance of the Welsh language, and still be
regarded as left wing. Put another way, one can agree with Lewis
that culture is all-important as a medium for transmitting values,
while at the same time strongly disagreeing with his objection to
the presence of doctors and dentists in schools.[121] This, in essence,
was Gwynfor Evans's position. Evans adopted Lewis's ideas

---

121 See Saunders Lewis, 'Gwanhau rhwymau'r teulu: tueddiadau gwleidyddol
y dydd', *Y Ddraig Goch*, January 1930, 1–2. The basis for his objection was his
presumption that their presence was a sign of the state reaching into areas which
were beyond its legitimate remit, thereby undermining the role of the family.

about the nature and value of the national community as well as the particular characteristics of the Welsh nation, but yoked them to a very different political sensibility. We observed a striking example of the resulting reorientation in our discussion of Plaid Cymru's constitutional objectives. Although they both favoured 'freedom not independence', for Saunders Lewis it was the association of the sovereign, independent state with modernity that was the problem, whereas Gwynfor Evans regarded independent states as old-fashioned. The core policy ('freedom not independence') may have made little sense in either context, nonetheless the impact of the political message being conveyed was clearly very different. We can observe the same process at work in Gwynfor Evans's evangelising in favour of self-government. 'A self-governing Wales', he asserted, 'would be as tenaciously radical as Norway or Sweden; for radicalism has been the Welsh political way of life, just as conservatism has been England's'.[122] It is impossible to imagine Saunders Lewis presenting the argument for home rule in such terms. This serves to underline once again how Gwynfor Evans succeeded in transposing some of Saunders Lewis's core political ideas from their original context into another that chimed more readily with mainstream political opinion in Wales.

Evans's position on the left-right spectrum was by no means the only difference between them. His theological views as well as his interpretation of Wales's history – his historiography – were also much closer to the mainstream in Wales; or if not exactly the mainstream, then to the views of a segment of Welsh society that at that time remained relatively strong and influential.

In today's secular age, the connection between theology and politics tends to be overlooked. In western Europe, at least, religion has retreated into the private domain. Politicians who acknowledge the connection between their religious beliefs and their views on contemporary issues, such as Tony Blair, make many uneasy by doing so. Gwynfor Evans was the product of a different era. Far from being embarrassed that his political beliefs were linked

---

122 Evans, *Land of my fathers*, p. 401.

to his religious convictions, he celebrated the fact; it was in no way a matter of embarrassment or something to be concealed, but rather the source of pride. Evans matured as a politician in a time when religion and theology still mattered in the public realm. In Saunders Lewis's case the consequences of this were very negative, and no one was more conscious than he of the damaging consequences for his party of his conversion to the Catholic Church. In contrast, Gwynfor Evans's enthusiastic Nonconformity was part of his appeal.

As far as his personal credo was concerned, Gwynfor Evans was very much part of the more liberal tendency that came to the fore within Welsh Nonconformity during its waning as a social force. On the evidence of a speech he delivered as president of the Welsh Congregational Union (Undeb yr Annibynwyr), he appears to have no particular interest in doctrinal matters per se.[123] His was rather an active, social theology. What is important in the present context, however, is the fact that Gwynfor Evans attracted enthusiastic support across the various theological and denominational divisions within Nonconformity. Thus, even if Pennar Davies and Tudur Jones can be located at opposite poles of the theological debates within Congregationalism – and Welsh-language Nonconformity more generally – both were also amongst Gwynfor Evans's closest friends and advisers. The chief representatives of Calvinism and neo-Pelagianism in Welsh-speaking Wales were united in their support for the president of Plaid Cymru.[124]

Also noteworthy is the fact that one of the principal political manifestations of Gwynfor Evans's religious beliefs, namely his uncompromising pacifism, was not a substantial stumbling block for his political career.[125] It is true that this was a source of constant

123 Evans, *Cristnogaeth a'r Gymdeithas Gymreig.*
124 As well as a generous tribute to both by Gwynfor Evans in *A National Future for Wales*, pp. 74–5, see D. Densil Morgan's outstanding discussion, *Pennar Davies* (Caerdydd: Gwasg Prifysgol Cymru, 2003).
125 For a statement on his pacifist convictions, see Gwynfor Evans, *Cenedlaetholdeb Di-drais*, trans. D. Alun Lloyd (Abertawe: Gwasg John Penry/ Cymdeithas y Cymod, 1973). See also Colin H. Williams, 'Christian witness and non-violent principles of nationalism', in Kristain Gerner et al. (eds), *Stat Nation Conflikt* (Lund: Bra Böcker, 1996), pp. 343–94. As part of his pacifist activity

tension between him and Saunders Lewis, and there is no doubt
either that it factored in Evans's decision not to become Plaid
Cymru's president until the Second World War had come to an
end. Nonetheless, if we widen the optic, it is clear that Gwynfor
Evans's pacifism and anti-militarism served to connect him to a
wider network in Wales – one that was particularly significant in
intellectual circles. It is important to remember, for example, how
people from both sides of the political spectrum in Wales united
to oppose compulsory conscription in the post-war period. Even
rabid anti-nationalists on the left of the Labour Party and in the
ranks of the Conservative Party accepted that there was a legitimate 'national' dimension to the argument that Wales should
be exempted from the relevant legislation.[126] Gwynfor Evans's
pacifism was not considered alien or outlandish even by those
Welsh people who disagreed with his views on the matter – this
in stark contrast to the responses evoked by Saunders Lewis's
Catholicism. Evans's Nonconformist beliefs and indeed prejudices also allowed him to generate an interpretation of Welsh history that the Welsh public found to be far more palatable.

At least until the publication of John Davies's magnum opus
Hanes Cymru/The History of Wales, there can be no doubt that
Gwynfor Evans was the most influential popular historian of
Wales in the final decades of the twentieth century.[127] His book
Aros Mae sold exceptionally well after publication in 1971 – which
was, according to Gwynfor Evans's own account, 'within seven
months to the day that I started writing it'.[128] The first edition,
with a print run of 5,000 copies, sold out within three or four

during the Second World War, Gwynfor Evans was editor of *Tystiolaeth y Plant*
(The Children's Witness) as part of the 'Pamffledi heddychwyr Cymru' series
(Dinbych: Gwasg Gee, n.d.). The pamphlet included a short essay by Pennar
Davies, (pp. 20–3) who by that point was quite a mature 'child' (b.1911)!

126 See L. V. Scott, *Conscription and the Attlee Governments: The Politics and Policy
of National Service 1945–1951* (Oxford: Oxford University Press, 1993), p. 123.
Reflecting the party's preoccupation with the issue, there are a large number of
possible sources detailing Plaid Cymru's attitude towards conscription including
Gwynfor Evans, Tudur Jones, Emrys P. Roberts and Lynn Moseley, *Wales Against
Conscription* (Cardiff: Plaid Cymru, 1956).

127 John Davies, *Hanes Cymru* (London: Allen Lane, 1990); *A History of Wales*
(London: Allen Lane, 1993).

128 Evans, *Aros Mae*, p. 14; translation.

months.[129] In 1973, he wrote a series of ten essays on the history of Wales drawing on the material that had appeared in *Aros Mae* for the *South Wales Echo*. The essays were later collected and published in a colourful and attractive volume that sold 20,000 copies; a Welsh-language version appeared later.[130] A translation of *Aros Mae* bearing the title *Land of My Fathers* was published in 1974.[131] It remains in print.[132]

Aros Mae, in its various forms, is Gwynfor Evans's most important and most influential work. It might also be his most personal and even regarded as akin to a confession of faith. In no way is it a book for the purist. Rather, it presents a view on the history of Wales that is wholly unapologetic in its commitment to a particular cause: it is subjective with a capital S. Neither does Gwynfor Evans hesitate to acknowledge this, declaring in the preface 'this is [not] an academic work that pretends to be unbiased'. Rather: 'What is here is my interpretation of the history of Wales: a personal sketch of our national story.' The purpose of the narrative is quite clear: 'Discussing the Welsh past can give strength in the determination to secure a national future.'[133] This is a didactic book which aims to persuade and incite its readers. Neither can there be any doubt about the precise conclusions that the author wishes his readers to draw: the book is full of obvious and rather unsubtle morality tales. A characteristic example can be found in Gwynfor Evans's 'conclusion' to his discussion of Wales's constitutional position between the tenth and twelfth centuries:

> In the tenth century the Welsh states were free and equal members of a loose association. What was important for Hywel [Dda] was the essential freedom of his position. Paying homage to the king of Wessex did not worry him at all since it did not take away any of his

---

129 Evans, *For the Sake of Wales*, p. 203.
130 Gwynfor Evans, *History of Wales* (Cardiff: *Western Mail and Echo*, 1973). Details of sales can be found in Evans, *For the Sake of Wales*, p. 203.
131 Gwynfor Evans, *Land of my fathers: 2000 years of Welsh history* (Swansea: John Penry Press, 1974).
132 Published by Y Lolfa press since 1992, the most recent impression (from 2022) is the ninth.
133 Evans, *Aros Mae*, p. 12; translation.

freedom, any more than recognising the crown today diminishes the freedom of the countries of the Commonwealth.[134]

And just in case the message remained unclear:

> The political autonomy envisaged by the princes [until the death of Llywelyn the Last] is remarkably like that of the Welsh nationalists today. They do not demand complete independence, but ask for Commonwealth status; they recognise the crown; and they do not want a military border, nor tolls between Wales and England. The consequence of operating this policy would be to create a close partnership between free and equal nations.[135]

So, the objective had been a Britannic Confederation all along!

Given that the book is replete with similar examples of unhistorical anachronism, it is perhaps no surprise that 'genuine' Welsh historians have tended to ignore *Aros Mae* or tut-tut it in private.[136] Evans's tendency to claim as fact things for which there is no validating evidence has also done little to convince historians that the work should be taken seriously. He insists, for example, that Arthur is a historical figure.[137] But despite this, it is a mistake to ignore Gwynfor Evans's historiographical contribution. For one thing, the narrative he offered of Wales's history has been enormously influential in terms of the broad brushstrokes he painted if not the fine details. That was precisely the intention. *Aros Mae* is a sketch: 'I tried to discover a pattern in the story and make it easy to remember.'[138] Evans was very aware that a kind of myth – or at least a very one-sided picture – would emerge from that 'pattern'. Yet he also believed that 'a people's sustenance is to be found in its history as a people, even among those who have only a tenuous grasp on it in the form of myth. We ought not to undervalue

---

134 Evans, *Land of my fathers*, p. 142.
135 Evans, *Land of my fathers*, pp. 182–3.
136 It should be noted that Gwynfor Evans saw things rather differently; see, for example, his reference to the praise he received from three famous Williamses in the field, Glanmor, David and Gwyn, in Evans, *For the Sake of Wales*, p. 202.
137 Evans, *Land of my fathers*, pp. 68–9.
138 Evans, *For the Sake of Wales*, p. 202.

the part played by national myth.'[139] It is important to acknowledge that Gwynfor Evans's understanding of history was highly
sophisticated in this regard. For it is not only postmodernists who
recognise the role of the subjective in determining the forms of
any historical narrative. Rather, this is now one of the starting
points for any consideration of historiography. Gwynfor Evans's
objective was to enthrone his own myth above other popular versions of Welsh history, be they British and / or socialist – versions
of Welsh history that are, in their own way, just as mythic.

Here, above all, lies Gwynfor Evans's originality and significance as a thinker. It is easy to identify different influences at work
on the narrative *Aros Mae*. As we might expect, the influence of
Saunders Lewis is obvious.[140] Arthur Wade-Evans's influence on
Gwynfor Evans's interpretation of Wales's connection with Rome
and its empire as well as Wales's relationship with the 'English'
before 1000AD is also clear.[141] In addition, it is possible to trace the
influence of those who contributed (alongside Evans himself) to
a volume published by Plaid Cymru in 1950 titled *The Historical
Basis of Welsh Nationalism* – a collection based on a series of lectures delivered at the party's Summer School in 1946.[142] In other
places Gwynfor Evans draws heavily on Ioan Bowen Rees and
the (brilliant) pamphlet he prepared for the party on *The Welsh
Political Tradition*.[143] But whatever the various influences upon
which it draws – and there are many more that might be mentioned – *Aros Mae* remains much more than the sum of its parts.
Working to explicitly nationalist ends, it provided a coherent and
pellucidly clear narrative encompassing and rendering easily
digestible the whole sweep of Welsh history. It was, moreover, a
nationalist historiography that was not only more transparent in

139 Evans, *For the Sake of Wales*, p. 202.
140 See, for example, Evans, *Land of my fathers*, pp. 310, 393.
141 See, for example, Evans, *Land of my fathers*, pp. 37–41, 63–5.
142 A. W. Wade-Evans, T. Pierce-Jones, Ceinwen Thomas, A. O. H. Jarman,
D. Gwenallt Jones and Gwynfor Evans, *The Historical Basis of Welsh Nationalism*
(Cardiff: Plaid Cymru, 1950). Also published in Welsh as *Seiliau Hanesyddol
Cenedlaetholdeb Cymreig*.
143 Ioan Bowen Rees, *The Welsh Political Tradition* (Cardiff: Plaid Cymru, 1962;
republished in 1975).

its political objectives but also much more likely to strike a popular note than anything that had come before it.

Matthew Levinger and Paula Franklin Lytle have highlighted what they term the 'triadic structure of nationalist rhetoric', demonstrating how nationalists seek to generate support on the basis of a rhetorical strategy that portrays the history of their nation in three distinct steps. A 'Golden Age' of the past is juxtaposed to a 'Fallen Present' but with the promise of a 'New Dawn' once the nation has revived itself.[144] They go on to show how the diagnosis of the reasons for the fall from better times provides the prescription which, if followed, will ensure the nation's full restoration.

Nationalists are hardly alone in reading history in this way. Indeed, part of the explanation for the appeal of this triadic rhetorical strategy may well be the extent to which it echoes the Judeo-Christian tradition's conception of time – the Purity and Innocence of Eden, the Sin of the present and the final Resurrection that will eventually come. A similar triadic structure is even observable in the rhetorical strategies adopted by some socialists and communists as they evangelised for their cause in the first decades of the twentieth century. Recall, for example, how Keir Hardie tried to inspire workers in the Celtic nations to demand a better future by comparing the hardship of the present with the riches and civilisation of the past, when property was held in common by the tribe.[145] We can also identify this triadic structure in nationalist historiography long before Gwynfor Evans produced *Aros Mae*. As we have already seen, for Saunders Lewis it was the loss of 'freedom' in the sixteenth century – at the end of Welsh culture's 'Canrif Fawr' (Great Century) – that explained Wales's parlous contemporary condition. Wales could be renewed only through regaining that freedom. What makes this interesting and unusual from

144 Matthew Levinger and Paula Franklin Lytle, 'Myth and mobilization: the triadic structure of nationalist rhetoric', *Nations and Nationalism*, 7 (2) (April 2001), 175–94.
145 'The Celts can never drive out of their blood that element of communism placed there by their wild free wandering forefathers who loved song and poetry during the thousands of years they lived with everything in common.'

the perspective of an interest in nationalism is the fact that it locates the 'golden age' of Welsh history as occurring after the English conquest and not before it. Implicit in Lewis's diagnosis of the reasons for the fall from grace is that forsaking the Catholic faith also damaged Wales – this despite the fact that Nonconformist Protestantism had since become one of the cornerstones of Welsh identity. Thus, even as Saunders Lewis's historiographical vision conformed in general terms to a triadic structure of nationalist rhetoric, the specific details of his interpretations made it very unlikely that they would appeal to a Welsh audience.

That same triadic structure is identifiable in O. M. Edwards's synoptic work, *Wales*, published in 1901.[146] But in this case the moral of the story, so to speak – the prescription offered to the Welsh people based on its diagnosis of the ills of the past – is loyalty to the British state and its empire. Llywelyn the Great is one of the heroes of *Wales*. In O. M. Edwards's view, 'The policy of Llywelyn is more modern than that of any native prince of Wales', because, '[H]e foresaw the eventual political fate of the country he had consolidated.'

> He saw that unity was impossible as long as any chief could appeal to a hostile king of England, and that the independence of Wales must be its independence as part of a more extensive kingdom. The experience of his long reign, so full in its intensity and variety, had enabled him to see very far into the future ... He had seen that the independence which is natural to Wales, and the unity which is natural to the islands of Britain, are not inconsistent.[147]

Although he would no doubt have chosen slightly different language, at first sight this may well remind readers of Gwynfor Evans's emphasis on the need to establish a Britannic

146 Owen M. Edwards, *Wales* (London: T. Fisher Unwin, 1901). Gwynfor Evans insisted that *Aros Mae* was 'the first attempt at portraying Welsh history in one book since the publication of *Wales* by O. M. Edwards in 1901': Evans, *Bywyd Cymro*, p. 284; translation. It is therefore particularly appropriate to compare both works.
147 Edwards, *Wales*, pp. 149–50.

Confederation. But in a passage that follows almost immediately on from this, we see the historical and political gulf that separated the first wave of Welsh nationalism as represented by O. M. Edwards from the second wave embodied by Gwynfor Evans. '[T]he ideas of Llywelyn', O. M. Edwards asserted,

> were finally realised by a statesman who may be regarded as one of his descendants. Llywelyn's daughter Gladys married Ralph Mortimer. Her descendant ... became the true heir to the throne of England and Wales. In spite of Glendower's help, he did not get the throne. But his claim was carried by his sister Anne to the House of York. Elizabeth of York was the mother of Henry VIII, who gave Wales a new unity and a voice in the Parliament of England and Wales.[148]

On Bosworth Field, the English crown was seized by Henry Tudor, 'a Welshman leading a Welsh army'.[149] With the so-called Acts of Union, Wales became a full participant – and also leaders via the Tudors – in a journey that would establish the Greatness of Britain.

Politically at least, the decline that followed in the wake of losing sight of Llywelyn the Great's ideals was reversed by the victory of the Welsh at Bosworth. In viewing Welsh history in this fashion, O. M. Edwards was much closer to the traditional Welsh historiography of the eighteenth and nineteenth centuries than he was to the narrative popularised by Gwynfor Evans through *Aros Mae*. Of course, that was not the end of the story for Edwards: the Acts of Union were not 'the end of history'. The great theme of his treatment of the following centuries was the awakening of the *Gwerin*. Indeed, from the perspective of his own times, it was here that the political impact of his historiography was most keenly felt. But in terms of the implications of *Wales* for its readers' understanding of the constitutional architecture within which they resided, the British state is portrayed as a medium for Wales's national revival rather than an obstacle to it. The message

148 Edwards, *Wales*, pp. 150–1.
149 Edwards, *Wales*, p. 303.

of *Aros Mae* is, of course, entirely different. Its discussion of the history of Wales incorporates aspects of earlier Welsh historiography such as the traditional emphasis on the continuing influence of the Roman empire as well as an O. M. Edwards-style celebration of the awakening of the *Gwerin*. Indeed, as already noted, Evans's ability to synthesise these disparate elements is one of the great strengths of his work (politically if not necessarily historically). He certainly did not reject everything that had come before. What he did do, however, was to interpret and reinterpret this raw material from a perspective that was totally opposed to the British state and its influence on Wales: a perspective that closely follows the triadic structure of Golden Age – Fallen Present – New Dawn.

The Golden Age – before the arrival of 'the barbarians' when the nation was free to develop in ways consonant with its own traits

Many portrayals of Welsh history – and, in particular, those Protestant historiographies that wanted, for their own reasons, to promote the era of the Celtic Church at the expense of the Catholic period that followed it – posit the Age of the Saints as a Golden Age. This was also Gwynfor Evans's view. The fifth and sixth centuries were 'the age of the saints and the age of the development of the Welsh language; the age which saw the spiritual revolution, and the age of the greatest intellectual energy experienced in Welsh history'.[150] Indeed, 'the two hundred years that followed the departure of Macsen Wledig (Magnus Maximus) was the period most like a golden age in the whole history of Wales'.[151] It is the creative energy of the era that Gwynfor Evans cherishes: 'Impressive industry is to be observed at that time: politically, intellectually and culturally, and above all in religion.'[152] By complete contrast with the civilised condition of Wales, this was a particularly dark and barbaric period in England.

[150] Evans, *Land of my fathers*, p. 71.
[151] Evans, *Land of my fathers*, p. 81.
[152] Evans, *Land of my fathers*, p. 81.

The Fall – when the nation's defences were breached and struck down

One thing that has united Welsh historiography throughout the ages is contempt for the ways in which the Saxons and, above all, the Normans, dealt with Wales. Gwynfor Evans is very much of the same view which he repeats with conviction. The voice of the nationalist and pacifist interweave in his condemnation of the Normans:

> The next two centuries are dominated by the fateful struggle between the powerful Normans, who had so completely demoralised the might of England, and the two hundred thousand people of the little Welsh nation ... Of all the countries of Europe in that period it was Normandy that created the strongest political order and was prepared for war ... The Normans ... had little culture at this time: the nobility could neither read nor write; there were no lawyers among them and hardly any professional men except for the priests. They hunted and organised, feasted and fought; these were pursuits dear to the hearts of the men who landed near Hastings on October the 4th, 1066.[153]

But in complete contrast with the popular historiographies of the past – even the Nonconformist, Cymru Fydd-inflected historical narratives from the turn of the twentieth century – Gwynfor Evans's condemnation of the effects of the Tudors on Wales was equally harsh. The following extended passage gives a flavour of his ire, as well as the sermonising that is so characteristic of *Aros Mae*:

> What Edward I had failed to do by defeating Llywelyn II; and what Henry V had failed to do in defeating Glyndŵr was now accomplished by the success of the Tudors. It led to the cynical acceptance of the Act of Union, and in the course of the two centuries following the Act it destroyed almost totally the heroic national spirit of the Welsh. The brave, vigorous, confident people of the centuries of the middle ages – people who knew they could stand on their own feet

---

153 Evans, *Land of my fathers*, p. 160.

and live their own national life, and who insisted on doing just that – were replaced by a servile, undignified people who believed their greatest honour was to die as a nation, and as individuals, so that Britain could be great; people who believed that it was their duty and their privilege to enrich and strengthen England: people who were so lacking in dignity that they could forsake their own language: people so lacking in confidence that they believed that as a nation they were unable to support even the degree of political freedom obtained in every one of the Swiss cantons. There is nothing despicable about the imperialist rape of the English. What is to be despised is that so many Welsh people themselves help them to ravage their nation.[154]

There was nothing to celebrate in the victory on Bosworth Field. Rather than auguring in a New Dawn, it was in fact one of the darkest hours in Welsh history.

Evans's treatment of the following centuries contains significant echoes of O. M. Edwards's version of Welsh history. Indeed, Edwards himself could hardly have improved on the following portrait of the eighteenth century:

The real hero of the century ... was the *gwerin* itself. It crowded the schools of Griffith Jones thirsting after knowledge; it swarmed to listen to Rowland, Harris and Williams in its longing for truth. It was completely transformed. It lost much, no doubt, in its music and dance; but it gained in dimension and purpose.[155]

That said, even while Evans spared nothing in his praise of the *Gwerin*, not even the brilliance of that class-which-is-above-class was sufficient to counteract the baleful effects of British influence

154 Evans, *Land of my fathers*, pp. 282–3.
155 Evans, *Land of my fathers*, p. 330. It is interesting to note how Gwynfor Evans used the 'nobility' as a bridge between Saunders's interpretation of history and O.M.'s rather different perspective. Discussing the nobility of the fourteenth century he claims that 'Membership of this big class depended entirely on descent and not in any way on wealth. In three centuries many of this class would be among the *gwerin* (folk), thereby enriching its quality' (p. 245). He goes on to argue that Griffith Jones's educational reforms of the start of the eighteenth century had led to a period of a century and a half when the *gwerin* fulfilled the 'functions of the aristocracy [*pendefigaeth*]' (p. 311).

on Wales. Wales continued in its fallen condition from the middle of the nineteenth century through the first sixty years of the twentieth century. Indeed, its position became even more desperate over time because, without a Welsh state, there was no means of withstanding the English/British tide, especially as the state played an ever-greater role in the life of society. He attributed particular importance to the development of the state education system after 1870 which was, consequently, 'a blacker year than 1282, and even 1536'.[156] This system thoroughly and systematically anglicised Welsh life, reflecting the fact that it was beholden to a state that did not prioritise its interests.

Gwynfor Evans identified the same pattern as characterising the history of Wales in the twentieth century: the heroic efforts of the Welsh to better their world proved ultimately in vain because of the failure to appreciate that salvation (worldly salvation, at least) was only possible by means of a Welsh state – a state that would also allow the nation to play its party in the worldwide battle for human dignity. He was quick to acknowledge the nobility of motivations that underpinned much of the activity of the labour movement. Alas, the tragedy of Wales's history was that 'the often heroic campaigns of the workers' movement for social justice was not combined with a Welsh national political programme'. If that had been the case, then both sides would have been strengthened immeasurably. But because this has not occurred, 'Wales continued to be exploited as a British province over the decades, with sad results for the workers and the national tradition'.[157]

Whatever the extraordinary virtues of the *Gwerin* and the Welsh working class, in a world of states, the fact that Wales did not have its own had left it defenceless. Its economic and social development had been distorted and, ultimately, frustrated. The nation had had no means of steering itself through the storms of the first half of the twentieth century, a period of bloody war and great hardship. As a result, it had been damaged to the point of almost complete destruction.

---

[156] Evans, *Land of my fathers*, p. 395.
[157] Evans, *Land of my fathers*, p. 358.

A New Dawn – when the nation succeeds in restoring its dignity and self-respect and begins the task of building a society that embodies the qualities of the previous Golden Age

Gwynfor Evans believed it was loss of independence / freedom that had brought Wales low. It was therefore only through their restoration that Wales's rehabilitation could begin in earnest. Nevertheless, he considered that Wales had started on that providential journey thanks to the national awakening that Wales had experienced in the second half of the nineteenth century, and in particular following the development of the national movement after 1925. It is little wonder that the president of Plaid Cymru considered the establishment of his own party as being particularly significant. But what is striking about the final chapter of *Aros Mae* is the emphasis placed on the contribution of members of Cymdeithas yr Iaith Gymraeg, 'the cream of Welsh youth … They are the new shepherds of these old hills. Because of their splendid commitment to the land of their fathers, Wales has a future as a nation.'[158]

> [L]iberty is something that has to be won, and won through hard work and sacrifice, and unyielding determination … With will and vision this nation can create her own environment. There are no economic and political powers in existence which her will cannot subdue. In the confident spirit and confidence of the young generation there is enough moral strength to ensure a free and just Wales which can transmit her civilisation to the future and make her worthy contribution to civilisation and the inter-national order.[159]

The achievement of a free, Welsh and just nation would complete the circle of our national history.

Gwynfor Evans was not an original political thinker; he rather synthesised the work of others. Indeed, when we consider his political thinking in the round, perhaps his greatest weakness was

---

158 Evans, *Land of my fathers*, p. 451.
159 Evans, *Land of my fathers*, p. 450. Interestingly, the original version refers to a 'free and just and Welsh Wales', see Evans, *Aros Mae*, p. 315.

that he was too catholic and too uncritical. He was too willing to try to force sometimes incompatible elements into a single narrative, and not willing enough to cast aside ideas and concepts that had long lost whatever purchase or relevance they may have previously possessed. But as a popular historian, Gwynfor Evans was far more successful. Whatever his deficiencies as a 'genuine' historian, through *Aros Mae* he was able to generate a popular narrative history of Wales that has proven to be invaluable to the national movement as it sought to motivate its supporters and draw others into the fold.[160]

Aros Mae offers a version of the nation's history that is, at first glance, simple and perhaps simplistic. But we should not underestimate the skill or intelligence that underpinned its production. Gwynfor Evans managed to weave together – and synthesise – important and influential elements of previous Welsh historiographies. Thus, there is room in his meta-narrative for some of the central elements from O. M. Edwards's liberal Nonconformist historiography as well as elements of subsequent Labour historiography. Space too for some of those historical narratives that have been so dear to previous generations, such as the longevity of the Roman influence in Wales and, relatedly, the contrast between the England of the dark ages and a civilised Wales. In this respect, the themes woven together by Gwynfor Evans were familiar. But the pattern he weaved with them was genuinely novel, because this was history written for the purposes of modern Welsh nationalism. He reoriented and reformed these familiar themes in a way that was consistent with his vision for the future of Wales. The book's central argument, of course, is that the only way to be true to the nation's past is by supporting the political and wider social movement to which Gwynfor Evans dedicated his life: the national movement. Reading between the lines of his autobiography, it appears that Gwynfor Evans was prouder of this book than of any other. It was, without question, his masterpiece.

---

160 Lest it have escaped the attention of some readers, Dafydd Iwan's 'Yma o Hyd' may be read as *Aros Mae* distilled into three verses.

The End of Britishness

Gwynfor Evans became president of Plaid Cymru on the first day of August 1945. He was to shoulder that responsibility until the final day of October 1981. Only a few weeks before his presidential term finally came to an end, he addressed a rally organised by his party in Port Talbot. The speech was published as *The End of Britishness* (his book bearing the Welsh version of the same title, *Diwedd Prydeindod*, was published the same month). To read the speech and to compare it with his first publications as president is to be struck by how little his message had changed during the intervening years. The context was of course different. There had been no mention of Margaret Thatcher, Trident missiles, the campaign for a Welsh television channel or Lord Beeching back in 1945. While memories of the Great Depression remained vivid in the 1940s, it was the impact of a new recession that demanded attention almost four decades later. Yet Gwynfor Evans continued to cling to the same beliefs and to many of the same tropes. Saunders Lewis's influence remained significant too. The latter's voice can be heard clearly in the following passage:

> This rally is concerned with language and work, 'iaith a gwaith'. Linking the two, far from being incongruous, is natural, for in Wales they are woven together in a seamless web. The Welsh language is not only our greatest tradition, it is *the* great tradition that Wales has, the only really great feature of world importance in our life. Its power is immense ... The state's attack on it has been part of an attack on the Welsh identity and on the national community of Wales. Today the assault on the steel, coal and other industries is the same as the assault on Welsh society and culture. Likewise the defence of the language is at one with the defence of the economy and the community. It is the defence of Welshmen as autonomous human persons and of their dignity against the onslaught of Britishness. We fight to prevent the conversion of Welshmen into abstract beings lost in a rootless mass.[161]

161 Gwynfor Evans, *The End of Britishness* (no publication details but Plaid Cymru, 1981), p. 3. It is noteworthy that although Gwynfor Evans himself claimed

Gwynfor Evans was still promoting those core ideas set out by Saunders Lewis well over half a century before.

Other influences were also obvious, above all the influence of D. J. Davies and the rest of the Scandinavian tendency within Plaid Cymru. Grundtvig and his Danish folk high schools are mentioned, for example – a man, an institution and indeed a country that would likely be less than familiar to the vast majority of the audience.[162] The wealth, abundance and civility of small countries (Scandinavian countries in particular) are compared with Wales's wretched condition, in order to 'prove' – at least to Gwynfor Evans's satisfaction – that 'Self-government is the main condition of successfully rebuilding the Welsh economy.'[163]

But in addition to the influence of others, we also see the workings of Gwynfor Evans's own interests and preoccupations. The fiendish dangers of militarism and the threat of nuclear annihilation are central themes. We also see how, during the second half of his presidency, Evans's political rhetoric became increasingly permeated by historical references. Indeed, with the passing of the years, he seems to have adopted what has been termed here the 'triadic structure of nationalist rhetoric' as a framework for his political declarations. The speech begins back in the Golden Age of the sixth century:

> We meet today on the western edge of the Vale of Glamorgan where Maelgwyn Gwynedd, the biggest political figure on the island in the 6th century, was educated at Llanilltud Fawr about the time that Arthur died of wounds received at the battle of Camlan, probably before the birth of St David. Maelgwyn Gwynedd came from Gwynedd to the Glamorgan coast through a country that had been united by nearly a thousand miles of Roman roads, and in which a sense of belonging was fostered by history, religion, language and traditions.[164]

that this was a rally for both work and language, only work – or the lack of it – is mentioned on the cover of the pamphlet: 'an Address ... to launch the party's campaign against unemployment'.

162 Evans, *The End of Britishness*, p. 1.
163 Evans, *The End of Britishness*, p. 6.
164 Evans, *The End of Britishness*, p. 1.

The speech concludes with a peroration that looks towards the future and the salvation that might yet be achieved through the national movement:

> By far the most exciting thing about Wales is her possibilities. In a people of such talent as the Welsh, with such a magnificent history and tradition, these are almost limitless, whether in the field of social justice, cultural vitality, intellectual endeavour, industrial venture or in terms of a contribution to European civilisation or world order. I may be wrong, but I think there is beginning to develop a new spirit which will enable the people of Wales to rise to the level of history, to respond to the harsh challenge of our day, and to create in the land of their fathers a society of which their children will be proud: a country free, just and Welsh.[165]

The central message of the lecture is that the past not only places a duty upon us in the present, but also offers a key to a better future provided, that is, that we embrace that duty. In the words of Prosser Rhys's great patriotic poem, 'Cymru', Gwynfor Evans sought to 'demand from our nation / A reconciliation with her fair past.'[166]

Ultimately Gwynfor Evans's chief contribution to Plaid Cymru was not as a thinker. Rather, it was his obstinate perseverance, his total commitment, the undoubted gravitas he brought to the role of president and, above all, his remarkable stamina that had the greatest influence. But his intellectual contribution should not be disregarded either. Yes, most of his core ideas about the nation and nationalism were derived from those of Saunders Lewis, and he remained true to them throughout his life. Many of his ideas about those policy areas that were most important to the party were also derived from the same source. Again, he remained remarkably committed to them. But he nonetheless did Plaid Cymru a great service by setting these

---

165 Evans, *The End of Britishness*, p. 12.
166 Translation: 'am fynnu o'n cenedl ni / Gymod â'i theg orffennol hi.' The poem was republished in Emyr Edwards (ed.), *Beirdd y Mynydd Bach* (Aberystwyth: Cyhoeddiadau Barddas, 1999), p. 162. The lines were quoted in Evans, *Rhagom i Ryddid*, p. 137.

words and themes to a very different tune – one that was much more appropriate for the tastes of some, at least, among the Welsh audience. Most importantly of all, the version of Wales's history that he produced and did so much to popularise remains a truly important contribution to the intellectual inheritance of Welsh nationalism.

4

More than *Dal Ati*?
The Era of the Two Dafydds[1]

There have been a number of pivotal moments in the history of Plaid Cymru, with the Fire at Penyberth and Gwynfor Evans's victory in the Carmarthen by-election among the most prominent. But in terms of the party's ideological development, the 1979 referendum result stands out as the most significant. It is hard to exaggerate the trauma generated by that result among Welsh nationalists. By rejecting the feeble devolution proposals contained in the Wales Act 1978 in such an overwhelming fashion, Wales's electors succeeded not only in shattering the dreams of generations of Plaid Cymru partisans, they also destroyed their self-confidence. They were left bitter, divided and contemplating their country's future in the bleakest possible terms. Indeed, many believed that Wales no longer had a future – the Welsh had voted themselves out of history. The final words of T. James Jones and Jon Dressel's *Cerddi Ianws Poems* give us a taste of the despair and hopelessness felt at the time:

> It is not unjust that we in turn are finally taken in ourselves.
> No one but us will ever grieve the difference,
> and even we will only grieve it for a while.
> A hundred winking springs from now,
> all that we feared the loss of will be with the loam of history,
> along with our dishonour.[2]

---

[1] *Dal Ati* is the title of the first volume of Dafydd Wigley's autobiography (Caernarfon: Gwasg Gwynedd, 1993). It is a very widely used colloquialism that might translate as 'keep going', 'keep on going' or 'persevere'.
[2] T. James Jones and Jon Dressel, *Cerddi Ianws Poems* (Llandysul: Gomer, 1979), p. 20. There is another apocalyptic interpretation of the implications of 1979

The words retain their power even now. The final defeat of the Welsh was at hand.

It is impossible to comprehend the full extent of the despair visited on Welsh nationalism after 1979 without understanding how the events of that year – a year in which the paralysing shock of the referendum defeat was followed by Margaret Thatcher's first general election victory – were interpreted by most Welsh nationalists. These developments might have been interpreted as a response to the specific context of the times: the unpopularity of a tired Labour government in the wake of the 'winter of discontent', for example, or the myriad other contextual explanations that could be offered. In the event, however, what might be termed an apocalyptic interpretation of the implications of '1979' was almost universally adopted by nationalists. For them, the referendum and election result were regarded as reflecting the outworkings of far more fundamental, long-term social processes; processes that were seen as threatening the continuation of any sense of Welsh identity.

One of these was the relentless march of anglicisation. By the end of the 1970s, it was obvious to all but the most naively optimistic that the prospects for the survival of *Y Fro Gymraeg* – those communities where the Welsh language remained the main medium of social intercourse – were now very bleak. This presented Plaid Cymru with an enormous challenge that was both ideological and strategic. What, for example, should its priorities be from now on? With the battle for self-government apparently lost, should the party not refocus all its energies on the struggle for linguistic and cultural survival? Even if it decided to continue to push for self-government, how could the party hope to craft a message that might appeal to the (diminishing) audience

in Gwyn A. Williams's memorable final chapter of *When was Wales?* (London: Penguin, 1991). It is interesting to compare Williams's despairing lyricism with the quiet confidence shown by his fellow historian Kenneth O. Morgan who, around the same time, argued that despite the 1979 defeat, Wales would inevitably return to the issue of self-government sooner or later (see Morgan's preface to David Foulkes, J. Barry Jones and R. A. Wilford (eds), *The Welsh Veto: The Wales Act 1978 and The Referendum* (Cardiff: University of Wales Press, 1983), pp. ix–xi). In this case, it was Morgan's Whiggish faith in progress rather than Williams's apocalypticism that was to prove correct.

in the Welsh-speaking heartlands – areas on which Plaid Cymru had become increasingly reliant – while also convincing electors who did not speak the language? This was not a new dilemma, of course. But when some of the most prominent spokespeople of English-speaking Wales, politicians such as Neil Kinnock and Leo Abse, had apparently managed to generate significant political capital by emphasising Wales's linguistic differences as part of their uncompromising and extremely effective opposition to devolution, this was a matter that could no longer be avoided. These questions were difficult enough in themselves, but the continuing decline of the language raised an even more fundamental issue for the party: given that the party's traditional thinking and doctrine had linked the Welsh language and Welsh identity so closely together, was there now any firm ground on which Welshness – and Plaid Cymru – could now stand?

Secularisation was another, related process that raised many of the same questions for party. By the end of the 1970s, Wales was a thoroughly secular country. Given how closely Nonconformist Protestantism had once been associated with Welsh identity, it is little wonder that process was also interpreted as a threat to the very essence of Welshness. It should be underlined that the secularisation of Welsh society presented a specific and very serious challenge to Plaid Cymru. After all, the party had become a force in Welsh society in large part through its association with Nonconformity. But as the Nonconformist denominations dwindled into shrunken husks of their former selves, the 'Christian nationalism' of Gwynfor Evans, Pennar Davies, Lewis Valentine and, in his own way, Saunders Lewis appeared increasingly anachronistic and irrelevant.[3] Was this to be the fate of Welsh nationalism more broadly?

As though the weakness of the form of Welshness from which Plaid Cymru had drawn its strength was not enough to cast the party's supporters into despair, it also became increasingly

---

[3] It is here worth recalling Dafydd Glyn Jones's astute observation that 'Saunders Lewis was a Catholic for Nonconformist Wales'. See Saunders Lewis, 'Sefwch gyda mi ...', selected by Dafydd Glyn Jones (Llanrwst: Gwasg Carreg Gwalch, 2000), p. 9; translation.

obvious in the months and years after St David's Day 1979 that the foundations of another form of Welshness were in the process of being completely undermined. The writing was on the wall for those heavy industries that had been so central to the Welsh economy long before they were swept aside in such a needlessly cruel manner by the recession of the early 1980s. Even so, their demise represented another shattering blow. While it may have been the case that there were some in the party's ranks that viewed industrial Wales with a certain ambiguity – as was the case with Saunders Lewis and Gwynfor Evans, for example – this did not equate with denying the fundamental Welshness of the inhabitants of the industrial valleys. Indeed, in the wake of Carmarthen, these were the electors that the party *knew* could be won over to the national cause. But with both *Y Fro Gymraeg* and Wales of the industrial valleys now in terminal decline, had not Wales itself reached the end of the road? This is what it was to be 'finally taken in ourselves'.

In retrospect it seems clear that the response to 1979, even if understandable, was somewhat hyperbolic. Specifically, the reductionism of equating Welshness with a particular social characteristic (for example, the Welsh language or the Welsh Nonconformist tradition) meant that many lost sight of the fact that national identity forms from a constellation of different features, institutions, ideas and experiences. It is, moreover, a constellation that is resilient enough to survive even the dimming or destruction of some of its individual elements. No doubt that some of the prophesising of doom was also intended to provoke a response and inspire resistance.[4] Then again, the wisdom of hindsight is an easy and insubstantial thing. Even those who were actively seeking to inspire a positive response through their apocalyptic warnings sincerely believed that Wales was faced with oblivion unless their efforts were successful. Thus, in the period that followed 1979, with the whole future of the

---

4 Witness the following comments by T. James Jones in his Welsh-language introduction to *Cerddi Ianws Poems* (p. 4): 'The poems offer a political point of view and urge the readers to take political action in order to protect our country and our language in the future'; translation.

country seemingly in the balance, Plaid Cymru was plunged into the most serious intellectual crisis in its history.

If continuity was the most striking feature of Plaid Cymru's political thought before 1979 – a period which had seen many of Saunders Lewis's core ideas incorporated into Gwynfor Evans's worldview – then, after 1979, everything was reassessed, including the party's aims, image and messaging. This was a painful and often querulous process. Many of the beliefs and presumptions that had previously been regarded as central were challenged. Some old shibboleths were completely cast aside. As will shortly be detailed further, the most important and long-lasting of the latter was the idea that Welsh nationalism could be considered to form a complete political ideology in its own right. Party figures as varied as Saunders Lewis, D. J. Davies and Gwynfor Evans had all shared the view that nationalism was a 'third way' between socialism and liberal capitalism. But in the wake of 1979, it was recognised that this 'third way' was in fact a cul-de-sac. From now on, Plaid would adopt more conventional and familiar political terminology and locate itself on the 'left' of the political spectrum. But of course, the left is itself a very, very broad category. Thus, rather than settling the argument about the party's ideological position, all this achieved in itself was to change the terms of that debate. From then on, the burning question was no longer whether or not the party was left wing – the key argument since the mid-1930s – but, rather, what kind of left-wing politics, what kind of socialism did the party represent? A host of potential answers were proposed. Yet even if there was no final agreement or consensus regarding the exact nature of Plaid Cymru's commitment to 'socialism', the fact that the rhetoric of the 'third way' had finally been cast aside represented a historic shift in the party's thinking.

As well as instigating far-reaching changes in the party's overall stance and ideological positioning, 1979 also served to revive old arguments about the methods that Plaid Cymru should adopt to advance its cause. Since conventional constitutional politics had failed so disastrously in the effort to secure even the weakest measure of self-government, how was Wales to be saved? Saved not only from the arrogant indifference of the British state, but from its most dangerous enemy of all, namely the servility and timidity of the Welsh themselves. Disagreement about which methods it should adopt had characterised Plaid Cymru from its very establishment, with significant support for unconstitutional direct action present throughout the party. It therefore is no surprise that their seeming failure had disheartened even the most ardent supporters of the 'parliamentary route' to national redemption. Yet, in all seriousness, what other route was available to the party?

In the wake of 1979, Plaid Cymru's leadership and membership were forced to reconsider their attitude towards Wales as well as their various presumptions about the role of their party. The various debates and arguments that emerged from that process are the subject matter of this chapter. The discussion is divided into four parts. First, we focus on the party's formal response to the 1979 disaster, namely the report of its Commission of Inquiry. Secondly, we focus on the debates on socialism that were such a prominent feature of the internal life of Plaid Cymru during the first half of the 1980s; arguments that came to a juddering halt in the wake of another great upheaval, namely the failure of the miners' strike. Thirdly, the discussion turns to an account of the various directions suggested as a way forward for the party in the second half of the 1980s. Fourth and finally, we focus on the party in the 1990s. It is here that we evaluate the political thinking of Dafydd Wigley as well as what we shall term the 'Ceredigion experiment', namely the efforts of Cynog Dafis and Phil Williams to paint the party green, so to speak, by yoking the national cause to green politics. This is also where the paradox of the 1990s is laid bare: a period when the nationalist cause in Wales was strengthening even while, intellectually speaking at least, the nationalist party appeared to be languishing. The chapter concludes with an evaluation of the wider significance of the years in question to the development of Plaid Cymru's political thought – a period which began in the depths of post-1979 despair but culminated in the euphoria of the remarkable, hair's breadth victory in the 1997 referendum.

Turning left: the end of the 'third way'

In a meeting held on 16 June 1979, the members of Plaid Cymru's national council agreed to establish a Commission of Inquiry that would review the standpoints, strategy, structures and financial foundations of the party, thus embarking on one of the most far-reaching internal reviews ever undertaken by a mainstream political party in the UK.[5] The commission was composed of five members. Reflecting the nature of Plaid Cymru at the time – and indeed, the nature of Welsh politics more generally – all were male, and all long-standing party stalwarts. Eurfyl ap Gwilym, Emrys Roberts, Owen John Thomas and Dafydd Wigley met regularly during the remainder of 1979 and throughout 1980. They were joined on occasion by Phil Williams, but the fact that he spent a substantial part of this time working abroad inevitably impacted on his ability to contribute to the work of the commission. Evidence was collected at party meetings and from individual meetings with its principal officers, the SNP was consulted to obtain its views, while the commissioners also received 'hundreds of written and oral observations'.[6] Their report – part of a publication of that stretched to 137 pages including a minority report by Phil Williams – was released in February 1981, only a few months before one of the commissioners, Dafydd Wigley, was elected president of the party for the first time.[7]

---

5   There is an outline of the formal proposal that led to the establishment of the commission in *Report of the Plaid Cymru Commission of Inquiry* (Plaid Cymru, 1981), pp. i–ii. See pp. 116–19 for the commission members' own interpretation of the terms of reference given to them.

6   *Report of the Plaid Cymru Commission of Inquiry*, p. ii.

7   It would be interesting to investigate further the process that persuaded Phil Williams to prepare his own minority report. In the preface to the main report, it was noted (quite accurately) that the Aberystwyth physicist had not attended the commission's meetings during the period in which the report was finalised (p. ii). The minority report is, however, very critical of the majority report (see pp. 94–115), and it is difficult to believe that it would have been possible to arrive at an agreed report even if Williams had not been isolated beyond the Arctic Circle in northern Sweden pursuing his academic research work. It is notable that Williams argued that it would have been more appropriate for the commission to have highlighted the different positions within Plaid Cymru rather than seek 'a form of words' to bridge between them (p. 94).

Reflecting the all-encompassing nature of its terms of refer-ence, the commission cast its net widely, discussing matters as diverse as fundraising activities, including whist drives and *cawl a chân* (soup and song) evenings, and the relationship between Plaid Cymru and the rest of the Welsh national movement.[8] But in context of the present discussion, two sections are of particular significance: those focused on Political Philosophy and Strategy.

Political philosophy
Traditionally, the leaders and principal thinkers of Plaid Cymru had rejected the 'left-right' divide as an appropriate means of characterising the different economic, social and political views of their party. Rather, they sought to find a means of escaping – or rising above – the terms of the ideological debate that had tended to define political discourse in Britain: they sought some kind of 'third way'. It is important to note that they did not view this third way as simply a middle road between left and right. This was not a 'split the difference' position. Rather their aim was more ambitious: they sought a political programme and as-sociated language that transcended the conventional left-right categories by incorporating and transforming the main themes associated with both, in order to generate a new synthesis. That was certainly the position adopted by Saunders Lewis and J. E. Daniel: the latter's pamphlet, *Welsh Nationalism: What it Stands for*, remains one of the most eloquent declarations of this point of view.[9] Despite the fact that both had been heavily influenced and inspired by Scandinavian social democracy, this was also the view of D. J. Davies and Gwynfor Evans. As such, both opposed the efforts of the self-conscious 'left' within the party to claim that the extensive overlap between Plaid Cymru and left-wing values and political positions – on internationalism, cooperation, indus-trial democracy, etc. – meant that the party should be considered a socialist party.[10]

8   *Report of the Plaid Cymru Commission of Inquiry*, pp. 85, 23–4.
9   J. E. Daniel, *Welsh Nationalism: What it Stands for* (London: Foyle's Welsh Co., n.d. [but 1937]).
10   See in this context Rhys Evans, *Gwynfor Evans: Rhag Pob Brad* (Talybont: Y Lolfa, 2005), p. 365.

Plaid Cymru's intellectual leaders were far from alone in their desire to signpost a third way. Even if their version of it led in very different directions, such rhetoric was heard across the (conventional) political spectrum – from the extreme right in the form of fascism, to the extreme left in the form of Trotskyism. So too in the centre ground, in the guise of the Catholic political philosophy developed mainly in continental Europe that was to influence Saunders Lewis. In post-war Britain, the Labour Party sought to present its 'democratic socialism' as a third way between American capitalism and Soviet Stalinism.[11] Given this context and the complexities that might result from embracing a rhetoric that could associate the party with any of these examples, it is perhaps not surprising that Plaid Cymru tended to avoid labelling its political philosophy as a 'third way'. While it published a pamphlet bearing that title in 1947 – written by Wilfred Wellock, former Labour MP for Stourbridge – other formulations were chosen to try to crystallise the party's distinctive position.[12] One was 'Cooperative nationalism', another 'Christian nationalism'. But while the various labels chosen are interesting, the point here is not the descriptions themselves but rather the fact that Plaid Cymru's leading lights were adamant that the conventional left/ right signifiers were not appropriate for describing the positions of their party. Similarly, they argued that the solutions proffered

11 It will be recalled that, for a short time at least, Tony Blair toyed with 'The Third Way' as a label for New Labour's political vision. In this context it is interesting to note that Blair acknowledged the influence of philosopher John Macmurray on his politics, a man who many years previously had been cited as an influence by Gwynfor Evans.

12 Wilfred Wellock, *The Third Way* (Plaid Cymru, n.d. [but 1947]). A Welsh-language version was published at the same time. In the introduction to his later pamphlet, *New Horizons: Build the Future Now!* (London: Housemans Bookshop, n.d. [but 1954–5?]), Wellock wrote: 'This brochure is dedicated to all those isolated persons and small groups in all lands who, in these restless days of self-indulgence and materialistic glorification, of conflicting ideologies and financial and military systems, and of threatening dooms, are labouring to bring to birth an era of creative faith and action in which the impulses of a cultured humanity will be directed to erecting a civilisation wherein justice, beauty and truth dwell in the harmony that is peace; and to all seekers after a better way' (p. 2). It is easy to understand the appeal of this kind of rhetoric for members of Plaid Cymru. It is also easy to understand Wellock's interest in Plaid Cymru. Even while small and isolated, it was nonetheless a political party with a genuine foothold in the intellectual life of its country. The struggle to be heard in England was of a greater order of magnitude.

by the self-styled left and right were inadequate for dealing with Wales's problems. An alternative approach was required – one animated by a different ideology.

Gwynfor Evans seems to have remained faithful to this view throughout his period as party president. In a letter published in the December 1980 issue of the party publication *Welsh Nation*, he reminded his fellow members that he considered the labels 'left' and 'right' – 'so beloved of British commentators' – to be 'unhelpful'.[13] It is a sign of Evans's waning influence that the members of the commission nonetheless chose to ignore both their president and decades of party tradition by declaring that 'any realistic evaluation of Plaid Cymru policy must conclude that it is socialist in nature'.[14] This was accompanied by an additional effort to definite precisely what was meant by this and – most importantly, perhaps – to differentiate the party's position from the British Labour Party's commitment to the centralist, centralising state and to imperialism. Specifically, the term 'decentralist' was introduced to qualify the commitment to socialism, this in reference to two ideological axes (left-right and centralist-decentralist) that the commission argued could be superimposed onto each other (see Figure 1):

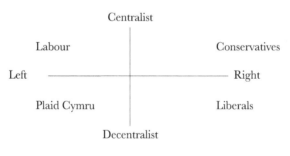

Figure 1.[15]

The commission's recommendation was that the party should espouse a 'decentralist, community-based form of socialism'.[16] This

13 *Welsh Nation*, December 1980, 5.
14 *Report of the Plaid Cymru Commission of Inquiry*, p. 14.
15 *Report of the Plaid Cymru Commission of Inquiry*, p. 14. The attempt to position other parties is also found in the original.
16 *Report of the Plaid Cymru Commission of Inquiry*, p. iii; see also pp. 12–16.

clarification and qualification was important, and we will return to its significance in due course. But what was much more significant from the perspective of Plaid Cymru's long-term intellectual development is that the members of the Commission of Inquiry had abandoned a nigh-on sixty-year effort by the party's leading thinkers to eschew traditional left-right labels and, instead, find an alternative way to characterise its position. While arguments over the party's positioning certainly did not end there, from that point on those arguments would take place on different terrain using a very different language.

Strategy

The party had become too respectable and overly concerned with electoral politics, with consensus and with the parliamentary game; it needed to adopt a bolder, more challenging and more radical approach. If there was a consensus position in the ranks of Plaid Cymru about what the 1979 debacle meant for the party, then it was this. In retrospect, the claim that the party's problem was its respectability seems a peculiar one, to say the least. The detailed polling regarding the attitudes of the Welsh electorate in 1979 showed clearly enough that the party was unpopular in part because, rightly or wrongly, a significant proportion of that electorate regarded it as an 'extremist' party.[17] It cannot be denied that a substantial part of the problem facing the party was the way that it was associated in the public mind with the activities of Cymdeithas yr Iaith Gymraeg. Yet despite this, the Commission of Inquiry's report praised the way that Cymdeithas yr Iaith Gymraeg had succeeded in bringing matters to a head in several of its campaigns, while acknowledging that, as a pressure group, it could act without needing to keep 'one eye on electoral popularity'.[18] Plaid Cymru itself had experienced impressive success in 1980 in the wake of Gwynfor Evans's threat to fast to death if the Thatcher government did not deliver on its manifesto

17   There is a discussion of the popular perception of Plaid Cymru in 1979, and the turnaround achieved by 1997, in Geoff Evans and Dafydd Trystan, 'Why was 1997 different?', in Bridget Taylor and Katarina Thomson (eds), *Scotland and Wales: Nations Again* (Cardiff: University of Wales Press, 1999), pp. 95–117.

18   *Report of the Plaid Cymru Commission of Inquiry*, p. 19.

commitment to a Welsh-language television channel – a threat that combined high principle with crude blackmail, and which had led the mainstream of Welsh nationalism far from the path of conventional party politics. It is little wonder, perhaps, that the commission considered pressure-group activity among the options for the party's future.

The commission gave detailed consideration to four potential strategies:

1. electoral politics;
2. pressure-group activity – activity that could include law-breaking, but not violence against individuals;
3. attempting to influence other movements from within – the kind of 'entryism' that had long been a familiar strategy for various Communist parties and by the 1980s was being championed by various Trotskyist groups;
4. building the 'alternative society' desired by the party by creating 'our own social and economic institutions', for example by establishing cooperative enterprises.

The commissioners were dismissive of the third option. Those Welsh nationalists who had joined the ranks of the Labour Party in the hope of ensuring effecting change were held up as a cautionary example of the failings of this approach – all had been smothered and captured by the party machine.[19] Beyond that, however, the Commission of Inquiry argued that the party – working alone or alongside other parts of the national movement – needed to combine options 1, 2 and 4 as part of a general, long-term plan for 'national restoration'.

The commission members, all experienced politicians, were fully aware of the tensions that were bound to emerge from these different strategies, and in particular between the first and second options – between a focus on electoral politics and pressure group activity. To try to mitigate these tensions, it was agreed that pressure-group activities should be extended

---

19 *Report of the Plaid Cymru Commission of Inquiry*, p. 20.

beyond the cultural sphere to include 'all aspects of Welsh life including industrial, economic and social problems'.[20] In fact, some party members had already been attempting to do so. The pages of *Y Ddraig Goch* and *Welsh Nation* in the early 1980s were full of stories of protests, whether demonstrations or attempts to occupy offices, and accounts of the various resulting court cases (successful prosecutions appear to have been relatively rare). The overwhelming majority of these demonstrations stemmed from the party's efforts to draw attention to the hardship that had resulted from the profound recession the country had experienced in recent times. In one sense, therefore, it can be said that the commission was acknowledging an already existing reality. Indeed, with the exception of entryism (recall how adamantly the party had opposed dual membership), these various approaches had all coexisted within Plaid Cymru since its earliest days, even if the main emphasis during the thirteen years after 1966 had been on electoral politics. The real significance of the Commission of Inquiry's efforts was that they prepared an intellectual framework which sought to justify and coordinate the use of all these different strategies by Plaid Cymru – and the rest of the Welsh national movement – at a time when very many members had 'become frustrated or disillusioned' by electoral politics.[21]

If the recommendation to embrace 'socialism' represented a revolutionary change in the history of Plaid Cymru, and if the willingness to promote other strategies alongside electoral politics also represented an obvious change of emphasis, other aspects of the report displayed far more continuity. Most strikingly, discussions around the inter-relationship between the individual, the community and the nation were orthodoxly Saundersian in both substance and style:

> Plaid Cymru believes in the importance of the individual and the individual's role as a member of the community. We look upon the nation as a community of communities made up of people sharing

20 *Report of the Plaid Cymru Commission of Inquiry*, p. 20.
21 *Report of the Plaid Cymru Commission of Inquiry*, p. 21.

common culture, experiences, history and aspirations. Because of this, Plaid Cymru believes that power – be it political and economic – should be centralised only when this is necessary for the good of the community of the nation as a whole … In economic terms, Plaid Cymru believes that as much power as possible should reside in the workplace and thus opposes the excessive centralising and authoritarian tendencies of both capitalist and communist systems. Plaid Cymru believes that a national and international order based on this philosophy will lead to a more just and satisfying way of life for the peoples of the world.[22]

Saunders Lewis may well have expressed all of this more eloquently: he – as well as Gwynfor Evans in his wake – would doubtless also have included 'the family' and 'civilisation' in their constellation of key concepts; and both would certainly have deplored the lack of reference to Christianity. Nonetheless, the sense here is of continuity and gradual evolution rather than some more fundamental rupture.

We see the same pattern repeated in the commissioners' treatment of the role of the Welsh language in Welsh identity. Again, it is worth quoting their exact words at some length in order to emphasise the degree of continuity in phraseology as well as content:

One obvious facet of Welshness is the Welsh language which makes a unique contribution to our national identity. Not only is it the carrier of our history, our culture and our traditions but also – both inside and outside Wales – it is taken as a symbol of our distinctiveness as a nation … Whilst the majority of Welsh people unfortunately do not speak the Welsh language, there exists a reserve of good will towards it. The party must take a leading role in bridging the gap between Welsh and non-Welsh speakers and ensuring that the non-Welsh speaking majority come to regard the language as an important part of their heritage.[23]

22 *Report of the Plaid Cymru Commission of Inquiry*, p. 13.
23 *Report of the Plaid Cymru Commission of Inquiry*, p. 10.

True, the commissioners also emphasised that the Welsh language is 'not the only test of our nationhood' and that 'we must accept that Wales means different things to different people'.[24] They also made it abundantly clear that Plaid Cymru's definition of nationhood was subjective in nature: it was about 'a sense of common identity, whatever its origins'.[25] That said, the core role attributed to the language as both a symbol of and medium for Welsh national identity is also very evident.

The influence on all of this of Saunders Lewis as interpreted by Gwynfor Evans is undeniable. It is also obvious in the report's account of the Wales that would emerge from the kind of national awakening championed by Plaid Cymru. The energies released, it is claimed, would result in a society free from the 'over-centralised bureaucracy which tends to dominate society and lead to social torpor', and free also from the 'excesses of individual greed and exploitation' that characterise capitalist society.[26] While they embraced 'decentralised socialism' as a description of the party's objective, and even as they considered different strategies for facilitating the journey towards that goal, much of the intellectual terrain traversed by the commissioners remains remarkably familiar.

Phil Williams's minority report was more a commentary on the main report rather than anything more rounded and complete.[27] He was critical of its conclusions regarding both political philosophy and strategy. Given that he was a dedicated socialist it is no surprise that Williams supported the decision to embrace 'decentralised socialism'. But he also regarded conflict between the two parts of this compound formulation as inevitable. Redistribution of wealth is surely an essential part of any socialist system worthy of the name? Does that not in turn entail the presence of some form of central authority that can enforce the transfer of resources from one place to another if required? Is that in turn not bound to contradict or undermine the principle of decentralising power? To be

---

24 *Report of the Plaid Cymru Commission of Inquiry*, p. 10.
25 *Report of the Plaid Cymru Commission of Inquiry*, p. 10.
26 *Report of the Plaid Cymru Commission of Inquiry*, p. 14.
27 *Report of the Plaid Cymru Commission of Inquiry*, pp. 94–115.

sure, he did not regard these tensions as a reason to reject efforts to reconcile the two principles, but Williams wanted to emphasise that 'when the two principles contradict it is to socialism we should give our highest priority'.[28] To be fair to the authors of the main report, even if they did not express the tension quite as crisply, they were clearly aware of its existence. Nevertheless, they avoided prioritising one principle over the other.[29]

Another of Phil Williams's criticisms of the main report was that its authors had failed to provide sufficient 'historical perspective' for their analysis of the present position of Wales and Plaid Cymru, as well as the prospects and possibilities for both country and party. As will become apparent, this became a regular complaint of the party's left in the early 1980s. It must be said, however, that is not entirely clear what Phil Williams means by it. At times, he seems to believe that the main report should have offered an 'honest and thorough' accounting of the past century in Welsh history; in other places he calls for a 'historical perspective to relate our situation with the pattern in other countries'; and in yet other places he appears to demand a comprehensive philosophy of history that would give nationalist supporters the same certainty that Communists derived from the (alleged) verities of dialectical materialism.[30] Yet it was hardly reasonable of him to expect a body such as the Commission of Inquiry to deliver on the first or second of these demands, while the third was always a pipe dream.

While those privileged to have known him can confirm that Phil Williams eschewed conventional 'respectability', he was nevertheless doubtful of the suggestion that Plaid Cymru should attempt to pursue several strategies at the same time by encompassing the role of political party, pressure group and an incubator of alternative institutions. He also opposed the idea that Plaid Cymru should – or indeed, could – coordinate and provide leadership to the national movement as a whole. Rather, he wanted Plaid Cymru to focus on the 'unheroic and unglamorous' but

28 *Report of the Plaid Cymru Commission of Inquiry*, p. 111.
29 See *Report of the Plaid Cymru Commission of Inquiry*, pp. 13–16.
30 See *Report of the Plaid Cymru Commission of Inquiry*, pp. 94–5.

'entirely essential' function of a political party. The point was to fulfil 'one role well', and that was not possible if energies were dissipated in other directions.[31]

Williams also highlighted the tensions that arose in a context in which Plaid Cymru was attempting to secure radical change to the political system (by promoting self-government) while at the same time seeking to improve Wales's position within the prevailing order (by gaining concessions such as compensation for quarrymen, the establishment of S4C, and so on). Didn't these objectives sometimes conflict? Without doubt, there was an element of refighting the battles of the second half of the 1970s at work in all of this – a period when Phil Williams felt that his party had sold its soul by lending unconditional support to Labour's plans to create a devolved assembly that would have been so weak 'that it could only discredit' Plaid Cymru's long-term aspirations for Wales.[32] The tension between reform and revolution is familiar to students of both progressive/revolutionary movements and critical social theory, and Phil Williams's proposed solution – focusing exclusively on changing the system – was hardly adequate. Then again, neither is denying the existence of this tension a sufficient response.

Although his observations about political philosophy and strategy are interesting and sometimes very perceptive, the main interest of the minority report lies in the manner in which Phil Williams rejects some central elements of the intellectual legacy bequeathed to his party by Saunders Lewis – elements that the authors of the main report had accepted. On the first page of his commentary, Williams claims that the term 'independence' is 'the only correct word to describe the constitutional status we seek'. Indeed, he went further. Independence, he argued:

> is the term understood throughout the world. I find the term 'self-government' pompous, moralistic and comic, with overtones

31 *Report of the Plaid Cymru Commission of Inquiry*, p. 109. It is also noteworthy that Phil Williams wanted the party to concentrate its efforts on local government. This was also Saunders Lewis's view, of course, and Williams justified his position on the matter in similar terms (see pp. 104–6).

32 *Report of the Plaid Cymru Commission of Inquiry*, p. 97.

of Samuel Smiles. Over 100 nations in the world have gained 'Independence' this century. Let Wales follow their example.[33]

In addition, he launched a vigorous attack on the central position allotted to the Welsh language, which the main report regarded as the 'carrier of our history, our culture and our traditions'. This, he said, was 'to ignore and insult a very large part of our history, culture and traditions'.[34] Phil Williams wanted to emphasise other foundation stones of Welsh identity in addition to the Welsh language, including the Welsh socialist tradition, an awareness of the history of Wales, Anglo-Welsh literature and a knowledge of the landscape and people of Wales, all of which were in his view equally valid.[35] Again, some of this criticism appears unfair. As we have seen, his fellow commissioners had adopted a broad, pluralistic and permissive definition of Welsh identity. Even so, Williams's criticism can perhaps be defended on the grounds that it was a fair characterisation of the general tone of the main report. It was certainly a fair characterisation of the general tone of Gwynfor Evans's leadership. He may well have been the true target of Williams's words.

In the same context, Phil Williams's stress on the socialist tradition as one of the cornerstones of Welsh national identity is also significant. Indeed, it is for him this tradition 'which still offers the greatest measure of national unity'.[36] Once again, such comments were obviously targeted at Gwynfor Evans and the kind of thinking for which he had been such a tireless spokesperson. A post-religious, anti-temperance, English-speaking and politically socialist Welshness was just as valid as the kind of Nonconformist, rural, Welsh-speaking Welshness feted by the man who, even then, remained Plaid Cymru president. Turning left, therefore, meant not only embracing the kind of values and worldview that Phil Williams and his like were passionate about. It also meant

---

[33] *Report of the Plaid Cymru Commission of Inquiry*, p. 94 n. Scottish-born Samuel Smiles (1812–1904), was the original celebrity self-help guru. His name has become a byword for self-righteousness.

[34] *Report of the Plaid Cymru Commission of Inquiry*, p. 102.

[35] *Report of the Plaid Cymru Commission of Inquiry*, pp. 102–3.

[36] *Report of the Plaid Cymru Commission of Inquiry*, p. 102.

embracing an alternative vision of Welshness: one that was in many ways more inclusive than the one championed by Saunders Lewis and by Gwynfor Evans in his wake. This was a vision which regarded the forms of Welshness that existed in Merthyr (if not quite in Radnorshire!) as being just as valid as those found in Meirionnydd. Thus, while the majority report had proposed that some of the party's old shibboleths – in particular, its commitment to a third way – should be cast aside, Phil Williams's minority report proposed going much further. He wanted to jettison the remainder of the Saundersian intellectual legacy as it pertained to understandings of Welsh identity. While the majority report could certainly be interpreted as allowing for large steps in the same direction, that was not sufficient for Phil Williams. He felt that it was past time for a clear public declaration that the party's understanding of Wales had changed and that Plaid Cymru had been completely transformed. An evolutionary adaptation of the party's previous attitudes and policies was not sufficient: what was required was much more fundamental than that.

This was also the central message of another left-wing critique of the report published in the spring of 1981, a critique that was utterly damning of the work of Dafydd Wigley and his fellow commissioners. Indeed, it was so damning that its publication will undoubtedly have occasioned (or further exacerbated) tensions within the party – after all, one of its joint authors was Wigley's fellow Member of Parliament, Dafydd Elis-Thomas.[37] He and his co-author Emyr Wynn Williams railed against its various deficiencies, time and again castigating the report and its authors for their 'extremely conservative stance', their 'intense conservatism' and, indeed, their 'utterly conservative stance'. They were also accused of 'nauseating paternalism', 'ideological dogmatism' and of providing an analysis that was 'utterly irrelevant and unreal'. Their

---

[37] Emyr W. Williams and Dafydd Elis-Thomas, 'Commissioning national liberation', *The Bulletin of Scottish Politics*, 2 (spring 1981), 139–55. Although this essay was published in Scotland, its impact was clearly felt among the upper echelons of Plaid Cymru and the Welsh national movement more generally. Dafydd Wigley's autobiography, for example, demonstrates that he was fully aware of its contents; see *Dal Ati*, p. 139. Interestingly, he fails to mention the essay's authors by name!

recommendation that the party should embrace 'decentralised socialism' as an objective is also dismissed. It was nothing more than a roundabout recognition of the strength of the party's left.[38] The commissioners were deemed to be trapped in the same-old ideological ruts of the past. While the minority report was more warmly received, there were substantial faults here too. Most fundamentally, Phil Williams was guilty of a 'fundamental misconception' regarding the nature and location of power within society.

Elis-Thomas and Emyr Wynn Williams believed that the task from now on was to ask 'the national question' in completely new terms:

> We are determined that the national question in Wales be no longer answered in the negative because it is couched merely in the narrowest of cultural terms. We are determined that it shall be asked of and by and for the Welsh working class on the basis of a Welsh class politics which seeks to confront and subvert the present social and economic system in Wales, by working through and beyond the Labour Party as the arbiter and container of the status quo … Our commitment is to the making of the future of Wales, not the safeguarding of its past.[39]

To ensure that this enormous task could be undertaken successfully, a fundamentally different Plaid Cymru had to be created:

> It is not a case of adopting positions which will 'appeal' to the Welsh working class. It is a case of positioning ourselves as a party at the service of that class. And, through that class, at the service of a new national and international economic and political order.[40]

In short, the nationalism of the past had to be abandoned and replaced by an analysis firmly anchored in Marxism.

---

38 Williams and Elis-Thomas, 'Commissioning national liberation', 146, 147, 152, 148, 143.
39 Williams and Elis-Thomas, 'Commissioning national liberation', 154.
40 Williams and Elis-Thomas, 'Commissioning national liberation', 155.

Plaid Cymru was divided about the way forward, with the party's two Members of Parliament associated with different factions. These divisions were further complicated and exacerbated by a tendency to adopt a deliberately aggressive language when engaging with different points of view. It was not enough to oppose arguments: doubt had to be cast as to the sincerity of their proposers. It was in this atmosphere that Plaid Cymru's annual conference met in Carmarthen later in 1981. There were two key items on the conference agenda. First, delegates had to discuss and decide upon a lengthy motion – and various related amendments to it – based on the Commission of Inquiry's recommendations concerning the organisation and objectives of Plaid Cymru. Secondly, they would choose a successor to Gwynfor Evans as party president, with Dafydd Wigley and Dafydd Elis-Thomas competing for that honour.

Few other conferences in the party's history can have been as dramatic – or confusing. Among the dramatis personae: Gwynfor Evans, in his own political backyard, attending his final conference as president and, unbeknownst to many of his most faithful supporters, about to make his final important contribution to deciding the ideological direction of his party – by performing an astonishing U-turn; representatives of the party's left who viewed 1979 as confirmation of the complete bankruptcy of Plaid Cymru's previous ideas and strategies and who were determined to seize the initiative; and representatives of the more traditional wing of the party who were stunned by the ferocity of the left's attacks on their alleged 'conservatism' and convinced that adopting its 'dogmatic' programme would only further weaken Plaid.

The left was victorious in the battle to decide the party's formal response to the recommendations of the Research Commission. It regarded committing the party to policies based on 'community socialist' values as insufficient. Rather, they pressed an amendment committing the party to the objective of establishing a 'devolved socialist state' for Wales. Over a decade later, Dafydd Wigley remained harshly critical of this change, believing that it gave the party's 'objectives an Eastern European flavour':

For me, Plaid Cymru's objective was a democratic state. Within such a state … we should, as a party, espouse community socialist policies. [But] it would be a matter for the people of Wales to choose the kind of government they would … A 'socialist state' raised doubt as to whether this right would exist.[41]

The biggest surprise for Wigley was that this fundamental revision to the party's aims was carried thanks to support from the unlikeliest of sources – no less than Gwynfor Evans! There has been much speculation as to why he was persuaded to support an amendment that went way beyond the commission's recommendation – which was itself heretical in the context of Gwynfor Evans's previous beliefs – and support the views of what was characterised as the 'hard left'.[42] But the net result was that Evans's support was enough to persuade many of his most loyal supporters to follow suit. As a result, the motion received the requisite two-thirds majority that would allow reform of the party's constitution.

But it was Wigley himself who won the vote to succeed Evans, defeating his fellow member of parliament by 273 votes to 212. It was a bruising campaign: Wigley himself admitted that 'there was too much enthusiasm on both sides'.[43] While the result was interpreted as a victory for the 'right', what is both ironic and very striking is that this was a battle fought on the left of the political spectrum by two prospective leaders who, for the first time in the party's history, were happy to define themselves in those terms. Witness, for example, the second priority Wigley outlined for his presidency (the first was returning self-government to the political agenda), namely to 'attract … wide support

---

41   Wigley, *Dal Ati*, p. 142. Note that Wigley speaks here of a 'socialist state' rather than a 'devolved socialist state' although the latter is the wording used in the successful amendment.

42   Gwynfor Evans's post hoc justification of his own actions – namely that the change was merely a matter of semantics because the policies remained unchanged – would have been more credible had he supported the Commission of Inquiry's position. But by embracing a 'devolved socialist state', he went much further than it had envisaged. Neither does Rhys Evans's excellent biography provide a definitive explanation for his behaviour (see *Gwynfor*, p. 455).

43   Wigley, *Dal Ati*, p. 143.

from the political centre-left for a programme of practical policies'. Thus, although the member for Caernarfon claimed that he had no 'interest in labels', and even as he committed himself to the 'peaceful, cooperative and internationalist values that Gwynfor worked so hard to promote', he nonetheless adopted conventional ideological labels to describe his and his own campaign's position on the political spectrum.[44] It was not only the party's leader that had changed.

In the aftermath of the conference, the editor of *Y Faner* – a weekly publication that was generally supportive of the left's case – sought to put the most positive possible gloss on the two results. According to Jennie Eirian Davies:

> From one perspective, it might be thought that what was witnessed in Carmarthen was strangely inconsistent: electing Dafydd Wigley as President, while incorporating Dafydd Elis-Thomas's ideology into the Constitution. But perhaps this is the very combination of elements that will ensure a successful composite whole ... It could be an exciting time in the history of Plaid if it now succeeds in harnessing the vision and energy of the two Dafydds. Because they both have a very special contribution to make.[45]

This was an extremely optimistic reading – more aspiration than analysis, perhaps. By then the intellectual tide within the party and wider national movement was flowing strongly in the direction of Dafydd Elis-Thomas and his supporters – 'a young, enthusiastic crowd', according to Wigley.[46] It was the member for Meirionnydd that 'expressed the spirit of the times'. Elis-Thomas and his followers regarded the Commission of Inquiry's adoption of conventional political language to describe Plaid Cymru's position, as well as their locating of the party on the left or the centre-left of the ideological spectrum, as thin gruel.[47] Something far more substantial than this would be required. Wigley went on

44 Wigley, *Dal Ati*, pp. 138, 136.
45 *Y Faner*, 6 November 1981, 2; translation.
46 Wigley, *Dal Ati*, p. 136.
47 Cynog Dafis, *Mab y Pregethwr* (Talybont: Y Lolfa, 2005), p. 155.

to experience a difficult, frustrating and rather unsuccessful time as president. The party was in an extremely difficult position after 1979; and he found himself in a difficult position within the party. In this sense – and in this sense only – it was perhaps fortunate that he remained in post for only a brief period. In the summer of 1984, he announced that he would be standing down as party president following a further deterioration in the health of two of his sons, both of whom suffered from a cruel, incurable illness.[48] In Plaid Cymru's annual conference held that year in Lampeter, Dafydd Elis-Thomas was duly elected to the presidency in his place. Not only was Plaid Cymru to be a determinedly left-wing party, it would also be led by a man who was (at that time) the chief spokesperson for that position.

Radical Wales

The left has always had a substantial presence in Plaid Cymru. A number of its earliest and most faithful members, such as D. J. Williams and Kate Roberts, were former members of the Independent Labour Party, and their commitment to the values represented by the ILP did not diminish after they changed their partisan allegiance. Indeed, as has already been discussed, there can be no doubt that the overwhelming majority of the party's members during the interwar period were on the left (or centre-left) of the left-right political spectrum, this even as the party's leader espoused a rather different position. After the war, the beliefs and views promoted by the party were those which we associate with the left or the liberal left. Nevertheless, even those prominent party figures who were most obviously progressive in terms of their political convictions – such as D. J. and Nöelle Davies, to name only two – strongly rejected any label that located them on the 'left' of the political spectrum. They did not consider themselves to be

---

48   Different aspects on this heart-rending story are recounted with an exceptional dignity in a radio interview with Elinor Bennett republished in *Arcade*, 5 March 1982, and in Dafydd Wigley, *O Ddifri* (Caernarfon: Gwasg Gwynedd, 1992), pp. 151–70.

socialists and neither did they wish to be called left wing. As we have seen, they tried to delineate a third way and most ordinary members were apparently content to follow them along this path. It is true that there were a few members including Dafydd Jenkins and Phil Williams, who were proud to call themselves socialists and who played prominent and respected roles in the life of the party. But neither they nor the activities of short-lived groups such as 'Mudiad Gwerin' succeed in weakening the party's faith in the righteousness of its alternative approach.[49] While there were signs by the second half of the 1970s that the self-declared left within Plaid Cymru was both strengthening and mobilising, there is nothing to suggest that their efforts would have been more successful were it not for the ideological vacuum created by 1979.[50] They certainly would not have been *as* successful. But the results of the referendum and subsequent general election meant that the previously dominant intellectual tradition within the party appeared completely broken. Only the left offered a way forward.

The left raised its banner very soon after the general election. Dafydd Elis-Thomas contributed an article to the summer 1979 issue of *Cyffro*, a journal published by the Communist Party in Wales, titled 'Cymru – Be nesa?' (Wales – What next?) In it he called on his fellow party members to adopt a left-wing analysis of the problems that faced their country.[51] The Plaid Cymru Summer School was held at Dolgellau in August to discuss the

49 The lack of support for Mudiad Gwerin may be partly explained by the fact that its views were quasi-Marxist – even quasi-Stalinist – in nature. If the Irish Free State was a primary source of inspiration for the bulk of party members in the interwar years and Denmark in the post-war period (see Volume Two of this study), then based on the evidence of Mudiad Gwerin's internal papers, it seems that its members regarded the Soviet Union as a model for emulation. The Mudiad Gwerin archive, including the book containing minutes from their meetings, is preserved in the library of Bangor University.

50 There is a revealing letter in Phil Williams's papers sent to him by Dafydd Wigley on 27 September 1977, referring to the dissatisfaction expressed to him by a group of councillors who had attended the Plaid Cymru conference on local government and been surprised by the 'extreme left-wing tone' of some of their fellow delegates. The councillors were considering establishing a 'Social Democrat movement within Plaid Cymru to withstand what they regard as the swing to the left'. It is clear from the letter that this was not the first time that Williams and Wigley had discussed the matter.

51 Dafydd Elis-Thomas, 'Cymru – Be nesa?', *Cyffro: Cylchgrawn Farcsaidd i Gymru*, summer 1979, 21–4.

way forward for the national movement. The answer had been foreseen in the nature of the programme arranged for the attendees: a lecture by Robin Okey on the lessons of Yugoslavia, a lecture by Merfyn Jones on the quarrymen of north Wales and a lecture by Robert Griffiths on S. O. Davies.[52] The way forward was to bridge the divide between socialism and nationalism. In September, a pamphlet was published by Gareth Miles and Robert Griffiths – including a foreword by Dafydd Elis-Thomas – titled *Socialism for the Welsh People*.[53] Even though its authors were commencing their journeys out of Plaid Cymru as it was being written and as a result did not play a direct role in the activities of the Plaid Cymru left in subsequent years, it was nonetheless a significant publication.[54] It set out what was, in effect, an intellectual agenda for the left. Abstracting a little from the text, the task of the nationalist left was:

1. to develop an alternative interpretation of Wales's situation (and the wider context within which Wales had existed historically). Crucially, this interpretation would include:
   - a critique of Plaid Cymru, and
   - a critique of the labour movement in Wales, and in particular the Labour Party;

---

[52] One of these contributions can be seen in Robin Okey, *The Lessons of Yugoslavia: Industrial Democracy for Wales* (Aberystwyth: Plaid Cymru, n.d.).

[53] Gareth Miles and Robert Griffiths, *Socialism for the Welsh People*, foreword by Dafydd Elis-Thomas (Caerdydd: Cyhoeddiadau Cleglen, 1979).

[54] *Socialism for the Welsh People* was the foundational document for the Welsh Socialist Republican Movement, a movement that dispersed in 1982 following pressure from the police. Miles and Griffiths subsequently joined the Communist Party; see 'Why I left Plaid Cymru … Gareth Miles is interviewed by Siân Edwards', *Radical Wales*, 1, winter 1983, 4–5. Miles had already published *Cymru Rydd, Cymru Gymraeg, Cymru Sosialaidd* under the auspices of Cymdeithas yr Iaith Gymraeg in 1972, a pamphlet translated into English and published 'on behalf' of Plaid Cymru in 1973 (Gareth Meils [*sic*], *A Free Wales, A Welsh Wales, A Socialist Wales* (Caerdydd: Cyhoeddiadau Cymru Cyf., n.d. [but 1973])). This reminds us that any comprehensive effort to trace the development of the political thought of the nationalist left in Wales during the period under consideration in this study must also address the relationships between different individuals and factions within, inter alia, Plaid Cymru, Cymdeithas yr Iaith Gymraeg, the Communist Party, the Labour Party, the Welsh Republicans, the Socialist Republicans and a myriad other small parties and groups. This is beyond the scope of the present work.

2. to outline an alternative political programme commensu-
   rate with the challenges faced by Wales. This would entail
   answering the following key and closely related questions,
   namely:
   - which social group or groups that had (potentially,
     at least) the means to implement this alternative pro-
     gramme? and
   - how might that group or groups be encouraged to do so?

The left's attitudes and proposed solutions to all of this evolved
over time. Indeed, the left's demise as a creative intellectual influence by the end of the 1980s can be attributed to increasing
doubts as to whether it could provide any credible answers to
the second set of challenges. The important point here, however, is that this – broadly speaking – was the left's *problematique*.
Engaging with it resulted in a notably ambitious intellectual project containing with it important historiographical and theoretical dimensions, as well as complex and sophisticated discussions
about appropriate strategy and tactics. Even if the project was
ultimately unsuccessful, it represented an exceptionally creative
period that continues to influence Plaid Cymru today.

Miles and Griffiths believed that Marxism held the key. The
Marxist interpretation of history allowed the dynamics of historical development to be revealed. In a few pages, they sketched
the history of Wales as viewed through its prism: a tribal Wales
conquered and absorbed by Edward I's more productive, feudal
order; Wales's failure to develop its own national bourgeoisie as
feudalism gave way to capitalism, this because the bourgeoisie
in Wales was either foreign or a segment of a native population
that had become thoroughly British because of the ways in which
the state-empire defended and guaranteed their class interests;
and the absence of a national bourgeoisie ensuring that it was the
petty-bourgeoisie who were the leaders in Welsh life during the
nineteenth century, with their efforts in the fields of religion and
education, in particular, serving to anglicise and render Wales
even more British. This analysis formed the basis for the authors'
critique of Plaid Cymru, a party that was established when a

section of the 'Welsh Nonconformist petty-bourgeoisie' rejected 'the traditional British allegiance of its class'.[55] Despite its 'socialist fringe', it had continued to be the party of the Nonconformist petty-bourgeoisie, and had thus continued to embody all its worst features: 'compromise, cowardice, vacillation, gradualism and opportunism'.[56] Brutal! That said, the treatment of the labour movement was perhaps even more severe. In the absence of a normal class structure in Wales (a national bourgeoisie competing with a Welsh proletariat within a framework of state institutions created through the efforts of the former), the Welsh working class was prey to all the pathologies of the British labour movement:

> *Economism* (an obsession within the trade union movement with wages and work conditions, to the exclusion of such matters as theory, and working-class history and culture), *Reformism* (bargaining in Parliament and the workplace for improvements within Capitalism, not fighting to install Socialism), *Philistinism* (an aversion to or sneering contempt for intellectualism and culture of any kind) and *British Nationalism* (a fear or dislike of 'foreigners' and an ignorance or animosity towards Welsh, Scottish and Irish nationhood).[57]

Because of these influences, the labour movement and the Labour Party in Wales abandoned their early interest in home rule. Instead, Labour itself became home to 'centralist, British Nationalist place-seekers'; a party that did more than any other party to undermine a Welsh identity.[58] The referendum result was a reflection of the destructive effects of this combination of a timid nationalism and a labour movement served only to reinforce the inferiority complex of Welsh.[59]

If Marxism was at the root of their diagnosis, it was also fundamental to the remedy that they proffered. According to Miles and

---

55 Miles and Griffiths, *Socialism for the Welsh People*, p. 12.
56 Miles and Griffiths, *Socialism for the Welsh People*, pp. 12, 25.
57 Miles and Griffiths, *Socialism for the Welsh People*, p. 14; emphasis in the original.
58 Miles and Griffiths, *Socialism for the Welsh People*, p. 16.
59 Miles and Griffiths, *Socialism for the Welsh People*, p. 24.

Griffiths, the working class is the only class in Wales whose interests are 'intrinsically in conflict' with the interests of the British
state.[60] The comfortable, 'good Welshmen' of the traditional
nationalist movement could be bought and corrupted. So too
could the leaders of the labour movement. Indeed, was it not the
case that a number of valleys Labour MPs lived in the south-east
of England? But this was not true of the working class itself. It
suffered the consequences of the ways in which the whole social,
economic and cultural life of their country has been distorted by
its role as an internal colony of the British state. Only by establishing their own independent and socialist Welsh state – a Welsh
republic – could they hope to change this. The words of Welsh
communist J. Roose Williams words were called in aid:

> Wales's misfortune is that the struggle for national freedom and the
> struggle for economic and social justice should have been separat-
> ed for the last fifty years and more. As a result, both sides have
> only won a crumb or two here and there. Very little will come of
> our efforts as socialists or nationalists unless we manage to unite
> both struggles. When we manage to harness together the two most
> dynamic forces in the life of the nation, the desire for freedom and
> the desire for a complete society, we will see some astounding
> changes.[61]

The task was, therefore, on the one hand, to convince nationalists
that there could be no future for Wales unless the working class
played the central role in the battle to secure it, and on the other
hand, to convince socialists that the national question was also
key to their struggle.

Easier said than done, of course. The authors hoped to bring
together all those in different parties who shared their vision
in an 'interim organisation', a Welsh socialist republican movement.[62] That movement's task would be to hold protests and
to organise educational and research programmes, all with the

60 Miles and Griffiths, *Socialism for the Welsh People*, p. 13.
61 Miles and Griffiths, *Socialism for the Welsh People*, p. 23.
62 Miles and Griffiths, *Socialism for the Welsh People*, p. 30.

aim of loosening the grip of the governing class on society and convincing the working class that the future was in its hands. Referring specifically to the Plaid Cymru left, and while wishing them well in their efforts to take the party in a thoroughly anti-British, socialist direction, Miles and Griffiths offer the following warning:

> in the event of the 'Rural Right' keeping its grip on the purse-strings and the internal levers of power, Socialists and Republicans in Plaid Cymru should have the courage – as well as the strength and organisation – to leave Plaid Cymru and contribute to the setting-up of an independent Welsh Socialist Party.[63]

As we shall see, this would not be the last time that such words would be uttered.

Dafydd Elis-Thomas clearly agreed with much of the content in *Socialism for the Welsh People*. The central theme of his preface to the pamphlet was the need for nationalists to identify with the struggle of the Welsh working class and for the left to acknowledge the importance and validity of the struggle for national freedom and thus create a new nationalist-left synthesis.[64] Although his admiring references to Rudolf Bahro, Raymond Williams and Jean-Paul Sartre were proof of the fact that he, unlike Miles and Griffiths, was no orthodox Marxist-Leninist – the appeal of Marxism is clear in Elis-Thomas's essay in *Cyffro*, where he suggested that it was time for cultural nationalists to develop a Marxist analysis of the situation facing the Welsh language and Wales.[65] Its appeal is also echoed in his castigation of his own party's weaknesses. Too many nationalists had forgotten that the working class made up the majority of the nation and had failed to extend their loyalty to the only group in society that had the ability to emancipate Wales. Too many ignored the economic reality faced by their fellow countrymen.[66] In an explosive review of D. Hywel Davies's work, *The*

---

63 Miles and Griffiths, *Socialism for the Welsh People*, p. 25.
64 Miles and Griffiths, *Socialism for the Welsh People*, pp. 3–4.
65 Elis-Thomas, 'Cymru – Be nesa?', 21 and *passim*.
66 For example, Dafydd Elis-Thomas, 'Let's cut out the ambiguity', *Arcade*, November 1980, 11.

Welsh Nationalist Party 1925–45: A Call to Nationhood, bearing the
suggestive title of 'Freud Cymru', he set out to discuss the party's
past in inflammatory terms:

> I'd always known it was bad from the bits of oral history picked
> up from my father's generation, but it's another thing to see ... that
> it was as bad as this ... Put ... bluntly ... these intellectual leaders
> were a bunch of ultra-reactionary 'fascist' sympathisers, as their
> contemporary critics alleged. After such a gruelling session of psy-
> chotherapy I will never let anyone get away with calling me a 'na-
> tionalist'. And I will never call myself that, if I ever did.[67]

One can only imagine the response of his own party's older generation to these words.

However, Elis-Thomas was equally scathing about the Labour
Party. He saw Labour not as the promoters of radical change but
rather as one of the main obstacles to any such change. Even the
great hero of the Labour left in the early 1980s, Tony Benn, was
no more than a spokesperson for a form of 'English nationalist
radical resistance'.[68] In Wales, Labour had maintained the Welsh
working class in a condition of 'servility' for two generations.[69]
Further afield, he condemned the failure of 'English Marxists and
their degenerate cousins in the Labour movement' to comprehend 'the liberating force of culture', while wondering in amaze-
ment at the 'mental flexibility and duplicity' which allowed them
to argue 'for the continued colonisation of the Welsh people in
the name of the unity of the working classes across Britain'. These
people were 'the most fiendish guardians of the status quo'.[70]

As we have seen, Elis-Thomas felt that the only way forward for
the national movement was to identify with the struggles of the
working class. Plaid Cymru's proper function was to offer its services to the working class and assist it in the task of emancipating

67 Dafydd Elis-Thomas, 'Freud Cymru', *Radical Wales*, 1 (winter 1983), p. 18.
As discussed further in Wyn Jones, *The Fascist Party in Wales?*
68 Dafydd Elis-Thomas, 'Blowing his own trumpet', *Arcade*, 2 October 1981, 13.
69 Dafydd Elis-Thomas is quoted in 'Plaid Conference', *Arcade*, 20 February
1981, 6.
70 Elis-Thomas, 'Cymru – be nesa?', p. 23; translation.

itself and thereby emancipating Wales.[71] This meant political action on several levels – as a conventional political party focused on gaining votes but also by throwing itself into the social and industrial battles of the working class. Responding to Dafydd Wigley's rebuke that the left was navel-gazing – obsessed with fruitless ideological discussions that had no connection with real-world problems – Dafydd Elis-Thomas emphasised the concrete implications of the left's beliefs: 'We have got very wet this year on account of our political ideology. On the People's March for Jobs, on picket lines, on factory closures, sit-ins, occupations, we have got very wet this year.'[72]

It need hardly be emphasised that all of this represented a completely new vision of both Wales and Plaid Cymru. Even so, it received widespread support across the party. In the minds of external observers – as well as internal opponents – Dafydd Elis-Thomas may well have been regarded as the embodiment of the party's left, but he was far from a lone voice. Almost all the party's intellectuals were supportive, a situation reflected in the fact that the movement's publications were in the hands of supporters of the left. It is important to emphasise, too, that the project was supported by both Welsh speakers and those who did not speak the language. There may have been substantial factions in both Carmarthen and Caernarfon who were suspicious, but there was support for the new direction in Meirionnydd (naturally) and Ceredigion. Plaid Cymru's leftward shift coincided with a similar shift to the left in Cymdeithas yr Iaith Gymraeg, a movement that enjoys a special symbolic status amongst nationalists. While there is a tendency to portray the ideological disputes within Plaid Cymru at the start of the 1980s as a battle between the Welsh-speaking rural 'right' and the industrial English-speaking 'left', this interpretation represents a grave misunderstanding of the dynamics of the time. Following the cataclysm of 1979, the

---

71 As well as Emyr W. Williams and Dafydd Elis-Thomas, 'Commissioning National liberation', see also the defiant statement of this belief in Dafydd Elis-Thomas, 'Sixties policies are old hat', *Welsh Nation*, July 1981, 3–4.
72 Elis-Thomas, 'Sixties policies are old hat', 4.

left was on the march throughout both the party and the wider national movement.

As well as an absence of any credible effort by the party's traditional leaders to map out an alternative direction, another development that gave the left credibility was that there were some in the Labour movement in the early 1980s who were willing to consider seriously the possibility of cooperating with the nationalists. In particular, some of those trade unionists under siege from the social and economic policies of the Conservative government and disappointed by the supine response of the Labour Party were willing to work alongside Plaid members. A good working relationship was developed with the Iron and Steel Trades Confederation (ISTC) and the National Union of Blastfurnacemen, Ore Miners, Coke Workers and Kindred Trades, during the steel dispute of the winter of 1979–80.[73] The Wales TUC even pondered the possibility of calling a general strike in Wales to oppose the impact of the government's policies on the country.[74] The same organisation also investigated the possibility of organising cooperative enterprises in Wales based on the model of the famous enterprises in Arrasate (Mondragón) in the Basque Country.[75] Although nothing came of the efforts to call a general strike, and even if the results of efforts to establish new cooperative enterprises were not particularly impressive, the fact that some of the leaders of a body as stolid and unadventurous as the Wales TUC were prepared to consider such options is itself proof of the ways in which the despair and frustration of the period was generating new and unexpected possibilities. It may well be that the nationalist left tended to read far too much into every positive hint from the unions, but in the aftermath of the 1979 referendum

[73] The *Welsh Steelman*, a paper supporting the steelworkers' strike, was published as an appendix to the March 1980 issue of *Welsh Nation*.

[74] See Joe England, *The Wales TUC 1974–2004: Devolution and Industrial Politics* (Cardiff: University of Wales Press, 2004), pp. 42–57. I am reliably informed – but cannot properly verify – that there were discussions between nationalists and some union activists about the possibility of organising joint law-breaking protests. If so, then nothing seems to have come from this.

[75] See, inter alia, 'A Mondragón is possible here', *Arcade*, 18 September 1981, 6–7.

and Thatcher's victory, there was a natural tendency to magnify the significance of every ray of light no matter how faint.

In June 1981 the Plaid Cymru left established its own internal organisation – the National Left (Chwith Genedlaethol) – to develop and promote its views. With Dafydd Elis-Thomas as one if its founders, and with Emyr Wynn Williams providing much of the intellectual energy and direction, it proved to be an influential force in the life of the party. Indeed, it was almost certainly the most effective internal pressure group in its history. Following the left's historic victory at the Carmarthen conference only a few months after its establishment, the National Left's activities focused on two main goals.

The first was the defensive. It sought to resist any efforts from the 'right', or more traditional wing of the party, to weaken or overturn Plaid Cymru's new commitment to a 'devolved socialist state'. Overturning was never a realistic possibility. As far as a 'right wing' existed within Plaid Cymru, it was weak both intellectually and organisationally. The internal pressure group Hydro, established in the aftermath of the 1982 party conference to counteract the influence of the National Left, was tiny.[76] Moreover, in calling on the party to return to a straightforward commitment to self-government without additional 'ideological' qualifications, it was calling for a 'return' to a standpoint that the party had never in fact embraced. Rather, as discussed in previous chapters, the party's main intellectual leaders from Saunders Lewis onwards had linked the cause of self-government to a much wider agenda – even if that was never described in conventional left-right terms. There was always much more to Plaid Cymru than a 'fundamentalist' focus on the constitutional question. In that respect, it was Hydro and not the National Left that was seeking to rub against the grain of party traditions.

The only real threats to the intellectual supremacy of the left were the efforts of the party's more traditional wing to dilute the

---

[76] The papers of the Hydro group – a body that remained in existence until 1987 – are in the National Library. According to the group's constitution, its principal aim was 'To re-establish self-government for Wales, unqualified by any ideological dogma, as the main aim of Plaid Cymru.'

new formal commitments by suggesting that the constitutional changes introduced at the Carmarthen conference did not, in fact, represent a fundamental change in programme or attitudes. This was an argument made by both Dafydd Wigley and Gwynfor Evans. In one of the volumes of his autobiography, Wigley mentions his desire at the time to persuade traditional supporters 'that there was no change in Carmarthen in terms of the body of our detailed policies, despite there having been a change in the wording of our aims'. Thus:

> While defending the fact that we were a 'socialist party' in the eyes of the world, I used the comparison of putting a label on a bottle of wine. The wine had not changed, for Plaid Cymru had always been a socialist party, rather than a capitalist one, from the very beginning, including during Saunders Lewis's time as leader. At the Carmarthen conference, Plaid voted to put a label on the bottle. This was done to help the people of Wales recognise the political wine held in the party's particular bottle. Those leaders familiar with every kind of political wine were able to recognise what we stood for a long time ago, but using the label made it easier for the rest of the citizens of Wales to know us as well, and therefore to trust us. This may have been a simple, superficial interpretation, but for a while it certainly helped to keep the party united.[77]

There was nothing simple about this, of course. Rather, it was part of a sophisticated strategy to repackage the events in Carmarthen in a way that made them consistent with the logic of the Commission of Inquiry's majority report. But for a left that had tasted victory in Carmarthen, such arguments were a source of anger and frustration. For them, the main purpose of their successful motions had been to denote a clear break with the past. They sought to make clear that the 'wine' of the Gwynfor Evans era – though orange juice would be more appropriate in his case – had been cast aside and replaced by a different, much headier brew. The very fact that Carmarthen was being interpreted

---

[77] Wigley, *Dal Ati*, pp. 146–7; translation.

in evolutionary rather than revolutionary terms – and that Saunders Lewis, of all people, was being presented as some kind of proto-socialist in order to facilitate that argument – was final evidence of the insincere and undemocratic attitudes of the 'traditionalists'. The left had to resist!

Doing this successfully, however, meant more than defending the changes achieved at Carmarthen. It was also necessary to develop the substance of the new commitments. This brings us to the second more positive aspect of the National Left's activities: its role in outlining a political vision and policy programme for the party, based on the left's analysis of Wales's past and present. The range of the left's intellectual ambitions is evident from the documents circulated among the National Left's members during 1982.[78] In 'Athroniaeth a rhaglen datblygiad y Chwith Genedlaethol' (The philosophy and development of the National Left) and 'Cymru annibynnol – 1983 a'r dyfodol pellach' (Independent Wales – 1983 and beyond), two pieces written by Emyr Wynn Williams, chair of the National Left, an attempt is made to lay the philosophical, historical and politico-economic foundations for an alternative version of Welsh nationalism.[79]

The first paper discusses the obstacles facing the National Left as it sought to establish its philosophic foundations, namely 'the skeletons of the ideas of the nationalist right' on the one hand, and the ideas of the 'revolutionary left, developed during the past 150 years and more' on the other. Both were 'by now either dead or calcified'.[80] This underlines an all-important point about the National Left: as well as delivering the (predictable) dig at the traditionalists of the national movement, the person who should be regarded as the main thinker of the National Left was always sharply critical of what still passed for Marxist orthodoxy. Thus,

[78] The following analysis is based on the large collection of National Left documents in Phil Williams's papers, now held in the National Library of Wales.

[79] The first paper was presented to a one-day conference organised by the National Left in Cardiff on 4 September 1982, and the second to the party's Summer School a few weeks previously which had 'devolved socialism' as its theme.

[80] Emyr Wynn Williams, 'Athroniaeth a rhaglen datblygiad y Chwith Genedlaethol', National Left conference, Cardiff (4 September 1982), p. 1; translation.

even as opponents of the new pressure group such as Gwynfor Evans tended to describe it as 'Marxist' – clearly as a means of belittling and marginalising – it was very clearly not Marxist-Leninist à la Miles and Griffiths.[81] Rather, what made the National Left such a creative intellectual force in the early 1980s was the fact that leading members did not feel constrained by a single dogmatic version of left-wing thought. Instead, they attempted to combine several different influences. As we shall see shortly, they were also prepared to analyse and interpret anew as circumstances changed. In short, their often-combative assertiveness was underpinned by a healthy dose of realism and pragmatism.

The structure of the argument presented in 'The philosophy and development of the National Left' echoes (one presumes unintentionally) the rhetorical form familiar from Gwynfor Evans's books and speeches. As with Evans, Williams's essays tended to commence from a historical discussion. In this case, emphasising the need to understand the state context within which Wales exists, he developed an analysis of the sixteenth-century Acts of Union seen as part of a process by which an imperial state set out to further marginalise both economically and culturally an already conquered nation. He goes onto champion the need to establish states on the basis of a 'national territorial unit' so as 'to enable the state to be an instrument for healthy economic and cultural policies'. The former party president of the party would have heartily approved of this, at least! He would also have approved of Williams's scorn towards metropolitan intellectuals – including those on the left – who remained indifferent in the face of imperialist oppression. But there were limits to the consensus. Williams was wary of those who saw 'the history of the nation as a linear development characterised by a constant battle to defend Welsh culture and attain a form of self-government' – or in other words, the approach to history embodied in *Aros Mae*. Rather, he emphasised that Wales had to understand and come to terms with the role it had played as 'a subordinate element within a state that was a metropolis for a global capitalist empire'. The

---

81 See Gwynfor Evans, 'Stirring things up', *Welsh Nation*, August 1981, 8.

imperialist nature of the British experience was not only of historic interest. In Williams's view, its effects continued to reverberate. For one thing, it had shaped the nature of the Labour Party, making it a fundamentally reactionary party; a party that hindered progressive developments both amongst the nations of the British state and internationally.[82]

'Independent Wales - 1983 and beyond' argues that the change in Plaid Cymru's objectives in 1981 represented a turning point in the history of the movement – at least insofar as it managed to withstand the efforts of the right to 'reinterpret the changes in the party's objectives adopted in Carmarthen in a way that diluted them completely'. One way of doing so was by providing a clear vision of the implications of the constitutional changes. In doing so, Emyr Wynn Williams focused on:

'the need for:
1. A WELSH SOCIALIST STATE promoting the development of;
2. A COMMUNITY SOCIALIST sector based on;
3. A NEW INTERNATIONAL ORDER.[83]

Mention of creating a 'decentralised socialist' sector within a Welsh state highlights an interesting aspect of the left's thinking in the early 1980s. As Dafydd Elis-Thomas evangelised on behalf of the left after 1979, he made regular mention of the size of the public sector in Wales.[84] If the number employed (at the time) in the nationalised industries were combined with the total of those employed by different parts of the state, he considered Wales to be home to one of the largest public sectors outside eastern Europe. Once the Carmarthen conference victory had made it necessary to ensure that there was some policy substance to the call for a 'devolved socialist state', there was discussion of the possibility of transforming this public sector in a way that would make it

---

[82] Williams, 'Athroniaeth a rhaglen datblygiad y Chwith Genedlaethol', pp. 2–3, 3, 6; translation.

[83] Emyr Wynn Williams, 'Cymru Annibynnol – 1983 a'r dyfodol pellach', Nationalist Left Summer School (1982), pp. 1, 3; translation, capitalisation in the original.

[84] See e.g. Dafydd Elis-Thomas, 'The state of the nation', *Arcade*, 6 March 1981, 15.

directly accountable to the people who worked in it, thereby creating the 'democratic socialist' nucleus within the new state. Even if the policy of breaking up the public sector materialising at the time had not rendered such ideas wholly academic, it is fair to say that no credible account of what this would actually mean in practice was ever formulated.

It is appropriate also to draw attention to two other elements of Williams's discussion. First, note the reference in the title of the paper to an 'Independent Wales'. In the first half of the 1980s, at least, the left was much more willing than the more traditional wing of the party to embrace the term 'independence' to describe the party's long-term objective. Indeed, it appears that their frequent use of the term was a means of differentiating themselves from – and tweaking the tail of – the 'petty-bourgeois' fuddy-duddies on the right. Another important element in Williams's commentary was the need for the left to decide on its attitude towards the leadership of the party (which remained, at the time, in the hands of Dafydd Wigley). It is in this context that we find this ambiguous if suggestive comment:

> As the only element within Plaid Cymru that takes the present objectives seriously, I believe it will be necessary for us to consider the stand we take in relation to the party leadership in three years' time. This should not, however, be a means of preventing us, in the meantime, from being active within it, but we must be aware of the limitations.[85]

In the dark days of the early 1980s, challenging for the party leadership – or even abandoning the party entirely – was never far from the left's agenda.

While Emyr Wynn Williams's extraordinary diligence made him unique – the term Stakhanovite would apply were it not for the Stalinist subtext – the left was able to call on impressive intellectual resources as it sought to give substance to decentralised socialism. Indeed, it is striking that the names associated

---

85 Williams, 'Cymru Annibynnol – 1983 a'r dyfodol pellach', p. 6; translation.

with the activities of the National Left, and the nationalist left in general, encompass a large swathe of a generation of humanities and social sciences academics in Wales, many of whom did not speak Welsh: Teresa Rees, Gareth Rees, Graham Day, Glyn Williams, Lynn Mainwaring, Gwyn A. Williams, David Reynolds, Charlotte Davies, and so on. If Penyberth was the key turning point in the relationship between Welsh-speaking intellectuals and Welsh nationalism, 1979 was a pivotal moment in the relationship between intellectuals who did not speak Welsh and the national movement.

One of the most important figures on the left was the economist, Phil Cooke. In 1983, he set about preparing a substantial discussion paper on the Welsh economy titled 'The decline must stop – let's build a new Wales', a document that became the basis for a motion on the party's economic policy passed at its annual conference in Treorchy later that year. The paper was a no-holds-barred critique of the state of Wales's economic foundations. Cooke's contention was that capitalists and those bureaucrats in charge of the nationalised industries were jointly responsible for the country's economic woes:

> The hard truth of the last twenty years is that Wales cannot afford Labourism any more than it can afford Capitalism … The private sector has been tried and found sadly wanting in Wales; more depressingly for a country with radical, collectivist traditions in its agricultural as well as industrial regions, state management … has been largely an exercise in black farce. The future of Wales now seems to lie in the force whose intelligence and imagination has been so sorely ignored in the past, the Welsh working classes.[86]

---

[86] Phil Cooke, 'The decline must stop – let's build a new Wales', National Left discussion paper, pp. 1–2; emphasis in the original. Elsewhere in the same document, it is interesting to note how suspicion of state control manifests itself in Cooke's views on housing policy. After criticising the bureaucracy and 'patronage' that was such an obvious characteristic of local council control over parts of the housing stock, he argued that a radical change 'from tenant to owner occupier' should be facilitated by reforming the way that houses are built, and ownership financed. This serves to underline yet again the extent to which the National Left was willing to challenge some of the views associated with the orthodox Marxist left.

But what did this mean on a practical level? In Cooke's view, it required the adoption of a three-part economic strategy that included:

1. an effort to revive Wales's coal and steel industries under the leadership of a Welsh Coal and Steel Board. A number of concrete ideas were proposed on the way forward, for example developing plans for producing oil and gas from coal, as well as producing for the international market with subsidies to allow the product to be sold at the international market price;
2. expanding the size of the public sector by developing more modern health and education facilities, providing appropriate housing for elderly people, and creating childcare provision for pre-school children;
3. providing support for job creation in the private sector by making subsidies conditional on an agreement by employers to provide fair conditions for the workforce – including worker participation in the management process.

In order to facilitate all of this, some kind of informal, central planning system would have to be created 'where upper and lower limits for output, prices, wages and employment are negotiated between worker representatives, the state in Wales, consumer groups and other special interest groups' including employers.[87] If all of this sounds simplistic and implausibly utopian in the current era of hyper-capitalism, it is only fair to note that, even at the time, there was an awareness of the potential problems with these recommendations. In an interesting speech at the Easter School of Plaid Cymru's youth movement in April 1984, Phil Cooke himself identified the deficiencies of decentralised socialism. Drawing on the experience of Hungary (at the time, the most prosperous economy in the eastern bloc), together with the work of economists like Alec Nove, he acknowledged the tension between efficiency and socialist values. In a socialist system where market discipline

87 Cooke, 'The decline must stop', p. 4.

was absent, the feckless could simply freeride on the efforts of the industrious. His conclusion, however, was that there was not one simple solution that could resolve every problem or tension. The world is imperfect. Although decentralised socialism would not usher in some human paradise, 'it might well be a realistic alternative to the current idleness, waste and alienation experienced by many under a declining capitalism'.[88] Given that Wales's economic life was in turmoil, with entire communities being thrown on the scrap heap as result, it is easy to understand the appeal of efforts to organise the economy on an alternative basis.

Another significant aspect of Cooke's economic ideas was his emphasis on sexual equality. In 'The decline must stop ...', he made clear that, 'Until women achieve an equal recognised standing (in reality not just in rhetoric) with men there can be no truly socialist state in Wales.'[89] This was an argument that the left (in particular) made with increasing insistency and consistency as the 1980s progressed. Generally speaking, equality between the sexes was not an issue to which the left nor the Welsh nationalist movement had paid much attention. It was largely absent from *Socialism for the Welsh People*, for example.[90] However, by 1981 a formal declaration committing Plaid Cymru to campaign for sexual equality was one of those reforms accepted by the party as a result of the left's successful intervention at the Carmarthen conference. At the same time, the party committed to promoting the status and position of women within the party itself through positive discrimination.[91]

One of the most energetic advocates of feminism in Plaid Cymru was that remarkable historian Gwyn A. Williams. When the former Communist joined the party on general election day in 1983, he brought with him many of the ideas of the Euro-Communists

88 The speech is available in Phil Williams's papers.
89 Cooke, 'The decline must stop', p. 8.
90 In fairness to Miles and Griffiths, they were clearly aware of the weaknesses of their pamphlet in this regard: 'The inferior position of women in different societies is worthy of far more attention than we can afford here': *Socialism for the Welsh People*, p. 28.
91 See 'Grassroots in the driving seat', *Arcade*, 13 November 1981, 6, and more generally Laura McAllister, *Plaid Cymru: The Emergence of a Political Party* (Bridgend: Seren, 2001), pp. 185–208.

as well as those of the 1960s New Left.[92] One of the most obvious characteristics of this kind of left-wing thinking was disillusionment with traditional Marxist view of the working class. For
orthodox Marxists, the working class was the Alpha and Omega
of socialism. Only this class possessed the means to revolutionise
society. More than that, it was the 'universal' or 'fundamental'
class whose emancipation would inevitably emancipate society
as a whole. Based on this assumption, Marxists tended to regard
every battle against social oppression as secondary to the class
struggle – this because emancipating the working class would
automatically eradicate every other form of oppression, be that
the oppression of women by men, the oppression of subject
nations by dominant ones, or oppression based on sexual prefer-
ence. Unsurprisingly, therefore, gaining the trust and support of
the working class was regarded as the only thing that mattered.

For the Euro-Communists, the kind of worldview and political
strategy that stemmed from this (ultimately metaphysical) belief
was simply not credible. Battles against forms of oppression were
equally valid and should not be subordinated to the class struggle. More than that, they argued that success in the class struggle
depended on the ability of the working class to ally itself effectively with other social groups. In short, there was more to the
emancipatory politics than the politics of class. The views of the
New Left were even more heretical: many thinkers associated
with it lost all faith in the ability of the working class to challenge the prevailing order – the working class had been absorbed
and tamed by it. Rather, they emphasised the leadership role that
other more marginal groups could play in the struggle to secure

92   Euro-Communism became an important influence within the communist
parties of western Europe towards the end of the 1970s. Its most important intellectual influences were the ideas of Antonio Gramsci and Enrico Berlinguer, the
leader of the Italian Communist Party between 1972 and 1982. As well as being
one of the first to discuss Gramsci's ideas in English, Williams contributed to the
journal *Marxism Today*, the most influential platform for Euro-Communist ideas in
the British Isles during the 1980s. There is an interesting discussion on Williams's
role in introducing Gramsci to a left-wing audience in Britain in David Forgacs,
'Gramsci and Marxism in Britain', *New Left Review*, I/176 (July–August 1989),
70–88.

radical social change, such as the unemployed, racial and ethnic minorities, students and so on.[93]

In an interview for the first issue of *Radical Wales* (winter 1983), Williams used his characteristic Gramsci-inflected language to emphasise the far-reaching potential of a coalition of women, the unemployed and those white-collar workers who were in boring and worthless jobs: 'They are all *disinherited* and are in theory a force which could shape themselves into a hegemonic bloc organised around the national terrain.'[94] With Gwyn A. Williams as an influential member of the journal's editorial board, along with Charlotte Davies, Siân Edwards and Jill Evans, three prominent feminists in the party's ranks, *Radical Wales* became an influential advocate for a 'synthesis' of feminist, socialist, pacifist and environmental themes.[95] The role of the first of these was regarded as absolutely central. In an editorial for a National Left newsletter circulated in 1984, Gwyn A. Williams went as far as referring to women as the 'fundamental class', around whom a new 'historical bloc' could be built.[96] Which was to suggest – translating from Gramscian – that it was women rather than the traditional working class who had the potential to be the focal point of an economic, political and social coalition that could overthrow the current order and build a better society.

In early winter 1984, with the miners' strike at its height, the most developed version of the left's vision for decentralised socialism was published in *Radical Wales* as 'Decentralism,

93   We should not overemphasise the *intellectual* differences between the New Left and the Euro-Communists for there was considerable overlap between their views.
94   'Gwyn Alf Williams interviewed by Phil Cooke', '… and why I joined!', *Radical Wales* (winter 1983), 6; emphasis from the original. It is interesting to note that Williams does not refer to the working class per se as part of this progressive coalition.
95   *Radical Wales* was published between winter 1983 and summer 1991. The editorial board included other respected academics such as Phil Cooke and Lynn Mainwaring. Plaid Cymru supported the publication financially even though it existed in an 'arm's length' relationship with the party. Two further issues appeared in 2000 and 2001, with many of the previous members of the editorial board associated with this revival. These later issues were not associated formally with Plaid Cymru; neither did they radiate the same élan or sense of direction that characterised the best issues of the original version. The absence of Gwyn A. Williams – who died in 1995 – may help explain this.
96   The National Left papers in Phil Williams's papers.

Socialism and Democracy' – with a Welsh-language version, 'Datganoli, Sosialaeth a Democratiaeth', published separately in pamphlet form.[97]

At its heart lay a rejection of the centralisation of power, be that economic, social or political. This was a sentiment with which both Saunders Lewis and Gwynfor Evans would have concurred. The essay's author, Phil Cooke, claimed that Wales – with its nationalised industries, its enormous and unaccountable public bureaucracy, and its degrading reliance on the state in the form of grants and unemployment benefits – was the most centralised country outside eastern Europe. Such centralisation was unhealthy and led to 'moral bankruptcy' by 'enfeebling imagination, creativity and will'. Indeed, underlining the point once again, 'Nowhere, other than perhaps in Eastern Europe, is this truer than in contemporary Wales.'[98] This could only be addressed by a political programme that would combine – in the words of the title – decentralism, socialism and democracy: a programme that aimed to undermine the power of both the capitalist class and the bureaucratic (often, Labourist) elite subjugating the Welsh people.

Restoring or reforming the welfare state was not enough. Cooke cited 'Swedish philosopher G. Olsson [who] had compared the statist welfare system with advising a freezing man to piss in his trousers – temporary relief at the expense of making the problem worse in the long term.'[99] (The older generation of party stalwarts may have blanched at the crudeness even while agreeing with the underlying sentiment.) What was needed was a more flexible and equal society. A society based on a mixed economy that took full advantage of the communications revolution; a society of 'active citizens' in which substantial power has been devolved to the level of local communes consisting of some

97 Phil Cooke, 'Decentralism, Socialism and Democracy', *Radical Wales*, 5 (winter 1984), 17–21 (also Phil Cooke, *Datganoli, Sosialaeth a Democratiaeth* (Aberystwyth: Plaid Cymru, 1984)). The editorial of that issue of *Radical Wales* makes clear that the intention of the article was to explain in more detail Plaid Cymru's objective of a 'decentralised, socialist, libertarian and independent [*sic*] state in Wales', p. 3.
98 Cooke, 'Decentralism, Socialism and Democracy', 18.
99 Cooke, 'Decentralism, Socialism and Democracy', 20.

20,000 to 50,000 people, and where the power of the central state has been reduced and reined in.[100]

Cooke believed that it was possible to form a coalition on the basis of such a political programme, a coalition that would transcend traditional class politics in the name of a 'new egalitarianism'. He foresaw three specific groups aligning. First, those within the present system who aspired to a better material life, that is, the working class (traditional or white collar), together with 'the vast army of the unemployed and semi-employed, young and old'. The second element of the coalition would be formed by those seeking equality within society, specifically women and ethnic minorities. As well as these two groups – described by Gwyn A. Williams as the 'real disinherited' – Cooke thought it would be possible to secure the support of the new 'knowledge-based class' for decentralised socialism. These were professionals 'operating in the post-industrial modes of production of the future'; a group that regarded the social and political patterns of the old industrial society as a fetter on the potential of the new forces of production. 'The demise of class politics and its replacement with a new egalitarianism, both more participatory and decentralised' was in the interests of both the 'real disinherited' and the 'knowledge-based' class.[101] This form of alternative politics was particularly relevant in the Welsh context. 'Perhaps Wales, with its peculiar combination of a large, declining working class, high unemployment, large numbers of alienated and exploited women, – a large public sector proletariat and its national consciousness, is the place where a mass movement can come together.'[102] Whatever the limitations and weaknesses of decentralised socialism – and to be fair to Cooke, he did not shy away from them – it was still 'morally superior to any other kind of social organisation I can think of'.[103] The task for Plaid Cymru – and for Wales – was to develop and implement it.

100 Cooke, 'Decentralism, Socialism and Democracy', 20–1.
101 The quotations in the above sentences derive from Cooke, 'Decentralism, Socialism and Democracy', 19.
102 Cooke, 'Decentralism, Socialism and Democracy', 19.
103 Cooke, 'Decentralism, Socialism and Democracy', 21.

The scope and ambition of Cooke's vision is undeniable. In this regard, it was characteristic of the intellectual contribution of the nationalist left during the first half of the 1980s. Casting our net widely, and recalling the agenda set out by Miles and Griffiths, we can identify notable contributions to our understanding of the ways in which contemporary Wales had been formed economically, socially and politically, with the work of Gwyn A. Williams among the most eminent. In addition, notable contributions to our understanding of the historical development of Welsh nationalism were made by Glyn Williams, Emyr Wynn Williams, John Davies and D. Hywel Davies.[104] *Radical Wales* itself made an important contribution by providing a platform for analyses of the current situation in Wales, with individual academics such as Charlotte Davies, Lynn Mainwaring and Phil Cooke all making their own signal contributions.[105] Indeed, it is difficult to imagine the academic social science periodical *Contemporary Wales* having survived the dark days of Thatcherism were it not for the existence and support of the nationalist left. In terms of setting out alternatives including different political programmes, there were other contributions in addition to those discussed over the previous pages. Some, such as Raymond Williams's, were particularly notable.[106] In summary, despite the almost unremittingly bleak context of the times, the post-1979 period was nonetheless characterised by a great deal of intellectual activity and creativity.

104 Glyn Williams, 'The ideological basis of Welsh nationalism in nineteenth-century Wales: the discourse of Michael D. Jones', in Glyn Williams (ed.), *Crisis of Economy and Ideology: Essays on Welsh Society, 1840–1980* (BSA Sociology of Wales Study Group, 1983), pp. 180–200; Emyr Wynn Williams, 'The politics of Welsh home rule 1886–1929: a sociological analysis'(PhD thesis, University of Wales, Aberystwyth, 1986) and 'D. J. Davies – a working class intellectual within Plaid Genedlaethol Cymru 1927–32', *Llafur*, 4 (4), 46–57; John Davies, *The Green and the Red: Nationalism and Ideology in Twentieth-century Wales* (Aberystwyth: Plaid Cymru, 1980); D. Hywel Davies, *The Welsh Nationalist Party 1925–1945: A Call to Nationhood* (Cardiff: University of Wales Press, 1983).
105 See, for example, Charlotte Aull Davies, *Welsh Nationalism in the Twentieth Century: The Ethnic Option and the Modern State* (New York: Praeger, 1989), and K. D. George and Lynn Mainwaring (eds), *The Welsh Economy* (Cardiff: University of Wales Press, 1988).
106 See Raymond Williams, *Who Speaks for Wales? Nation, Culture, Identity*, ed. Daniel Williams (Cardiff: University of Wales Press, 2003).

It is difficult to overemphasise the significance of all this. The 1979 referendum had smashed the hopes of generations of Welsh nationalists, and it would have been very easy for Welsh nationalism to develop into a wholly negative and even nihilistic force. It was primarily the left that ensured this did not happen through its role in setting out an alternative vision and vocabulary that (once again) connected trends in Wales with international developments. A generation of new members was given inspiration, direction and sense of purpose as a result. Even though the nationalist left's programme proved to be an electoral failure – the party's results in the 1983 general election were disastrous, and the results in some by-elections nothing short of calamitous – it remains difficult to believe that the decision to abandon the search for a third way and adopt a more conventional description of the desired direction for Wales did not prove beneficial to the party over the longer term.

That said, it is important not to over-romanticise the left's contribution nor pass over its less positive sides. The querulous, rancorous tone of the internal battles within Plaid Cymru during the 1980s has already been noted. Neither side in those battles was without blame. It can nevertheless be argued that the left's structural position caused it to overemphasise differences, both real and imagined, between it and the 'right', as the left insisted on referring to the party's more traditional supporters. In doing so, the left was seeking to highlight the far-reaching changes to the party's constitution and programme following the 1979 debacle. On this view, these reforms saw Plaid Cymru abandon its 'petty bourgeois' (or worse) past and embrace its role as a party that a different target audience (be that the working class or some other combination of social groups) could now embrace. Distancing a party or movement's past from its present is a familiar move in politics. Consider, for example, the efforts of Tony Blair, Gordon Brown and their colleagues to distance New Labour from 'Old Labour'. Although they may not appreciate the comparison, is this not in part what the left within Plaid Cymru was also seeking to achieve in the early 1980s? In order to rebuild a new Plaid Cymru on alternative foundations, it was first necessary to cast aside the old Plaid Cymru. But this was, of course, a painful experience for that old party. Little wonder, then, that Gwynfor Evans and Dafydd Wigley wanted to emphasise continuity rather than transformation – evolution rather than revolution – even as this served to fuel resentment on the left.

In addition, there were 'internal' intellectual problems inherent to the left's programme. The most prominent of these regarded the role of Plaid Cymru as a political party in promoting the desired process of the social change. This was a general problem for both the New Left and the Euro-Communist left; a problem with both theoretical and practical dimensions. In the Welsh context, particularly problematic were questions around the nature of the relationships the nationalist left should form with other left-wing political formations in Wales, especially the Labour Party. In 1983, for example, Phil Cooke proposed that the National Left should call on the Plaid Cymru constituency party in Cardiff North West not to contest a forthcoming by-election but rather support the Labour Party candidate, Jane Hutt.[107] This because, 'in broad terms, she agrees with many of our policies'. The proposal was furiously rejected by Emyr Wynn Williams. All that would be achieved '[B]y trying to suck up to Cardiff "TRENDY LEFTIES"' would be:

> to prove to everyone within the nationalist movement and outside it, how 'naive' we are as a movement … By recommending that members support a Labour candidate, the proposal suggests that what is needed to solve the problems in Wales is not a strong national liberation movement to gain independence for Wales, but rather a strong left wing in the Labour Party.

Although Williams's view prevailed on this occasion, the question – and fundamental strategic dilemma – remained. Later that year, Jonathan Evans and Lynn Mainwaring asked their fellow members of the National Left whether they could in all seriousness

---

107   A writ for this by-election was moved but was overtaken by the Conservative government's decision to call an early general election. The constituency itself was abolished at that election.

afford 'the luxury of locating our socialist policies outside the Labour Party?'[108]

In the end, however, it was not these internal arguments or even the objections of the 'right' that caused the intellectual ferment that had characterised the Plaid Cymru left in the first half of the 1980s to dissipate, but rather the result of another great upheaval – the failure of the 1984–5 miners' strike.

A parliament and Europe – again

It is hard to exaggerate the scale of the investment made by Plaid Cymru's left – and, indeed, the wider nationalist left – in the coalmining communities' epic struggle between March 1984 and March 1985. It was as much an emotional investment as it was an investment of time and energy. No one invested as extensively and generously as the party's president, Dafydd Elis-Thomas. His efforts were tireless: he gave speeches, lobbied and marched from one end of Wales to the other and beyond. Whether or not he had private doubts about the strategy adopted by the leadership of National Union of Mineworkers, his public support for the striking miners and their families was absolute and unwavering. Indeed, he was very critical of what he saw as the failure of parts of his own party to follow the lead of the left and throw all their energies behind the miners' struggle.[109]

Apart from a general desire to stand in solidarity with the miners in their battle against the Thatcher government, there were many specific aspects of the strike that caused the nationalist left to support it with particular enthusiasm. One was the way in which the strike seemed to confirm that it was indeed possible to build the kind of coalition of social groups that

108 The National Left's papers in Phil Williams's papers; capitalisation in the original.
109 See 'Interview with Dafydd Elis-Thomas', *Penderyn* (autumn 1984), 8–10. Elis-Thomas was particularly critical of the way many in the party continued to be marked by 'the worst aspects of the Nonconformist tradition'. He berated the Nonconformist denominations for their role during the strike: 'they opened their vestries to the police but scarcely one denomination organised collections for the miners in their chapels' (p. 9).

left-wing thinkers had long hankered for. The prominent role of miners' wives – and the women of mining communities more generally – was the most significant and hopeful example of this. An editorial in *Radical Wales* waxed lyrical about the unity between 'the miners of Wales, traditionally a vanguard, and the women of Wales, today's vanguard'.[110] Special significance was attributed to the establishment the 'Wales Congress in Support of Mining Communities' in the summer of 1984, namely a coalition of different groups and parties that supported the cause of the miners. It was seen as an example of alternative politics which moved beyond the 'narrow, male trade union, class-based politics of which South Wales Labourism is a classic expression'. The congress was interpreted as an example of weaving together 'coalitions of very different interests, new social movements, extra-parliamentary activities as well as diverse, formal parties'.[111] It was, in short, an embodiment of the nationalist left's aspirations for an alternative model of political organisation. No wonder, therefore, that Dafydd Elis-Thomas promoted the strike to the status of a 'national struggle', arguing that to play a part in that struggle was a much more important matter for the national movement than 'yakking on about an Assembly in Cardiff'.[112] If the opportunity to collaborate as part of a coalition of other political forces was not enough, the tensions within the labour movement around the strike – in particular between the Labour Party establishment and the miners and their supporters – also appeared to offer a golden political opportunity for the party. Surely this was the moment at which the Welsh electorate's faith in Labour would finally be shaken?

All these hopes proved in vain. After the total failure of the strike, the alternative coalition soon disintegrated. The congress was neutered, shattering the hopes of those who believed that it might develop into a grassroots, popular version of the devolved Assembly rejected in 1979. Nor was there any evidence of lasting

110 *Radical Wales*, 5 (winter 1984), 3. The reference to 'vanguard' is clearly a deliberate echo of Marxist-Leninist doctrine.
111 Phil Cooke, Siân Edwards, Gerald Howells and Dafydd Elis-Thomas, 'Congress at the crossroads', *Radical Wales*, 7 (summer 1985), 14.
112 'Interview with Dafydd Elis-Thomas', 10.

damage to Labour's standing in the valleys. In addition, its victory in the dispute served to render the UK government's position even stronger, dashing all hopes that it might be successfully challenged from the left (traditional or otherwise). Suffice it to say that the defeat of the strike proved as heavy a blow to the left as the 1979 referendum result had been to the approach embodied by Gwynfor Evans. It responded with dismay, disappointment and – in due course – a rethinking of strategy.

Tensions within the left were revealed in an editorial article by Emyr Wynn Williams in the National Left's newsletter in August 1985. In Williams's opinion, Dafydd Elis-Thomas was guilty of adopting a *'Romantic idealist* approach', which focused on the promotion of ideals rather than on developing a party offering a 'practical political alternative'. Hence, Plaid Cymru's identity and programme were diluted 'in favour of an identification with serious pressure groups within Welsh and British politics'. Furthermore, Elis-Thomas's unwillingness to acknowledge his leadership role as president of the party was doing active harm to it. By maintaining that he was no more than a spokesperson, rather than leader, the party's membership was being deprived of the opportunity to have a serious debate about its direction.[113] Given that one of the key criticisms of the-then leaders of Plaid Cymru by Williams and Elis-Thomas had been that they were too traditional and 'elitist' in their approach to leadership, it was deeply ironic that Williams was now calling on his former co-author to behave in a more traditional manner. A sign, perhaps, of the frustrations of the period?

After the *Western Mail* had seized on Williams's remarks, it also published a response from Elis-Thomas. In it he acknowledged that he was a romantic idealist in the mould of Gwynfor Evans, Saunders Lewis and W. J. Gruffydd. He accepted, too, that he had spent more time recently on pressure-group politics and that this needed to change. But he also made clear his view that his work had forged a more positive attitude towards the party across the '[C]entre-left of Welsh politics': 'The task now until the general

---

[113]   The quotations are from Emyr Wynn Williams, 'Golygyddol', *Cylchlythyr y Chwith Genedlaethol*, August 1985; translation, with emphasis in the original.

election is to turn the positive attitude into active support.'[114]
There was a hint of how the party president hoped to turn these
positive attitudes into genuine support in a remarkably revealing
essay that he and David Reynolds contributed to in the winter
1985 issue of *Radical Wales*: an essay that attempted to evaluate
Plaid Cymru's progress since the Carmarthen conference in 1981
and to suggest a direction for the future.

By embracing decentralised socialism in 1981, Plaid Cymru
had taken a historic gamble, which had two aspects to it:

> that enough momentum and members would be gained from cross-
> over Labour voters to outweigh any losses of enthusiasm among
> conventional nationalists, and that the new politics would be in-
> tellectually coherent, publicly understood and therefore capable of
> winning the political battle of ideas in Wales.[115]

Although the new direction had brought some success, it was not
without its problems. They proceeded to make specific reference
to some. First, the new approach was too abstract as the party
had failed to prepare a clear and credible blueprint of the kind of
Wales it intended to create. Although this was wholly consistent
with the party's position of seeking to empower communities to
set their own course and make their own decisions instead of imposing ideas from the centre, it created a substantial practical political problem: 'A political future which is in the hands of oneself
and one's neighbours without any blueprint or prior guidance is
perhaps a future that only the most secure could welcome without
reservations.'[116] Which is to say, only the most privileged could
afford such uncertainty. The second problem with the strategy
adopted by the party after 1981 was that it was more successful

[114] *Western Mail*, 25 September 1985, 8. Note the way the 'left' of the early 1980s
had mutated into 'centre-left', the term used by Wigley during the leadership contest between the two in 1981! Many arguments were now in the process of being
turned on their heads.
[115] David Reynolds and Dafydd Elis-Thomas, 'Four years on: charting Plaid's
new direction', *Radical Wales*, 9 (winter 1985), 18. It is noteworthy that the same
issue of Radical Wales contained a learned and sympathetic appreciation of
Saunders Lewis also by Dafydd Elis-Thomas ('A Tribute to Saunders Lewis', 24–5)
[116] Reynolds and Elis-Thomas, 'Four years on', 18.

in attracting members than votes. A third was that Plaid Cymru had become too closely aligned with other left-wing parties and was thus in danger of losing its identity. Finally, other parties, particularly the SDP-Liberal Alliance and the Conservatives, had succeeded in targeting some of the party's traditional supporters.

What was to be done? The party's rhetoric had to be given tangible form to render it 'street credible and street understandable'.[117] In addition, a Welsh dimension to the party's politics had to be rediscovered – a rather startling admission, to say the least. In addition, it was necessary to acknowledge and respond to the danger of the Alliance by emphasising the differences between the two parties 'on nuclear disarmament, on economic policy and on the issue of Welsh independence [*sic*], where the Alliance's devolution proposals offer Wales merely limbo status between integration and independence'.[118] More fundamentally still, it had to be acknowledged that hatred of Thatcherism alone was insufficient to persuade those groups which had the potential to create an alternative political coalition to collaborate successfully with each other:

> the groups that now uneasily co-exist within the Welsh resistance movement must themselves be brought into a closer relationship. For socialists, only through the conventional idea of independence will one ever get the chance of a socialist Welsh state. For 'cultural nationalists' … it is *only* through Wales' control of its own economy that we can stop the ditching of the language by young people forced into the English job market. Socialists must be nationalists – nationalists must also appreciate socialism. The green of nationalism, the red of socialism and the white of pacifism belong together in our Welsh rainbow coalition.[119]

The gamble had not failed, but a lot more work was required before it could be proclaimed a success.

---

117 Reynolds and Elis-Thomas, 'Four years on', 18.
118 Reynolds and Elis-Thomas, 'Four years on', 19.
119 Reynolds and Dafydd Elis-Thomas, 'Four years on', 18.

In one respect, Reynolds and Elis-Thomas were merely restating some of the familiar ideas – and tropes – of the nationalist left. The need to bring socialism and Welsh nationalism together was an argument that long predated 1979, even it had been heard more insistently since. Even so, the tone was different, as if the experience of the previous years had imposed a sobering influence on the authors. The reference to the threat posed by the Alliance also indicated a pragmatism and political realism than had not always been obvious. But perhaps the most striking part of their argument is the authors' acknowledgement of the need to 'discover again a Welsh dimension'. The big question, of course, is what exactly might that entail? As we shall see, there were two elements to the answer that was eventually proposed for that question (although neither was mentioned in the Reynolds/Elis-Thomas essay). A plan for a devolved parliament for Wales and a renewed emphasis on the European context – both of which, ironically enough, were positions that would ensure that Plaid Cymru would inhabit the same political terrain as the Alliance! In addition, attempts were made to strengthen the party's electoral credibility by planning an electoral union with the SNP ahead of the 1987 election.[120] The fact that Plaid had come to an agreement with a party that many on the left still considered – not without cause, perhaps – to be rather right wing and opportunistic, is a clear indication of how quickly its fortunes had ebbed after 1984–5.

The view that Plaid Cymru had either forgotten or watered down its commitment to self-government as it turned left after 1979 is entirely without basis. In fact, the constitutional discourse of the left was characterised by the (deliberately heretical) use of the word 'independence' and the kind of absolutism – 'independence' or nothing – that we encounter in Reynolds and Elis-Thomas's essay. After all, what hope was there of establishing a socialist state in Wales without a far-reaching measure of home rule? What was abandoned after the disappointment of 1979 was

---

120 The content of the agreement exists as an appendix to Plaid Cymru's manifesto for the election; see *Ennill dros Gymru/Winning for Wales* (Plaid Cymru, 1987), pp. 29, 31.

any faith in the notion that 'devolution' might prove a step in the right direction. But in December 1985, the party's executive committee invited Emyr Wynn Williams to draft new constitutional proposals on its behalf. That draft formed the basis for further discussion by a special sub-committee of senior party members – Gwynfor Evans, Dafydd Elis-Thomas, Phil Williams, Dafydd Huws and Emyr Wynn Williams. The end result was the formation of a plan for a 'Senate' for Wales that would be the basis for Plaid Cymru's campaign for the 1987 general election.[121] In the words of the election manifesto, although 'an independent Welsh government answerable to no-one except the people of Wales' remained the objective of the party, the 'crisis was so dire, the problems so difficult, the injustice so great that the work has to be started at once'.[122] It urged that the powers of the Welsh Office should be transferred to an elected Welsh Senate that would concentrate above all on reviving the economy.

The proposed Senate would be formed of 100 members elected by proportional representation. It would inherit the authority of the Secretary of State to determine public expenditure priorities in Wales as well as reform local government, nominate members to public bodies, and so on. The proposed scheme of legislative empowerment was so convoluted and obviously nonsensical as to make the various schemes that would underpin the first few terms of the National Assembly for Wales seem – almost – sensible! Here is the attempt of the editorial article in the summer 1987 issue of *Radical Wales* to explain what the party was recommending:

> The Senate will have the power to initiate legislation of particular relevance to Wales. It will not, however, have the power of unconditional implementation – the final reading will still be at Westminster. On the other hand, where Westminster-initiated legislation is of specific relevance to Wales, the Senate will take over the functions of the House of Lords and thus have the power to delay

121 See, in particular, Emyr Wynn Williams, *The Welsh Senate and Regeneration of Wales* (Plaid Cymru, n.d. [but 1986/7]); *Ennill dros Gymru/Winning for Wales*, pp. 25, 27.
122 *Ennill dros Gymru/Winning for Wales*, p. 25.

or suggest amendments to such legislation (but not, at the end of the day, to block it all together).[123]

Considering that most of Westminster's legislative programme could in one way or another be regarded as being of 'specific relevance' to Wales, it is not clear whether the authors of the plan seriously believed that a Welsh Senate could develop into, in effect, a second chamber to the House of Commons? Once again, Plaid Cymru's grasp of constitutional questions appears to have been less than certain. Then again, it was not the detail of Plaid's plan for a Senate developed between 1985 and 1987 that mattered. The plan was significant – not only for the party, but also for politics in Wales generally – because of the way that the arguments in favour of it were framed by Emyr Wynn Williams.

Williams's central argument was that Wales now possessed very many state institutions – that is, that a form of Welsh state existed – but these institutions were not accountable to the people of Wales. This was not in itself a new argument. The need to democratise Wales's already existing governmental and administrative structures had been one of the arguments used to press the case for devolution back in the 1970s. But there are two important points to note. First, democratising existing structures had not been the main argument in favour of devolution at that time and – in particular – during the unsuccessful 'Yes' campaign ahead of the referendum. Secondly, whatever its role at the time, because of the completeness of the failure in 1979, the argument appears to have been largely discarded in the aftermath. Williams revived it on the basis of a relatively detailed description and analysis of the nature of this undemocratic 'Welsh state' to make it the central plank of his argument in favour of devolution. Not only that, but he was able to crystallise the deficiencies of the current system by exemplifying the ways in which the Conservative Party was using its powers of patronage to place those public bodies that formed the Welsh state into the hands of its own unelected and unrepresentative supporters. For example, at least six of the

[123] 'Independence and the Senate' [Editorial], *Radical Wales*, 15 (summer 1987), 5–6.

twelve board members of the Welsh Development Agency were Conservative members.[124]

The clearest statement of Williams's analysis was provided in a paper circulated to supporters of the National Left in early 1988. After tracing institutional developments in Wales, he concluded in the following terms:

> In their totality I believe that these developments illustrate quite clearly that the tide of history is flowing very strongly in favour of Wales, and that the constructive processes at work far outweigh the destructive cross-currents which are also evident … Wales has survived the era of British centralism and nationalism which reached its peak around 1934, and now experiences a political reconstruction … If we contrast the current situation with that which existed during the early 1930s it is abundantly apparent that a transformation of revolutionary proportions has occurred. Whereas during the early '30s the existence of Wales was being challenged … we now live in a situation in which the Welsh state not only exists but also has developed a tremendous impetus of its own. By now the concept of the Welsh state intervening in order to nurture the regeneration of Wales is becoming the central concept of Welsh politics. Moreover to state that Wales is run by a Governor General is to fail to comprehend the extent of the autonomy inherent in the post of Secretary of State for Wales. A far more appropriate concept would be to view Wales as being governed by a Prime Minister whose role is restricted by the absence of a Welsh Senate having a legislative and financial autonomy.[125]

This passage summarises the main lines of argument used by devolutionists of all parties to plead their cause during the 1990s. It even presages the language used to make those arguments. As far as one can judge, it was the work of Emyr Wynn Williams between 1985 and 1989 which laid the intellectual and rhetorical

[124] Williams, *The Welsh Senate and the Regeneration of Wales*, pp. 36–8.
[125] A paper by Emyr Wynn Williams delivered before members of the London branch of Plaid Cymru on 23 March 1988 and circulated later amongst members of the National Left, p. 3; see the National Left papers in Phil Williams's papers.

foundations for nationalist politics in the 1990s. His efforts have not received the recognition they deserve.

What is also striking about this passage is its optimism: despite the pain and misery of 1979, the tendencies of the age were running in Wales's favour after all. This was also the conclusion drawn from the second all-important element of the process of reflection and reconsideration in which the Plaid Cymru left engaged in the wake of 1984–5: this time in relation to Europe.[126]

Despite the fact that some individuals connected with the nationalist left had adopted a very different position – Raymond Williams and Ned Thomas were two prominent examples – most of their associates in Plaid Cymru had tended to portray the European Community as a capitalist club, or to ignore it completely as if it were somehow peripheral to the real issues of the day.[127] As such, their attitude was entirely characteristic of the British left more generally. However, in 1988, there was a rather dramatic volte-face. The spring issue of *Radical Wales* included an article by Syd Morgan – a prominent figure on the left – calling on the party to focus on Europe and European Parliament elections on the basis that it was here that the party's enemies were at their weakest.[128] The same issue also contained an article by Jill Evans – also prominent on the left and a key link in the party's European and wider international connections – extolling the possibilities now being revealed at the European level. The concept of a 'Europe of the peoples', combining an emphasis on transferring power to the lowest level possible with establishing

126 For a discussion on Plaid Cymru's attitudes towards European integration see Anwen Elias, 'From "full national status" to "independence" in Europe: the case of Plaid Cymru – the party of Wales', in Michael Keating and John McGarry (eds), *European Integration and the Nationalities Question* (London: Routledge, 2006), pp. 193–215.
127 As a comparatively late example of the former tendency, see Lynn Mainwaring, 'The European community [*sic*] – a new colonialism?', *Radical Wales*, 3 (summer 1984), 8–10. Mainwaring, Plaid's economic spokesperson at the time, was doubtful about what he regarded as a tendency to romanticise the EU's progressiveness: 'The fact is that socialism has about as much chance of realisation in the European proto-state as it does in the British super-state' (p. 10) – which is to say, none! As has already been noted, there was no reference to the European dimension in Reynolds and Elis-Thomas's 1985 essay.
128 Syd Morgan, 'Plaid Cymru: crisis and resolution', *Radical Wales*, 17 (spring 1988), 9–11.

democratic assemblies at regional level, was obviously relevant to Wales. In addition, a coalition was beginning to form at a European level that could bring such a Europe into being; a coalition that included 'the "new thinking" European left', peace movements, environmentalist parties and movements, and national and regional parties like Plaid Cymru.[129] Or in the words of a later essay by the same author, Plaid Cymru would no longer be a small party on the margins, but rather part of a 'new and progressive force' within European politics.[130]

By the winter of 1988, four members of Plaid Cymru, all connected with the left in their various ways, had been selected as candidates for the following year's European elections. One of them, no less than Dafydd Elis-Thomas himself, provided the clearest account of the basis for the party's newfound Europhilia.[131] The president's view was that the 1979 referendum result reflected the fact that the Welsh electorate thought in British terms and had evaluated the devolution proposals through that prism. Now, however, Britain was being integrated within the European Community, which in turn meant a change in the terms of the pro-devolution argument – in ways that were favourable for 'political nationalism'. The objective now was to show how Wales could benefit from the existence of a layer of national democratic government 'with direct access from the Cardiff capital to the community capitals and the institutions of Europe'.[132] Furthermore, although the two most important manifestations of Welshness during the twentieth century were in crisis, with both Labourist industrial Wales and Nonconformist Wales in terminal decline, this did not mean the end of Wales (nor even the end of the Welsh language).[133] Adopting a European

129 Jill Evans, 'A shared experience: Wales and the European free alliance', *Radical Wales*, 17 (spring 1988), 17.
130 Jill Evans, 'Self-governing Wales in Europe: a community charter for change', *Radical Wales*, 21 (spring 1989), 9.
131 The three other candidates were Phil Williams, Jill Evans and Peter Keelan (it should be remembered that Wales at the time was divided into four constituencies for the purpose of the European Parliament elections).
132 Dafydd Elis-Thomas, 'A sense of Europe', *Radical Wales*, 20 (winter 1988), 19.
133 Note here his description of the miners' strike as 'the last great celebration of that tradition of solidarity' that characterised Labourist industrial Wales: 'The march back to Maerdy symbolised the end of a tradition' (p. 19).

framing and perspective provided a means of recreating afresh an understanding of Welshness that was relevant, progressive and running with the grain of wider international developments: a Wales in which devolution could be mooted without raising the spectre of 'separatism'; a Wales where bilingualism and multilingualism on the European pattern was the norm; a Wales where many different experiences and manifestations of Welsh national identity co-existed; a Wales that was once again aware that it had always been part of European cultural life 'from its Celtic beginnings through its Anglo-Norman influences, into Calvinism and Communism'.[134] Saunders Lewis and Gwynfor Evans may not have agreed with all of this, but both – and in particular the former – would have applauded the way in which the European context was being used to frame the analysis of Wales's current situation and future prospects. Lewis would surely have approved the essay's peroration:

> For Scotland, the SNP is embracing a notion of independence within Europe. Interdependence within Europe would be a more acceptable slogan, but I think we understand the point. It seems to me quite clear that the only road for greater self-government for Wales is through relating what happens in Wales to what happens in Europe. If we succeed in replacing the British dimension with a European dimension in our thinking, then we will have become already the Welsh European internationalists that we always were in our hearts.[135]

Yes, Plaid Cymru had turned (back) to Europe.

This new, very positive attitude towards Europe was echoed in speeches and articles by Dafydd Elis-Thomas, Gwyn A. Williams, Jill Evans and others, and proved significant for several reasons.[136] First, the significance of the European context became

134 Elis-Thomas, 'A sense of Europe', 18.
135 Elis-Thomas, 'A sense of Europe', 18–20.
136 Space precludes a wider discussion here, but any account of the development of pro-European sentiment on the nationalist left in the second half of the 1980s would need to give due consideration to the central role played by Gwyn A. Williams. See, inter alia, his speech to the launch meeting of the Assembly for

an important part of the intellectual and rhetorical framework for pro-devolution arguments during the 1990s. Once again, Plaid Cymru provided some of the ammunition for devolutionists from all parties for the struggles of the decade. Second, after one of the routes to 'freedom' had been closed off by the referendum result and another by the subsequent failure of the miners' strike another, the 'Europe of the peoples', gave the party a new sense of intellectual direction. Key here is that this was a direction that could unite all (or nearly all) of the party. The most traditional elements within Plaid Cymru regarded this new Europeanism as echoing classical Saundersian themes. The constitutional aspirations that emerged from the 'Europe of the peoples' project were also wholly consistent with traditional injunction against 'independence' – an injunction that the left had challenged during the first half of the 1980s but had never managed to overturn. Dafydd Wigley had also been passionately supportive of European integration long before the left converted to the same view (with the characteristic conviction of the late convert). Indeed, as the plan for a 'Senate' and a new emphasis on Europe had to all intents and purposes displaced class politics from the nationalist left's programme, Plaid Cymru was more intellectually united by the end of the 1980s than it had been for many years.

It is ironic, therefore, that the end of the 1980s and the early 1990s was (another) difficult time for party. For one thing, the animosities of the first half of the 1980s had left their mark.[137] With those divisions having forced different factions into the trenches so to speak, it was difficult for all concerned to acknowledge what would have been apparent to any external observer, namely that by around 1987 or 1988 there was very little that divided them in terms of political philosophy. In truth, the supposed differences between the left and the rest of the party in the early 1980s were never as great as many imagined at the time, with the principal difference being the left's desire to denote and highlight a

Wales Campaign in Merthyr in November 1988 printed in the spring 1989 issue of *Radical Wales*, 11–13.

[137] For a striking example of this animosity, note Emyr Wynn Williams's reference to the 'right' within Plaid Cymru as the party's 'flag waving "Nuremberg Tendency"' in an editorial for the National Left's newsletter in December 1988.

symbolic break between the 'old Plaid Cymru' and the new, progressive version. Be that as it may, after 1985 any objective gap between the different factions closed rapidly. Indicative of this shift was a motion debated at the party's annual conference in Holyhead in 1985, which would revise the declaration of the party's aims as follows:

> as the national party of Wales, its aims will be:
>
> to secure self-government for Wales and a democratic state based on socialist principles:
>
> to safeguard and foster the culture, language, traditions, the environment and economic life of Wales through devolved socialist policies.

This was passed more or less unanimously, with none of the high drama experienced in Carmarthen in 1981. In the 1987 general election, the doyen of the left, Gwyn A. Williams spoke at the campaign launch meeting for the member for Caernarfon, Dafydd Wigley. But, despite such developments, the rather toxic legacy of the first half of the decade continued to make itself apparent.

Many felt that Plaid Cymru lacked direction. This apprehension was at the root of Wigley's journey to Dolgellau in September 1989 to ask Dafydd Elis-Thomas '[W]hat, in simple terms, was the "game plan"?' Wigley feared that the president did not have 'any type of strategy'.[138] Significantly, former colleagues of Elis-Thomas on the left shared the same concern. A few months before, in December 1988, Emyr Wynn Williams told his fellow members of the National Left that it was 'essential that Dafydd Elis-Thomas gets his act together'.[139] But discontent with the leader was not the only sign of the dissatisfaction in the ranks. Perhaps the most striking indication were the recurrent rumours that one wing or other of Plaid Cymru was engaged in behind-the-scenes

---

[138] Wigley, *Dal Ati*, p. 309.
[139] Editorial ('Was that really the Plaid Cymru Conference?') in the National Left newsletter, December 1988.

conversations with other parties or party factions with a view to forming an alliance or even, more ambitiously, attempting a complete restructuring of the party system in Wales. The left was suspicious of the alleged connections between prominent members on the 'right' – such as the party's chief executive, Dafydd Williams, and vice-president, Dafydd Huws – with the Alliance and, later, the newly merged Liberal Democrats.[140] These suspicions intensified following a bizarre episode in October 1987 when an anonymous copy of a letter was sent to five members of Plaid Cymru's national council that appeared to reveal discussions between Williams and Richard Livsey, the Alliance Member of Parliament for Brecon and Radnorshire; a letter that was condemned as a forgery by Plaid.[141] For their part, more traditional elements within the party were suspicious of the connections between the Plaid left and other left-wing factions in Wales and further afield.[142] It is difficult to evaluate just how much truth there was in all of this, but it is clear that the various suspicions were not without substance. Although those individuals who were part of the various discussions remain reluctant to confirm the details (many remain active in Plaid Cymru), we can be certain that there were conversations with prominent members of the Alliance about the possibility of collaboration between both parties. Indeed, Dafydd Wigley has confirmed that Dafydd Elis-Thomas and Richard Livsey discussed some form of cooperative arrangement between the two parties in the early 1990s.[143] It also appears highly probable that discussions took place in the late 1980s between some of the most prominent figures of the party's left and other groupings

---

140   The National Left papers in Phil Williams's papers.
141   See *Daily Post*, 9 October 1987.
142   The suspicions on both sides dated back to the beginning of the 1980s, when the left alleged that the 'right' was conspiring with the Liberals or the SDP, and the more traditional elements were suspicious of the left's alleged connections with the Bennites in the Labour Party; see, for example, the letter column of *Arcade*, 4 September 1981, 13, where there was a letter from Dafydd Wigley denying that there were ongoing discussions about an electoral arrangement between Plaid and the SDP in Caernarfon and another letter by Emyr Wynn Williams also denying that discussions were happening between the National Left and Tony Benn's supporters in the Labour Party.
143   Wigley, *Dal Ati*, p. 342.

on the left of the Labour Party and the SNP.[144] But again, nothing seems to have resulted. Indeed, one of the consequences of the Labour Party's vicious attacks on Plaid Cymru during the 1989 Pontypridd by-election campaign was that the nationalist left lost faith in the possibility of building bridges between it and the left of the Labour Party. (Plaid's left seems to have been unable to recognise that it, too, was guilty of using much the same inappropriate language in its internal struggles with their own party's so-called 'right-wing culturalists' as Labour's campaigners had used to vilify Plaid Cymru more generally.[145]) In truth, however, the fact that different parts of the party were willing to consider creating different sorts of agreements was hardly a sign of some fundamental lack of loyalty to the party's programme. Although it cannot be denied that there were some fractious elements in the party, neither was the somewhat querulous tone of the period a sign that this was a particularly divisive or divided organisation. The basic problem was rather Plaid Cymru's lack of electoral success.

Although Ieuan Wyn Jones's victory in Ynys Môn in the 1987 general election lifted spirits, it was not enough to hide the fact that the party's total number of votes had declined in every county outside Gwynedd. Nor was there any way of hiding the disappointment of the 1989 European election result, especially in north Wales where there had been real hope that Dafydd Elis-Thomas's wholehearted campaign could dislodge the Conservative Beata Brooks. In the event, the party president came third – with Labour's candidate, the unremarkable Joe Wilson, claiming the seat. The Labour Party was back as a serious electoral force, this even though many Plaid Cymru members had been prophesising its demise since 1979. ('THERE WILL NEVER AGAIN BE A LABOUR GOVERNMENT IN OUR LIFETIME', had been Gwyn A. Williams's confident prediction on St David's

---

144 It seems, for example, that at least one meeting between the three groups took place in the Manchester area.
145 The term 'right-wing culturalists' comes from a report on the April 1988 National Left meeting in one of the movement's internal newsletters found in Phil Williams's papers.

Day, 1987.[146]) Worse still, the Greens – a party with no meaning-ful presence across most of Wales – saw a remarkable increase in their vote, winning more votes than Plaid Cymru in three of the four Welsh constituencies. Thus, even though the party was more united ideologically than it had been for a long time, and despite opinion poll evidence that support for devolution was increasing amongst voters in Wales, it was clear that Plaid Cymru had stalled. Indeed, beyond Gwynedd, it was continuing to lose ground.

In his autobiography, Dafydd Wigley reports that the European election result was a particularly heavy blow for Dafydd Elis-Thomas. In the aftermath, the party president 'soured towards the Labour Party' and 'also became increasingly close to [Conservative Welsh Office Minister] Wyn Roberts'.[147] More importantly, it seems that the 1989 result fired the starting gun for the Meirionnydd MP's journey from the House of Commons into the House of Lords and his chairmanship of the Welsh Language Board, the quango established in the wake of the Welsh Language Act 1993. There was ample evidence before 1989 that Elis-Thomas was becoming disillusioned with conventional party politics. In a lecture published in 1986 in the journal *Radical Scotland*, for exam-ple, he argued that anyone who wished to achieve fundamental social change should not fear the disappearance of 'traditional party forms'. This because political parties were far too often con-servative forces that hindered rather than encouraged progres-sive efforts. This was true even for the nationalist parties in Wales and Scotland: 'In their determination to seek representation in the British state, these parties too often find themselves replicat-ing the internal organisational forms of conventional political parties.'[148] Elis-Thomas was notably more positive about social movements and, in particular, the women's movement, the green movement and the peace movement. It is not difficult to see how this general disillusionment with party politics – and with the

146 Gwyn A. Williams, *Towards the Commonwealth of Wales* (Cardiff: Plaid Cymru, 1987), final page (pages are not numbered); emphasis in the original.
147 Wigley, *Dal Ati*, pp. 307–9.
148 Dafydd Elis-Thomas, 'Socialism and nationalism for our time', *Radical Scotland*, 22 (August/September 1986), 25.

politics of Plaid Cymru – combined with the interpretation of the actually existing Welsh state pioneered, above all, by Emyr Wynn Williams, to underpin an alternative political strategy which he revealed to Dafydd Wigley in September 1989.

When Wigley asked Elis-Thomas for his 'game plan' for Plaid Cymru, the answer he was given was 'Quango Wales': 'Because the Tories are creating countless numbers of them, this will now become be the new layer of government in Wales: and if they exist, we need to take them over, and press for their democratisation.'[149] Here was the acceptable, nationalist version of *entryism* as practised by sections of the British left and rejected by the Commission of Inquiry at the start of the decade. In one sense, it was a logical enough strategy. It is certainly not difficult to understand its appeal to a man who had been seeking a way forward politically for Wales since 1974 with so little success. Doubtless, attempting to implement such a strategy would raise all kinds of practical difficulties, but with the party's electoral prospects so poor – and with no sign of any improvement on the horizon – every option available to Welsh nationalists (or 'post-nationalists' for that matter) was freighted with challenges.[150] At least the quangos were real bodies wielding real power over large parts of Welsh life. As such, was not 'the long march through the institutions' – as Dafydd Elis-Thomas described his version of nationalist entryism – likely to prove a substantially shorter journey than any march to power via the ballot box?[151] After all, that particular long march was already sixty years in the making, with only three MPs – all in Gwynedd – the reward for all the effort and sacrifice involved.

---

149 Wigley, *Dal Ati*, p. 309. Wigley is not an unbiased observer, and his relationship with his fellow MP was clearly a difficult one. Having said that, Wigley's version of Elis-Thomas's thinking is perfectly consistent with Elis-Thomas's actions. Moreover, Dafydd Elis-Thomas has never sought to cast doubt on Wigley's version of their conversation.
150 On some of the inherent problems and limitations of the Quango Wales strategy see Richard Wyn Jones, 'From "Community Socialism" to Quango Wales: The Amazing Odyssey of Dafydd Elis Thomas', trans. Meg Elis and Richard Wyn Jones, *Planet: The Welsh Internationalist*, 119 (1996), 59–70.
151 For an insight into Dafydd Elis-Thomas's worldview during his period as chairman of the Welsh Language Board, see 'Adeiladu'r Wladwriaeth Gymreig', *Tu Chwith*, 5 (summer 1996), 24–38. The 'long march through the institutions' is taken from Raymond Williams.

But of course, the Quango Wales strategy was an entirely indi-
vidualistic one; a strategy in which only the elite could hope to
play an active role. Despite the extent of Wales's quango state,
there were not *that* many jobs on the various governing bodies. It
was certainly not a strategy for a political party. Yet, this was the
strategy the president of the Plaid Cymru was now recommending. The position was clearly unsustainable, and one senses that
it came as a relief to all concerned when Dafydd Elis-Thomas's
announced that he would be giving up the presidency in 1991
and would leave the House of Commons at the next general election.[152] By 1992 he would be taking his seat in 'the other place'
with his contribution to Plaid Cymru's political thinking at an
end – for the time being, at least.

Wigley, Ceredigion and the paradox of the 1990s

Dafydd Wigley's first period as president of Plaid Cymru between 1981 and 1984 was neither happy nor fruitful. It would
have been difficult for anyone seeking to take over the reins from
Gwynfor Evans. The long shadow of the 1979 debacle was sufficient to have ensured that. But Wigley's position was made nigh-
on impossible due to a combination of heartbreaking personal
circumstances and the fact that the ideological tide within Plaid
Cymru was flowing so strongly in the direction of the 'hard' left.
But by 1991 that tide had turned. After 1986, the party focused
increasingly on the constitution as opposed to class politics. This,
combined with the enthusiasm for European integration that
swept through the ranks two years later, led to Plaid Cymru as a
whole embracing the same ideas and priorities that had always
been central to Dafydd Wigley's political vision. If Dafydd Elis-
Thomas represented the 'spirit of the age' within Plaid in the first
half of the 1980s, then without doubt it was Dafydd Wigley who
represented the spirit of the 1990s. Partly as a result, his second

[152] We should note Dafydd Wigley's generous recognition of the way in which
Dafydd Elis-Thomas handed over both the presidency as well as his Meirionnydd
constituency; see *Dal Ati*, p. 329.

period as president was a much happier and much more successful one. It was crowned by what were arguably the two biggest
achievements so far in the history of Plaid Cymru – the results
of the 1997 referendum and the first election to the National
Assembly of Wales in 1999.

It is perhaps not his contribution as a political thinker that
springs most readily to mind in any consideration of Dafydd
Wigley's contribution to the life of his party or Wales. Indeed, his
political ideas have received next to no attention from commentators. Rather the focus has tended to be on his charisma and popular appeal; his untiring work as a constituency representative;
his passionate commitment to the disabled, etc. One suspects that
Wigley will not be overly disappointed at this. He has always
presented himself as a practical politician in search of practical
solutions rather than some abstract dreamer. It is almost certainly
true that he has never had the same inherent interest in political
thought as Saunders Lewis and Dafydd Elis-Thomas. It would
nonetheless be a mistake to ignore his political beliefs. Wigley has
adhered to a core of set of principles and values throughout his
political career – sustaining him through some very dark times.
More than that, Dafydd Wigley's political ideas were also a key
influence on the political thinking of Plaid Cymru during the
1990s.

Three dimensions of his political thought are particularly relevant in the present context. We have already referred to the first,
namely his enthusiastic Europeanism. The second is his emphasis on winning the valleys for Plaid Cymru, an emphasis which
reflects his view of Welsh identity as much as his strategic priorities. Third is the way in which he has consistently sought to link
the argument for self-government to wider arguments about the
material benefits that would accrue to the people of Wales with
its advent.

Dafydd Wigley was way ahead of his time on Europe. So far
ahead, in fact, that in the first half of the 1970s he was left almost
totally isolated within Plaid Cymru because of what we might
term his premature Europeanism. This was a period in which
the more traditional elements within the party joined forces with

the left to oppose membership of the European Community and support a 'No' vote in the 1975 referendum. A number of factors combined to persuade the overwhelming majority of Plaid Cymru members of this view: fears that such a community would develop into a military – even nuclear – power; fear of loss of sovereignty; the belief that the community was nothing more than a capitalist club; a sense that the place of a Free Wales was alongside the small Scandinavian countries as part of the European Free Trade Area (EFTA); and so on.

Wigley's alternative position was premised on very different views and calculations. In the most complete discussion of the matter, he notes the influence of Leopold Kohr and Saunders Lewis on his ideas, and the way that this contributed towards making him a European of conviction.[153] But there were also more pragmatic considerations at play. The European dimension offered a way of 'turning the tables' on those political enemies castigating Plaid Cymru as separatists. If the party were to 'recommend, positively, tearing down barriers and creating a wider, multilingual community, thus bridging old divisions' – that is, if it were to embrace the European project – then this would expose 'the introverted, narrow, monolingual and isolationist Britishness' of so many of its opponents.[154] In addition, once British membership was a fact, arguments to the effect that the Free Wales of the future should distance itself from the community were surely unsustainable? Rather, the proper place for the party was to stand alongside the 'democratic forces of other micro-nations' in a battle to devolve power within the European state he foresaw developing on the foundation of the Community: 'Since the problems associated with central control are bound to become a growing worry for many communities, Plaid politics will become a part of the mainstream of European development.'[155] He wrote these words in 1972. At the time, his fellow party members simply turned a deaf ear. By the end of the 1980s, however, his position – and many of his arguments – were part of the intellectual

---

153 See Wigley, *O Ddifri*, pp. 302–11.
154 Wigley, *O Ddifri*, pp. 311–12; translation.
155 Dafydd Wigley, 'Rethink on Europe', *Welsh Nation*, 22 September 1972, 2.

mainstream within Plaid Cymru. The high tide of this new Euro-enthusiasm was reached at the party's annual conference in 1990 when a motion was passed committing the party to constitutional aims that linked self-government to European integration. Plaid Cymru's objective would be to establish a Senate for Wales within five years and secure a voice for Wales within a European Community, which itself would have been democratised though the establishment of a 'Senate of the Regions' that would act as a second chamber to a more powerful European Parliament. In the long term, the aim was to ensure that Wales gained 'full political status' within the European Community with power being shared between Wales and the European levels – and with the British level losing all influence. This was now a party ready to be led by Dafydd Wigley.

If Wigley's Europeanism was orthodox Saunders – he sought and received solace at the old man's Penarth home in 1975, 'a period when I felt exceptionally lonely within Plaid Cymru' – the same cannot be said of his understanding of Welsh identity.[156] For the avoidance of doubt, it should be underlined that Wigley has worked exceptionally hard throughout his political career to secure measures to promote the Welsh language. Indeed, few if any politicians can ever have been as committed to that cause. But in contrast to Saunders Lewis and Gwynfor Evans, Wigley's commitment to the Welsh language was never accompanied by even a hint of ambiguity about the Welshness of those who did not speak the language. They are Welsh, full stop. In Wigley's view, it was among these Welsh people – and in the valleys in particular – that Plaid Cymru should be concentrating its efforts.[157]

In all of this, there was considerable overlap between the views of the two Dafydds. That said, the underpinning logic of their positions was somewhat different. While Wigley's zeal for social justice was no less ardent than that of Elis-Thomas, he did not understand politics in term of class struggle. It was not, therefore, the class consciousness of the old industrial Wales that caused

---

156 Wigley, *O Ddifri*, p. 321; translation.
157 This theme is repeated almost ad nauseum in the second volume of his autobiography (in particular), *Dal Ati*.

him to place the valleys at the heart of his political programme, but rather the combination of the Welsh identity and the disadvantaged conditions that he saw and experienced there. Despite Elis-Thomas being perceived as the most radical of the two (at least, before his elevation to the Lords), Wigley was at least as well placed to have a direct impact on the politics of the valleys. He both lived and was involved in local politics there before becoming the Plaid Cymru candidate in Caernarfon.[158] It should also be recalled that far from every Plaid member in the valleys was in favour of the kind of left-wing agenda embraced by Elis-Thomas. But be that as it may, by the time of the 1989 Pontypridd by-election – with both 'right' and 'left' uniting behind (left-wing) candidate, Syd Morgan, to create the most effective electoral campaign that Plaid had seen for many years – it seems that internal bickering had lost much of its appeal. Again, the net result was that the conditions were now ripe for Dafydd Wigley to lead Plaid Cymru. The party was ready to back his strategy of trying to maintain and strengthen its hold on the constituencies with the highest proportion of Welsh speakers while attempting – somehow – to make its mark on voters in the valleys as well.

But how to achieve this? Wigley did not claim to have identified a magic formula for electoral success. To the contrary, he emphasised the need for perseverance and unceasing efforts in the attempt to convince the people of Wales of the value of its message.[159] In other words, there were no substitutes or shortcuts available. Self-government had to be brought alive, not simply by appealing to national identity, but by convincing electors that their prosperity ultimately depended on it. Even if Dafydd Wigley has almost certainly never heard of Miroslav Hroch, his understanding of the conditions of success for political nationalism was in perfect harmony with Hroch's work as outlined in Chapter 1.

---

[158] Wigley discusses his time living and being involved in politics in Merthyr in *O Ddifri*, pp. 113–41.

[159] See, in particular, one of the most passionate pieces of prose produced by Dafydd Wigley, namely the final chapter of *Dal Ati* (pp. 448–68).

Wigley was not the first to try to argue in favour of self-government on the basis that it was only constitutional change that might rescue Wales from its myriad economic problems, but he may well have been the most consistent advocate for this position. Indeed, it can be argued that Wigley, alongside his gifted friend and colleague Phil Williams, did more than anyone else in the history of Plaid Cymru to render that argument credible.[160] After the Carmarthen victory in 1966, both played a central role in the activities of Plaid Cymru's research group, a unit which not only provided an all-important support system for Gwynfor Evans during his time at Westminster but, by 1970, had produced the party's celebrated *Economic Plan for Wales*. As they made clear in their preface to that ambitious work, the aim was to outline the steps that a self-governing Wales could take to address the nation's economic problems. To summarise an extensive report much more brutally than is deserved, their answer was that a Welsh government should identify approximately ten growth centres across Wales, equip those areas with the required modern infrastructure, and instruct a 'National Development Authority' to promote appropriate industrial and business developments within them.[161] The authors foresaw a mixed economy, and although this type of economic planning was a feature of governments of both the left and right at this time, the model for the proposed Welsh government clearly derived from efforts of governments in small European and Scandinavian countries.

It is unlikely that the economic plan was widely read – at least in its entirety. Only a select few will have waded through a document that was almost three hundred pages long and weighed

160 The pioneer was, of course, D. J. Davies, whose contribution to the party during its first decades was of vital importance. What makes the contributions of Wigley and Williams so crucial was the fact that they were so detailed – through their own work and by coordinating and building on the work of others, they succeeded in fleshing out the argument in a way that had not previously been achieved.

161 There is a remarkable similarity between the Economic Plan and the Spatial Plan adopted by the Welsh Government in 2004. Indeed, future historians of attempts to develop Wales's economy are likely to be struck by the similarity of the various plans promoted by Plaid Cymru and those adopted (often many years later) by various public bodies.

down by a slew of statistical tables. Nonetheless, for the remainder of the decade it was an all-important weapon for the party. It gave Plaid Cymru members confidence. Its mere existence was proof that it was Plaid that had the answers. More than that, the fact that the task of drawing up such a fundamentally important document had been left to Plaid's talented amateurs served to underline the complete bankruptcy of the prevailing order and the value of Plaid Cymru to the life of the nation.[162] Bearing this in mind, and given Wigley's central role in putting the plan together, it may appear surprising that no effort was made in the 1980s – especially during Wigley's first period as president – to update or redesign an economic plan for the very different social and economic circumstances of that era.

It seems that a number of factors combined to ensure that this did not occur. Most obviously perhaps, after the debacle of 1979, what was the point of spending time and effort setting out detailed plans for a self-governing Wales that seemed further away than ever? But in addition, parts of the left had principled objections to any such effort. For them, planning reeked of the Labourist and Stalinist tendency to allow the state to impose on the working class rather than allowing workers to decide for themselves. This was the basis of Lynn Mainwaring's objections to the efforts made by Phil Williams (with Wigley's blessing?) to encourage the party to draw up a new economic plan at the beginning of the 1980s.[163] But by this point, it may well be that doubts about the whole approach would have extended beyond the ranks of the 'hard' left. It is hard to deny that the kind of *dirigiste* economic policies fashionable in the mid-1960s, and which formed the basis for the 1970 economic plan, had by then lost much of their lustre. How could an economic plan be drawn up to ensure the prosperity of a self-governing Wales if there was now no credible strategy for economic development to put at its centre?

---

[162] This was a point reiterated several times in the plan itself, see for example, *Economic Plan for Wales* (Plaid Cymru, 1970), p. 287.
[163] See Dafis, *Mab y Pregethwr*, p. 157. See also the different internal discussions of the National Left in Phil Williams's papers.

The answer would come from Ceredigion, in the form of an important and influential experiment at the beginning of the 1990s to yoke the ideas of the green movement to the ideas and ideals of Welsh nationalism. It was this experiment that led to the extraordinary triumph of a Plaid Cymru/Green coalition in the Ceredigion and Pembroke North constituency at the 1992 general election. Even more importantly, it was this experiment that allowed Plaid Cymru to develop a new argument about the relationship between self-government and prosperity; an argument that connected self-government to a new concept of 'prosperity' based on a green analysis of human society and its relationship with the planet on which we reside.

The history of the 'Greening of Plaid Cymru' has been told by Cynog Dafis, the victor of Ceredigion and the Plaid member who did most – alongside Phil Williams – to lead the two sides to the altar.[164] The 'startling' result of the Greens in the 1989 European elections served as the catalyst for the start of a far-reaching conversation between both parties.[165] The Greens were invited to set out a critique of Plaid's policy programme at the latter's annual conference in the autumn of 1989. Under the leadership of Phil Williams, that policy programme was subsequently refashioned and rebuilt on green foundations in time for the 1990 conference, forming the basis of the Plaid Cymru manifesto for the 1992 general election.[166] At a local level, discussions were held between the Greens and Plaid Cymru about the possibility of creating electoral pacts in specific constituencies; discussions that led to startling success in Ceredigion and Pembroke North.

The formal relationship between two parties in Ceredigion proved to be only short-lived, albeit fruitful. The chaos of the Green Party's internal constitutional arrangements combined with the belligerence and intolerance of a small handful of its local members undermined the credibility of the coalition in the eyes of its chief advocates in both parties. But there was nothing

---

164 See Dafis, *Mab y Pregethwr*, pp. 206 and 174–209 passim.
165 Dafis, *Mab y Pregethwr*, p. 175.
166 *Tuag at 2000: Rhaglen Plaid Cymru ar gyfer Ewrop/Towards 2000: Plaid Cymru's Programme for Wales in Europe* (Plaid Cymru, 1992).

short-lived about Plaid's engagement with green ideas and principles. It continued throughout the 1990s and, indeed, continues today. There are two important points to make in this context. First, accepting that pragmatic considerations following the performance of the Greens in 1989 were an important driver in the 'Greening of Plaid Cymru', this was a process with much deeper and more resilient roots. Intellectual leaders such as Cynog Dafis, Phil Williams, Peter Keelan and Dafydd Elis-Thomas had long been interested in the green movements and its ideas. In fact, it is not too great a leap to claim that many of Plaid Cymru's fundamental ideas – an emphasis on the advantages of smaller units most obvious amongst them – were wholly consistent with those of green politics. In this sense, at least, it can be claimed that Saunders Lewis and Gwynfor Evans were greens *avant la lettre*. Cynog Dafis may also have been correct when he pointed out that the 'moralising tone' [collfarn moesol] characteristic of the green movement was one with which the substantial numbers of Welsh nationalists brought up 'to the sound of Puritanical values' were comfortable – himself included.[167]

Secondly and relatedly, it is important to underscore the extent to which the appeal of green ideas was felt right across the party – transcending both the ideological divisions of the early 1980s and any internal cultural differences. After the collapse of the left's project in the mid-1980s, many of its stalwarts turned towards green politics. This was, of course, the Welsh manifestation of a much wider international intellectual journey. Here as elsewhere, one of the all-important influences was the success of the German Greens – *Die Grünen*. Indeed, *Radical Wales* had already published a speech by Petra Kelly, one of the most prominent leaders of that party, in 1984.[168] Going Green appealed just as much to the Welsh-language intellectuals – left wing or otherwise – that formed the backbone of Plaid Cymru's machinery in Ceredigion. Another key point was that Dafydd Wigley also became persuaded of the new direction.

---

167 Dafis, *Mab y Pregethwr*, p. 174; translation.
168 Petra Kelly, 'The scandal of Europe', *Radical Wales*, 3 (summer 1984), 6–7.

As Wigley was later to acknowledge, he required some convincing of the wisdom of forming electoral pacts with the Greens.[169] But this appears to have been a case of being concerned at the wisdom of associating too closely with the Green Party rather than one of objecting to green arguments. The evidence suggests that he was strongly supportive of both the direction and tone of the manifesto Phil Williams had prepared ahead of the 1992 general election, a manifesto that Wigley was later to describe as the 'best ever presented by any party for Wales'.[170] By 1994, his own grasp of green arguments – and his understanding of how these fused with the argument for self-government – had matured to such an extent that he reserved one of the best and most powerful presidential speeches he ever gave to the subject.

The starting point for Dafydd Wigley's argument in 'The Challenge to Wales' was the need to think afresh about our understanding of economic development. In particular, it was time to embrace a more rounded emphasis on the quality of life rather than continue to focus on narrower, more traditional measures of economic growth. 'The measurement of well-being in terms of economic growth – "the growth of GDP" – is to ignore every other consideration. What about social growth, cultural growth, community growth, moral growth, personal growth, and the growth of character?'[171] Indeed, efforts to promote economic growth through unsustainable methods may even undermine rather than improve the quality of life.[172] He argued that this obsession with growth, as measured by the crude and misleading metrics of the past, had rendered us blind to the growth of poverty and the opening of a vast and immoral gulf between the poor and the wealthiest in society.

But how could we break this vicious circle in which policies meant to promote development were undermining the quality of life? There would be no deliverance from Westminster. 'Politics

169 Wigley, *Dal Ati*, p. 344. In fairness, it should be noted that Cynog Dafis is clear that Wigley was very supportive in the aftermath of the agreement with the Greens in Ceredigion; see *Mab y Pregethwr*, p. 206.
170 Wigley, *Dal Ati*, p. 347; translation.
171 Dafydd Wigley, *The Challenge to Wales/Yr Her i Gymru* (Plaid Cymru, 1994), p. 8.
172 Wigley, *The Challenge to Wales/Yr Her i Gymru*, p. 8.

at Westminster are still in a time warp', and this, according to Wigley, was just as true of Tony Blair's New Labour as it was of the Tories:

> It is incredible that the Labour Party's new agenda should ignore the biggest shift in economic-political thought for 200 years. Tony Blair says that economic growth is a precondition of social justice. We say that social justice is a precondition of sustainable economic development.[173]

But a Welsh Senate offered a route to deliverance. A Senate with legislative and tax-raising powers could implement economic policies based on principles of sustainability aimed at improving the quality of life. Such policies would not only be aligned with the needs of the age, but also wholly in accord with the egalitarian and radical values of Wales. On establishing such a Senate, Wales would have taken the first step towards realising Plaid Cymru's final constitutional aim of attaining full self-government and a 'strong, independent and equal constitutional position within the European Union'.[174]

By acknowledging what he called the biggest shift in economic-political thought in 200 years, Dafydd Wigley was also acknowledging the inadequacy of the type of ideas and attitudes that formed the basis for the 1970 economic plan. He nonetheless remained determined to demonstrate how self-government would create a context in which Wales could address its challenges. In 1995, the party published an outline of a plan for creating 100,000 jobs in Wales which was based on sustainable development principles.[175] His later recollections about it are revealing. The plan, he said, was:

---

173 Wigley, *The Challenge to Wales/Yr Her i Gymru*, p. 11.
174 Wigley, *The Challenge to Wales/Yr Her i Gymru*, p. 16. For details of Plaid Cymru's constitutional stance in the mid-1990s, see *A Democratic Wales in an United Europe* that includes an introduction by Dafydd Wigley (Caernarfon: Plaid Cymru, 1995).
175 *100,000 Answers ... to Conquer Unemployment in Wales*, preface by Dafydd Wigley (summer 1995).

part of the process of developing detailed policy recommendations, relevant to the nineties and for the century to come, as was the case with our Economic Plan a quarter of a century earlier. Today, as in the sixties, I am totally convinced that we as a party have to show the people of Wales that we are doing our homework, that our recommendations are relevant to their concerns, have been costed and that they can be implemented.[176]

In short, the people of Wales had to be shown that self-government was the key to their long-term prosperity, whether that prosperity was measured by the standards of the 1960s or by the very different green yardstick of the 1990s.

By the 1990s, therefore, Plaid Cymru was united around a single economic, social and constitutional programme. Although it was characterised by elements of continuity – in particular, the party remained wedded to the Saundersian prohibition against 'independence' – the programme nonetheless did much more than simply rehash the previous stances of the 1960s and the 1970s; the 1980s had left their mark. Plaid Cymru had embraced a bilingual Wales with none of the ambiguities of the past. It had enthusiastically embraced Europe and the process of European integration.[177] The green agenda had not only been embraced but placed at the heart of the party's policy programme. At the same time, the party had abandoned the search for a third way and identified its position on the conventional right-left ideological spectrum. Plaid Cymru was a party on the left or the centre left. It is also significant that the party was now consistently presenting its message as one that was focused on the future and on future prosperity (in its broadest sense), rather than one which harked back to a past that had long since been lost.

Not only was Plaid Cymru's policy programme of the mid-1990s different, but there was every sign that its contents chimed with mainstream popular opinion in Wales. Opinion polls

176 Dafydd Wigley, *Maen i'r Wal* (Caernarfon: Gwasg Gwynedd, 2001), p. 37; translation.
177 Indeed, its attitude may well be characterised as overly enthusiastic; see Ned Thomas's salutary warning, 'Against europhoria', *Radical Wales*, 30 (summer 1991), 10–12.

certainly suggested that support for devolution had increased substantially since the nadir of 1979. One 1994 poll conducted on behalf of the BBC suggested that 37 per cent of the electorate supported 'Independence within the European Union'.[178] One swallow does not make a summer of course, but auguries suggested that the grip of the long winter of the 1980s was at last starting to loosen. In addition, there was ample evidence of the popular appeal of green themes, with political parties and even commercial enterprises seeking to convince the public of their commitment to the environment. Regardless of the sincerity of those making the claims, the fact that they were being heard so frequently was an indication that environmental concerns were no longer the preserve of the social and political fringe. Another advantage for Plaid Cymru during this period was that its programme had popular spokespeople – with Dafydd Wigley, in particular, having developed a special rapport with the electorate. His appeal was highlighted by the result of the 1994 European election – an election at which Labour performed particularly strongly – when he won 34 per cent of the vote in the North Wales constituency. Given all of this, it is easy to understand Cynog Dafis's retrospective view that: '[T]hroughout the nineties it seemed as though the ideological and political wind was in our sails.'[179]

In reality, it was rather more complicated than this. Yes, Plaid Cymru's programme seemed to be an attractive one, and its leader one of the most popular politicians in Wales. Nevertheless, with rare exceptions such as the leader's performance in the 1994 European elections and Cynog Dafis's victory in Ceredigion and Pembroke North, Plaid Cymru still struggled to make an electoral impression. Consider the result of the May 1997 general election, for example: only a few months before the referendum

178   It was of course the BBC and not Plaid Cymru that chose the question wording! For an accessible summary of the results of the opinion polls of the period see John Osmond, *Welsh Europeans* (Bridgend: Seren, 1995), p. 32. On the evolution of public attitudes towards devolution see Richard Wyn Jones and Roger Scully, *Wales says Yes: Devolution and the 2011 Welsh referendum* (Cardiff: University of Wales Press, 2012), pp. 57–76.

179   Dafis, *Mab y Pregethwr*, p. 209; translation.

Plaid Cymru lost its deposit in 15 of the 40 Welsh constituencies and in 10 of those the Plaid Cymru candidate placed fifth or sixth behind candidates from fringe and short-lived parties such as Jimmy Goldsmith's Referendum Party or Arthur Scargill's Socialist Labour Party. It was not only electoral outcomes that were disappointing. Despite the undoubted substance of the 1992 and 1997 election manifestos, there were clear signs that the party was losing its intellectual vitality. The publication of *Radical Wales* was abandoned in the summer of 1991. And after a period of intermittent publication, the party stopped publishing *Y Ddraig Goch* and *Welsh Nation* as separate papers. In fact, Plaid more-or-less stopped publishing. There is no doubt that this partly reflected social changes far beyond the party's control. Society was changing, and so, too, was the nature of politics. Nonetheless, it remains surprising that Plaid Cymru was losing vitality precisely at the point at which there were genuine prospects of realising the old dream of a Welsh parliament. The contrast between this period and the 1940s and 1950s – when, objectively, the prospects for any success were very much bleaker – is particularly striking.

Here we confront the paradox that the 1990s represented for Plaid Cymru. This was a period in which the cause of Welsh nationalism was strengthening. Support for devolution was increasing both among the public at large and in other political parties. Welsh-medium education was on the rise. There was increasing interest in Welsh history, thanks in large part to the efforts of two party members, Gwyn A. Williams and John Davies.[180] The meta-narratives of Welsh history that they offered, and which were consumed with relish by their fellow countrywomen and men, were consistent with the teachings of the national movement. Meanwhile, the process of national institution building continued and even deepened. All of these represented developments that previous generations of nationalists had fervently longed for. Yet while Welsh nationalism in its broadest sense was a growing force, the Welsh

---

180 Gwyn A. Williams's *When was Wales?* was published in 1985 followed by John Davies's magnum opus, *Hanes Cymru*, in 1990 – with the English translation, *A History of Wales* (London: Allen Lane), appearing in 1993.

nationalist party, Plaid Cymru, was largely stagnant, unable to benefit electorally from what appeared to be the propitious circumstances of the period.

There are a number of factors that help explain this paradox: the fact that the Westminster electoral context and voting system are particularly unfavourable for Plaid Cymru – meaning that the party is likely to underperform its 'real' level of support in such elections; the fact that the national movement is more than just Plaid Cymru; and the fact that Plaid Cymru has never been the only political home of Welsh nationalists, such that any attempt to evaluate the social and political influence of Welsh nationalism as a whole would also need to consider the role of these nationalists. There is another (paradoxical) fact that should also be recognised. Even if Plaid Cymru was not advancing electorally, it was nevertheless playing an important political role that would make a substantial contribution to reversing the result of the 1979 St David's Day referendum in September 1997.

Dafydd Elis-Thomas was proven partially correct in the late 1980s when he predicted that, in the next decade, devolution would become a matter of elite politics. At least until the summer of 1997 that was indeed the case. But *pace* Elis-Thomas, it was not those in charge of the quangos that mattered, but rather the leadership of the Labour Party. All of the important arguments about the principle of devolution and the form that devolution might take would happen within that small group, with efforts to broaden the conversation determinately rebuffed.[181] In such a context, the role of particular individuals was absolutely key, none more so than Ron Davies. There is evidence that Dafydd Wigley became an important source of external support for Davies during Labour's internal wrangling on the matter. There is certainly

[181] See Richard Wyn Jones and Bethan Lewis, 'The 1997 Welsh devolution referendum', *Politics*, 19 (1999), 37–46; David McCrone and Bethan Lewis, 'The Scottish and Welsh referendum campaigns', in Taylor and Thomson (eds), *Scotland and Wales*, pp. 17–39; Lindsay Paterson and Richard Wyn Jones, 'Does civil society drive constitutional change? The cases of Scotland and Wales', in Taylor and Thomson (eds), *Scotland and Wales*, pp. 169–97; Kevin Morgan and Geoff Mungham, *Redesigning Democracy: The Making of the Welsh Assembly* (Bridgend: Seren, 2000). For a later, more systematic discussion, see Wyn Jones and Scully, *Wales says yes*, pp. 26–56.

no doubt that the two met together on a fairly regular basis after 1995.[182] The exact content of those discussions is not known. Thus, for example, we do not know to what extent (if any) Davies was influenced by Wigley's ideas. But given that the Plaid Cymru president had spent much longer arguing the case for some form of home rule than the then MP for Caerphilly, it would be surprising if the former did not exert at least some influence. What is abundantly clear is that a relationship of trust developed between the most prominent devolutionists within the Labour Party and the leaders of Plaid Cymru. That relationship was in turn wholly essential to the successful Yes campaign in 1997; indeed, it formed the very foundation of that campaign.[183]

Plaid Cymru contributed to the 1997 referendum result in other important ways. Its efforts helped ensure that one part of the Welsh electorate – Welsh speakers – became a bastion of support for devolution. Fluent Welsh speakers were much more likely to turn out to vote in the referendum and were much more likely to vote 'Yes' than those who did not speak the language.[184] But Plaid's contribution went beyond that. One of its most significant contributions during the 1990s was to draw the sting from the accusation of 'extremism' which had long plagued it. While our knowledge about the attitudes of the Welsh electorate before 1997 is very patchy, we know that Plaid Cymru was the most unpopular party in Wales at the time of the 1979 general election. It is also clear that the main reason for this was a sense among a large proportion of the Welsh population that Plaid Cymru was an 'extremist' party. This changed dramatically by 1997 – by which time Plaid was enjoying levels of popularity akin to those of the dominant Labour Party. It was now the

182 Wigley, *Maen i'r Wal*, p. 115. For a good example of the two meeting and holding talks in a period that was very difficult politically for Davies, see also pp. 80–1.
183 Not all the details of the collaboration and cooperation are yet known. In addition to Wigley and Davies, Ieuan Wyn Jones and Peter Hain also worked closely together on behalf of their respective parties. The third volume of Dafydd Wigley's autobiography (*Maen i'r Wal*) treads very gingerly over this sensitive ground.
184 Richard Wyn Jones and Dafydd Trystan, 'The Welsh devolution referendum', in Taylor and Thomson (eds), *Scotland and Wales*, pp. 65–93.

post-Thatcher Conservatives who had taken over the mantle of the most despised party in Wales.

Thatcher almost certainly played an important if inadvertent role in bringing about this shift in public opinion. Thatcherism succeeded in uniting the people of Wales far more effectively than any nationalist, with rivals discovering that they had more in common with each other than they had imagined when faced by a far more dangerous external threat. But Plaid Cymru itself played its own part in that process as well, not least because of the cumulative impact of its ability to 'keep on going'. With Plaid Cymru's representatives a constant presence at Westminster, and the party a permanent (albeit marginal) part of Wales's political landscape, the public had ample opportunity to become acclimatised to it. In the process, much of the sense of exotic otherness – as well as perceptions of extremism – that had once surrounded the party, receded. It became much easier in due course for electors to look afresh at a policy that had been so closely associated with Plaid.

Although it is impossible to be definitive on the matter, it seems likely that Plaid's shifting political vocabulary also played a role in changing perceptions, and in particular the decision to adopt the familiar terminology of the left-right spectrum to describe the policy positions of the party and of Welsh nationalism more generally. Even if the social and political values of the bulk of the Welsh electorate are not as left wing and radical as suggested by the dominant political discourse in Wales, the perception that Wales is a progressive, left-wing country is nonetheless important.[185] By associating itself so explicitly with the left and centre-left, Plaid Cymru succeeded in creating a new space for itself and its core messages. In the process, many on the left in Wales became convinced that the constitutional question was part of a progressive political project rather than its negation: a crucial turning point in Wales's political history.

* * *

185 For brief discussions of the evidence see Richard Wyn Jones, 'Dŵr coch croyw', *Barn* (June 2004), and 'Y traddodiad radicalaidd Cymreig?', *Barn* (July/ August 2004).

'… no day like this
for seven hundred years.'

Such was T. James Jones and Jon Dressel's apocalyptic rendering of the implications of the 1979 referendum result. They went on to describe a country where 'The land is rotten. Rotten to its bowels. The trees ooze corruption. The hedges drip with it.'[186] The perspective was very different after 18 September 1997. Then the bardic response combined joy with a palpable sense of surprise and relief.[187] Perhaps it was Dafydd John Pritchard who best crystallised the mood:

> Despite the pains of long hours expecting
> your unwilling birth,
> all the voices and all the talk –
> one muffled cry was enough.[188]

'One muffled cry was enough': there was nothing triumphal about the tone adopted; no mock-heroic chest slapping. It was very much more modest. The swing between the 1979 and the 1997 votes may have been an enormous one in electoral terms – fully 30 percentage points. But that left a winning margin of a mere 6,721 votes, corresponding to a tiny 0.3 per cent of the Welsh electorate. Triumphalism would hardly have been appropriate. Neither was it political heroics in the tradition of Nelson Mandela or Martin Luther King that finally led us to this outcome.

---

186   Jones and Dressel, *Cerddi Ianws Poems*, p. 16.
187   Branwen Niclas (ed.), *1997: Sut Oedd Hi i Ti?* (Llanrwst: Gwasg Carreg Gwalch, 1998) contains a collection of responses to the referendum. See also the poem 'Ie' by Rhys Dafis in *Stwff y Stomp* (Llanrwst: Gwasg Carreg Gwalch, 2002): 'Ni ail-law, gwastraff o le; / Y ni, o bawb, â'n "Ie"!' (Us the weathered, waste of space / Us, of all people, with our 'Yes!'); and 'Dydd Iau, Medi 18fed 1997' by Tudur Dylan Jones in Myrddin ap Dafydd (ed.), *Cywyddau Cyhoedddus 3* (Llanrwst: Gwasg Carreg Gwalch, 1998) pp. 126–7: 'A wyddost y bydd dyddiad / y deunawfed o Fedi / un dydd yn dy gynnal di?' (Do you know that the date, / the eighteenth of September, / will one day sustain you?)
188   'Er poenau'r oriau hirion a disgwyl / dy esgor anfodlon, / y lleisiau oll a'r holl sôn – / un waedd egwan oedd ddigon': in Niclas (ed.), *1997*, p. 108; translation.

To be sure, Plaid Cymru's history during the 1980s and 1990s was not a heroic one either, even if there is an element of quiet heroism in the determination to keep on going – dal ati – after the disaster of 1979. Indeed, there is little doubt that some will interpret the shifts in Plaid Cymru's political thinking witnessed during these decades – and, in particular, the fundamental changes in the views of prominent individuals like Dafydd Elis-Thomas – as nothing more than insincere opportunism. The assessment advanced in this chapter is more generous. Without the efforts of some of the leaders and members of Plaid Cymru to find a way forward for the party and the wider national movement after 1979, Welsh political nationalism might easily have vanished completely or succumbed to a violent nihilism. They deserve recognition for ensuring that this did not happen. But more than this, Plaid Cymru's behaviour during the period in question was surely wholly rational. Small parties like Plaid Cymru are not able to shape and reshape the political landscape that surrounds them in the same way that larger parties sometimes can. Rather, they are required to respond to a political terrain that is being shaped by others. In these circumstances, it is entirely reasonable that they seek to identify and exploit any opportunities that may appear to arise. Is this not exactly what Plaid Cymru attempted to do during the era of the two Dafydds? Indeed, viewed from this angle, it is not the change and inconsistency of the 1980s and 1990s that is surprising or difficult to explain, but rather the degree of continuity that characterised the political thinking of Plaid Cymru from the party's formation until 1979.

Index

Aberystwyth 25, 26f, 121, 140, 171, 226f
Acts of Union, the 67f, 68, 183, 209, 256
Adorno, Theodor 96
Africa 25
Alliance, the (political party) 273, 274, 283
Anarchism 48
Anderson, Benedict 28f, 55, 56
Anderson, Perry 65, 66, 72
Anglican Church, the 104
Arraste (Mondragón) 252
ap Gwilym, Eurfyl 226
ap Iwan, Emrys 51, 55
Armenians 41
Arthur (King) 154, 205, 217
Austro-Hungarian Empire 26

Bahro, Rudolf 249
Bala, Y 37
Balkans 38
Baner ac Amserau Cymru (Y Faner) 136, 147, 242
Bangor 84, 85, 134, 244f
Basque Country 252
BBC (British Broadcasting Corporation) 299
Bebb, Ambrose 88, 90, 109f, 133, 134
Beeching, Lord 216
Beethoven, Ludwig van 38
Beijing 44
Bell, David A. 29
Benjamin, Walter 96

Benn, Tony 250, 283f
Billig, Michael 47
Blair, Tony 46, 75, 125, 201, 228f, 267, 297
Bloch, Ernst 96
Boer War, the 74
Bosnia 38
Bosworth, Battle of (1485) 209, 212
Britannic Confederation 186, 187, 191, 205, 208
British Empire 68, 72–5, 129–30, 182, 191, 208
British nationalism 27, 42–3, 46–8, 73, 137, 168, 247, 277
Brooks, Beata 284
Brown, Gordon 42, 46, 267
Brubaker, Rogers 35f, 40

Caernarfon 83, 84f, 132, 134, 147, 162, 242, 251, 282, 283f, 291
    byelection (1929) 82, 112, 117, 127
Caerphilly 142, 302
Calvinism 202, 280
campaign for Welsh language TV channel 216, 231
Cardiff 255f, 268, 270, 279
Carmarthen 110, 162, 172, 251
    byelection (1966) 141–3, 168–9, 220, 223, 292
    Plaid Cymru conference in (1981) 240–2, 253–5, 257, 261, 272, 282
Catalunya 64
Catholicism 102–4, 106, 203, 208, 210, 222f, 228

Celtic Church, the 210
Celticism 156
Ceredigion 225, 251, 287, 294–8
Charles, Prince 162
China 110
Christianity 46, 93, 95, 102, 126, 144, 155, 157, 184, 202, 207, 222–3, 228
Churchill, Winston 139, 180
Cole, G. D. H. 148
Colley, Linda 66, 74
Common Wealth (political party) 185
Commonwealth; British Commonwealth (international organisation) 75, 182–5, 187, 191, 205, 234
communism 26, 39, 113, 207, 231, 233, 235, 244, 249, 262, 268, 280
Communist Party 190, 244–5, 261
conservatism 48, 57, 58, 116, 238
Conservative Party 46, 139, 203, 252, 268, 272, 276–7, 284–5, 303
Contemporary Wales 266
Cook, A. J. 11
Cooke, Phil 259–61, 263f, 264–8
Cwmllynfell 175
Cyffro 244, 249
Cymdeithas yr Iaith Gymraeg (Welsh Language Society) 161–2, 214, 230, 245f, 251
Cymru Fydd (Young Wales) 54, 59, 87, 99, 211
Cymru Well 83

Dafis, Cynog 225, 294–6, 299
Daniel, Catherine 80
Daniel, J. E. 80, 154f, 227
Darian, Y 127
Davies, Aneirin Talfan 146
Davies, Charlotte 259, 263, 266
Davies, D. Hywel 88f, 111–12, 130f, 132, 249, 266
Davies, D. J. 107, 114, 120–4, 128, 135, 147–9, 170–1, 175–6, 178f, 195, 217, 224, 243, 292f
  The Economics of Welsh Self-Government 121–2

Davies, George M. Ll. 148
Davies, Jennie Eirian 242
Davies, John 51, 63f, 158, 300
Davies, Noëlle 107, 122, 170, 172f, 176, 195, 243
Davies, Pennar 142f, 145, 202, 222
Davies, Ron 301–2
Davies, S. O. 245
Day, Graham 259
Ddraig Goch, Y 82, 109–11, 115f, 117–19, 121–3, 128, 133–5, 147, 232, 300
de Saint-Etienne, Jean-Paulo Raubaut 29
De Valera, Éamon 87, 168
Declaration of Arbroath 36
Denmark 121–2, 217, 244
Devolution 43, 60, 66, 94, 128–9, 140, 144, 149, 195, 220, 222, 272, 275–81, 285, 299–302
Dolgellau 244, 282
Dominion Status 126–30, 180–2, 191, 194, 208–10, 212, 215
Dressel, John 220, 304
Dublin 187

East Timor 44
Edwards, Hywel Teifi 67
Edwards, Ness 58
Edwards, Nicholas 58
Edwards, O. M. 99–101, 104–5
Edwards, Siân 262
Eliot, T. S. 96
Elis-Thomas, Dafydd 58, 238–87, 288, 290–1, 295, 301, 305
  Miners' Strike 269
  Quango Wales 286–7
Ellis, T. E. 55
Encyclopaedia Britannica 63, 196
England 63–76, 90, 93–5, 106f, 110, 121, 127, 153, 175–6, 185–7, 194, 201, 205, 208–15, 228f, 248, 229–87
euro-communism 261–3, 268, 40
Europe 23, 28–9, 32f, 36, 47, 51–5, 66, 69f, 75, 136, 156–7, 177, 179, 184, 189–92, 201, 211, 218, 228, 262f, 269–87, 292, 298
  Common Market 187–91

eastern Europe 240, 257, 264
European Community / Union
187, 191, 289–90, 297
European Free Trade Area
(EFTA) 289
European parliament and
European parliamentary
elections 284–5, 294, 299
Europeanism 149, 188, 288
in Saunders Lewis's political
thought 92–106, 152–4
Evans, Beriah Gwynfe 87
Evans, Gwynfor 80–1, 107, 113,
135, 139–220, 222–4, 227–30,
233–4, 237–9, 240–2, 254, 256,
264, 268, 271, 275, 280, 287, 290,
292, 295
A National Future for Wales
162–3, 178
'Court of Llangadog' 142
Aros Mae (Land of my Fathers)
183, 198–215, 256
*Bywyd Cymro (For the sake of
Wales)* 148–50
End of Britishness 216–18
Eu Hiaith a Gadwant 163
Our Three Nations 185–7
Plaid Cymru and Wales 169–71
Rhagom i Ryddid 164, 169, 172,
181, 183
Wales can Win 147, 164, 178
Evans, Jill 263, 278–80
Evans, Jonathan 268
Evans, Rhys 143–4, 241

Fascism 26, 104, 192f, 228
federalism 36, 60, 128, 186, 191–2
feudalism 24, 246
Ffransis, Meinir (née Evans) 162
Fianna Fáil 187
Finland 64
Fire in Llŷn (Tân yn Llŷn) *see*
Penyberth
First World War (the Great War)
38, 53, 88f
Foster, R. F. 61
France 29, 48, 64, 67, 87,
106f

Free Wales Army 149, 162
French revolution 29, 143
Freud, Sigmund 96, 250

Gaudí, Antoni 38
Gellner, Ernest 25–33, 60f
General Elections 301
1929 82, 112, 117, 127
1945 174
1970 143, 162
1979 244, 302
1983 125, 261, 267, 268f
1987 274–5, 282, 284
1992 294, 296, 300
1997 299–300
Germany 36, 93
Gilcriest, Margaret 88f, 106
Glyndŵr, Owain 68, 126, 211
Goethe, Johann Wofgang 29
Goldsmith, Jimmy 300
Gramsci, Antonio 49–51, 56–7,
262–3, 266
Green Party, the 285, 294–6
green movement / politics 178,
225, 273, 285, 298–9
Greene, Graham 96
Greenfeld, Liah 29, 65f
Griffith, Arthur 89
Griffiths, Robert 190, 245–9, 256,
261f
Gruffydd, Elis 34
Gruffydd, W. J. 103
Grundtvig, N. F. S. 217
Gwerin 85–6, 100–1, 105, 136,
209–13
Gwynedd 217, 284–6
Gymdeithas Genedlaethol
Gymreig, y (Y Tair G) (the
National Welsh Society) 84–6

Hardie, Keir 207
Hegelianism 110
Hobsbawm, Eric 32–3, 51, 55–6
Hollywood 156
Holyhead 282
House of Commons 43f, 69, 131,
172, 188, 276, 285, 287
House of Lords 277, 285, 291

Hroch, Miroslav 23–4, 33, 51–5, 62, 179, 291
Hungary 260
Hunter, Jerry 34
Hutt, Jane 268
Huws, Dafydd 275, 283
Hydro 253
Hywel Dda (Hywel the Good) 126, 169, 204

independence 90, 84, 97–8, 126–9, 130, 171, 180–4, 187, 191–4, 201, 205, 208, 214, 236–7, 258, 268, 273–4, 280, 299
Independent Labour Party (ILP) 115, 243
India 182
Indonesia 44
industrial revolution 29, 71–2, 165f
Ingham, Geoffrey 72
Internationalism 26, 38–9, 227
Ireland 61, 85, 116, 122f, 126, 130, 168, 170, 172f, 186–7, 196, 244f
Irish language, the 168
Iron and Steel Trades Confederation (ISTC) 252
Iwan, Dafydd 31, 215

Jamaica 171
Janus 60, 63
Japan 36
Jedlicki, Jerzy 71
Jenkins, Dafydd 244
Jenkins, R. T. 100
Jews 41
John, E .T. 88f
Jones, Dafydd Glyn 222f
Jones, Francis 134
Jones, Fred 88
Jones, Griffith 212
Jones, Gwilym R. 82
Jones, H. R. 79, 83–91, 117–18, 126–7, 130, 134, 159
Jones, Ieuan Wyn 284, 302f
Jones, J. E. 117, 128–9
Jones, J. R. 38
Jones, Merfyn 245
Jones, Michael D. 51, 55

Jones, R. Tudur 107, 202, 203f
Jones, R. M. (Bobi) 198
Jones, T. Gwynn 38
Jones, T. James 220, 223
Jones, Walter S. (Gwallter Llyfnwy) 84
Joyce, James 96

Keelan, Peter 279f, 295
King, Martin Luther 304
Kinnock, Neil 43, 58, 222
Kohn, Hans 40
Kohr, Leopold 289
Korea 36
Kosovo 38
Kraus, Karl 61

labourism 65f, 66, 115f, 259, 264, 270, 279, 293
labour movement, the 131, 175, 213, 247–8, 250, 252
Labour Party, the 39, 46, 65f, 66, 75, 84f, 106, 115, 125, 136, 139, 143, 144f, 173–5, 196, 203, 221, 228–9, 231, 236, 239, 245, 248, 250, 252, 257, 268–72, 283–5
New Labour 267
Lampeter 243
League of Nations, the 95, 110, 130, 181
Lenin, Vladimir Ilich 39–40
Levinger, Matthew 207
Lewis, Saunders 31, 46, 54, 58, 79–138, 139, 141, 144–61, 163, 169f, 173, 177, 180–1, 183–4, 188, 191–4, 197–203, 206–8, 216–18, 222–4, 227–8, 233–4, 236, 238, 253–5, 264, 271–2, 280, 288–90, 295
Buchedd Garmon 31, 81
Principles of Nationalism (*Egwyddorion Cenedlaetholdeb*) 82, 90, 92–101
The Case for Welsh National Development Council 124, 173
The Fate of the Language (*Tynged yr Iaith*) 80, 146
Liberal Democrats 143, 283

Liberal Party 101, 129, 131, 137, 171, 229, 273, 283f
liberalism 26, 40, 48, 58, 115, 215
List, Fredrich 56–7
Livsey, Richard 283
Lloyd George, David 60, 87, 108
Lloyd, D. Tecwyn 104, 132
Llywelyn Fawr (the Great) (Llywelyn I) 126, 208–9
Llywelyn the Last (Llywelyn II) 183, 205, 211
Llywelyn-Williams, Alun 61–2
Luther, Martin 93, 103, 106f
Lytle, Paula Franklin 207

Machiavelli, Niccolò 93, 103, 106, 144
Machynlleth 82, 92, 126, 129
Macmurray, John 228f
Mainwaring, Lynn 259, 263f, 266, 268, 278f, 293
Mandela, Nelson 304
Mann, Michael 28, 30
Marx, Karl 99, 119–20
Marxism 32, 49, 57, 115f, 134, 153–4, 199, 239, 244f, 246–50, 255–6, 259f, 262, 270f
Masaryk, Tomáš 125
Maximus, Magnus 210
Mazzini, Guiseppe 148
McCrone, David 26
Meirionnydd 166, 238, 242, 251, 285, 287
Merthyr Tydfil 71f, 142–3, 238, 281f, 291f
Methodist Revival, the 95, 102
Mexico 48
Middle Ages, the 24, 93, 95–8, 211
Miles, Gareth 245–9, 256, 261, 266
Mill, John Stuart 56–7
Miners' Strike (1926) 110–11
Miners' Strike (1984–85) 225, 263, 269–70, 279f, 281
Morgan, Kenneth O. 196, 221f
Morgan, Syd 278, 291
Morrises of Ynys Môn 51
Mudiad Amddiffyn Cymru 162

Mudiad Cymreig, y (the Welsh Society) 79, 87–90, 117
Mudiad Gwerin 134–5, 174f, 244

Nairn, Tom 27, 29–31, 33–4, 39f, 45, 51, 60, 65–8, 72
Nanmor, Dafydd 95f, 154f
National Assembly for Wales 24, 52f, 143, 275, 288
National Left, the (Chwith Genedlaethol) 253–9, 263, 268, 271, 277, 282, 284f
National Union of Blastfurnacemen, Ore Miners, Coke Workers and Kindred Trades 252
National Union of Mineworkers 269
National Welsh Society, the see Gymdeithas Genedlaethol Gymreig, y
Neo-Pelagianism 202
Nevin, Edward 170–2
New Left, the 65, 178, 262, 268
New Zealand 180
Nicholas, T. E. (Niclas y Glais) 48f
Nonconformism 96, 100, 102, 104–6, 202, 222
Normans, the 211
Northern Ireland 38, 47, 63, 69, 74, 128
Norway 201
Nove, Alec 260f

O'Leary, Brendan 30, 35, 48, 56–7
Okey, Robin 245
Olsson, G. 264
Owen, Evan Alwyn 82–6, 89–91, 159

Pacifism 135, 140f, 185, 187f, 195, 202–3, 211, 263, 273
Parry-Williams, T. H. 40, 43
Parry, R. Williams 104
Parry, Thomas 84
Pearse, Pádraig 168

Penarth 88, 90, 151, 290
Penyberth 79–80, 82, 131–4, 136, 147, 220, 259
Perchentyaeth 123–6, 135, 169–70
Philip, Alan Butt 142–3
Pius IX 103
Plaid Cymru
　Commission of Inquiry 225–42, 254, 286
　Conferences 134–5, 140, 185, 199, 240, 272, 282, 290, 294
　Research Group 190, 292–3
　Summer Schools 82, 92, 107, 122, 133–5, 181, 206, 244, 255f, 257, 259
　Youth Movement 260
Plamenatz, John 40
PONT 165
Pontypridd byelection (1989) 284, 291
Port Talbot 216
Pound, Ezra 96
Protestantism 29–30, 100, 102–4, 126, 208, 210, 222
Prussia 29
Pwllheli 79, 87, 91, 117, 127–8, 136

Radical Scotland 285
Radical Wales 243, 263–6, 270, 272, 275, 278, 295, 300
Radnorshire 166, 238, 283
Rees, Gareth 259
Rees, Ioan Bowen 206
Rees, Teresa 259
Referendum, Common Market (1975) 189–90, 289
referendum, devolution (1979) 43, 196, 220–1, 244, 247, 252, 267, 271, 276, 281, 301, 304
referendum, devolution (1997) 140, 225, 288, 299–304
referendum, further powers (2011) 185
Referendum Party 300
Reynolds, David 259, 272–4, 278f
Rhondda 142

Rhyd-ddu 82, 86f
Rhys, Prosser 109f, 136, 218
Roberts, Emrys 226
Roberts, Kate 133, 243
Roberts, Mai 88f
Roberts, William 105
Roberts, Wyn 285
Rokkan, Stein 69
Roma 55
Roman Empire 93, 210, 215
Roosevelt, F. D. 173
Rousseau, Jean-Jacques 56–7
Russia 39, 64
Rwanda 38

Sardinia 56
Sartre, Jean-Paul 249
Saxons, the 211
Scandinavia 38, 63, 211, 200, 217, 227, 289, 292
Scargill, Arthur 300
Scotland 36, 66, 69, 73–4, 143, 185, 189, 196, 238
　nationalism in 42, 48, 187, 280, 285
Scottish National Party (SNP) 42, 163, 185, 226, 274, 280, 284
Second World War 38, 80, 108, 135, 137, 157f, 170, 173, 180, 182, 195, 203
Shakespeare, William 150
Shaw, George Bernard 139
Sinn Féin 83, 85, 87, 89
Smith, Anthony D. 59
Socialism for the Welsh People 245–9, 261
Socialism 26, 58, 115, 123, 153–4, 159, 224–5, 228–30, 232, 234–5, 239, 245–78
Socialist Labour Party 300
South Wales Daily News 87
South Wales Echo 204
Soviet Union 27, 35, 228, 244f
Spain 64
Speenhamland 57
Stalin, Joseph 25
Statute of Westminster 130, 180
Stormont 128

Stourbridge 228
Swansea 133–4
Sweden 48, 64, 201, 226f

Tennessee Valley Authority 173
Thatcher, Margaret 46, 75, 139,
    176, 216, 221, 230, 253, 266, 266,
    269, 273, 303
'The City' 72
Third World, the 71
Thomas, Ben Bowen 88
Thomas, George 148–9
Thomas, Ned 44f
Thomas, Owen 105
Thomas, Owen John 226
Tibet 44
Tonypandy Riots 132
Treorchy 259
Triban 171
Trident 216
Trotskyism 228, 231
Tudors, the 93, 103, 106f, 120, 209,
    211
Tutsi 41

United Kingdom of Great Britain
    and Northern Ireland, the 27,
    47, 63, 143, 180
    nature of the state 68–70
United States of America 47, 67,
    75–6, 173
University of Wales 80

Valentine, Lewis 79, 81, 84, 86–7,
    127–8, 132–3, 222
Valleys, the 223, 248, 272, 288,
    290–1
Valmy, Battle of (1792) 29

Wade-Evans, A. W. 206
Wales Act, the (1978) 196, 220
Wales Congress in Support of
    Mining Communities 270
Wales TUC 252
Webb, Harri 126f, 167, 185f
Weber, Max 56–7
Weil, Simone 96
Wellock, Wilfred 228

Welsh Coal and Steel Board 260
Welsh Congregational Union
    (Undeb yr Annibynwyr) 202
Welsh Development Agency
    (WDA) 124, 173–4, 277
Welsh Language Act (1993) 285
Welsh Language Board, The 285
Welsh Language Society, the
    see Cymdeithas yr Iaith
    Gymraeg
Welsh Nation 171, 229, 232, 300
Welsh Office, the 275, 285
Welsh parliament 43, 129–30,
    161–2, 176f, 195–6, 274–6, 300
Welsh Republicans, the 185f, 245
Welsh Socialist Republican
    Movement 190, 245, 248
Western Mail 90, 271
Westminster 89, 148, 275–6, 292,
    296–7, 301, 303
    see also Statute of Westminster
Westphalia, Peace of 97–8
Wigley, Dafydd 41–2, 139, 172,
    225–6, 238, 240–4, 251, 254, 258,
    268, 272f, 281–3, 285–97, 299,
    301–2
    Europeanism of 287–90
Williams, Abi 140
Williams, Dafydd 283
Williams, D. J. 80, 90, 133
Williams, Edward (Iolo
    Morganwg) 51
Williams, Elisabeth 88
Williams, Emyr Wynn 124f, 238–9,
    253–9, 266, 268, 271, 275–7, 281f,
    286
Williams, G. J. 88
Williams, Glyn 259, 266
Williams, Gwyn A. 49, 86f, 220–1f,
    261–6, 280, 282, 284–5, 300
Williams, J. Roose 248
Williams, L. J. 71
Williams, Phil 58, 142f, 167, 172,
    178f, 190, 225–6, 234–9, 244f,
    275, 279f, 292–6
Williams, Raymond 249, 266, 278,
    286f, 278
Williams, Waldo 41, 43

Williams, William (Pantycelyn)
102–3, 212
Wilson, Harold 139
Wilson, Joe 284
Wordsworth, William 143
working class 32, 53, 121, 213, 239,
247–51, 259, 262–3, 265, 267, 293

Yeats, W. B. 96
Yma o Hyd 31, 215f
Ynys Môn 51, 284
Young Wales *see* Cymru Fydd
Yugoslavia 245

Zedong, Mao 25